AN
HONORABLE TITAN

AN
HONORABLE TITAN

A Biographical Study of

ADOLPH S. OCHS

BY

GERALD W. JOHNSON

HARPER & BROTHERS PUBLISHERS

NEW YORK · LONDON

Personal Book shop

2.10

2-28-47 fm

4-15-47 fm

CONTENTS

[v]

CONTENTS

PREFACE

HERE is no history of the New York *Times*. It is true that just fifty years ago, as this book is published, the *Times* became the life of Adolph S. Ochs and so remained for thirty-nine years. It is true that under him the *Times* recaptured all its ancient glory and more. It is true that many men, including some brilliant journalists, had tried to revive the *Times* and had failed, so it is not fantastic to assume that he was the one man of his period capable of accomplishing the task. It is true that during his long service he devoted his energies exclusively to the *Times*, consistently refusing to engage in any business enterprise not directly connected with his newspaper.

But while the *Times* was his life, he would have have regarded himself as a failure if his life had been the history of the *Times*, even from 1896 to 1935. His purpose, to which he held tenaciously, was to create an institution greater than any individual connected with it and not dependent for its existence upon any individual. His success is evidenced by the fact that although he has been in the grave for nearly a dozen years, the *Times* survives. In those things that can be measured by statistics, indeed, it is not diminished but greater than it was when he left it, and while there is no statistical measurement of such imponderables as prestige and power, it is an erratic mind that would deny them to the *Times* in 1946.

An institution greater than the man who created it is obviously not to be comprehended in a description of the man. This explanation is necessary in justice, first, to the reader, and then to many men, living and dead, whose labor went to the building of the newspaper. Some of the greatest journalistic achievements of the institution are given scant attention or none at all in this volume, and some of the *Times's* most brilliant servants are not even named. This was not done inadvertently, but because those things are another story. This one deals with a single extraordinary man who was, indeed, chief of the *Times*, but whose denial was swift and indignant whenever it was intimated that he was the whole newspaper.

This man, however, is worthy of study because he had certain qualities of mind and heart and was subjected to certain experiences that, apart from his craftsmanship, illuminate a phase of American history none too well understood yet important for its significance in our own time. Although he was in some ways unique, he was not an isolated phenomenon, but an integral part of a pattern of great magnitude and, perhaps, of a magnificence not yet fully revealed. To understand him, even incompletely, is to gain a clue to understanding, not merely the New York *Times*, but also many other men, institutions and events of the vastly significant period between Lincoln and the second Roosevelt.

It may not be important historically but the writer cannot forbear adding that study of this particular representative of that period proved to be exceptionally rewarding because of the impression left by the man upon his surviving colleagues. The biographer's labor was lightened immeasurably by the eagerness to be of assistance exhibited by everyone who had come into contact with the subject. That some of this was due to amiability may be granted; but for the most part it is attributable solely to a strong desire to see justice done to the memory of one whom they regard as indubitably a great man. As a monument to the human qualities of the publisher this enduring loyalty is more impressive than the New York *Times* itself.

Documentary sources are identified in footnotes as they are cited, but to name individually all who have assisted in the work would be to call the roster of the people who knew Mr. Ochs, both in New York and in Chattanooga. Special mention must be made, however, of Messrs. G. E. Govan and J. W. Livingood, who not only made available the results of their researches in the early history of Chattanooga, but were prodigal of their time and patience in answering questions, many of which must have seemed to them inept; and to Mrs. L. K.

PREFACE

Lang, of New York, for years Mr. Och's private secretary. To Colonel and Mrs. Milton B. Ochs, of Chattanooga, and to Mr. and Mrs. Arthur Hays Sulzberger, of New York, surviving members of Mr. Och's immediate family, thanks are due not merely for assistance in the work, but for many personal courtesies.

Finally, to every member of the staff of the New York *Times* with whom the writer came in contact: all thanks.

GERALD W. JOHNSON

Baltimore, January 1, 1946

AN
HONORABLE TITAN

A Discourse on Titans, Which the Gentle Reader May Skip as Preliminary, but Not Essential to the Story.

WHEN Adolph S. Ochs, publisher of the New York *Times*, died in 1935 the mayor of New York proclaimed a day of public mourning, the President of the United States sent a magnificent wreath, all over the continent the wires of the Associated Press were stilled for two minutes and tributes poured in from the illustrious of many nations.

But in the office of the *Times* someone said to a printer who had recently come to the paper, "You didn't know Mr. Ochs, did you?"

"Sure, I did," replied the printer. "He was the little man who went about turning off the lights."

The printer was wrong. The man with the habit of turning off the lights was Lucien Frank, head of the Purchasing Department, who bore a strong resemblance to the publisher except that he was lighter. The printer, therefore, had a better excuse than many who have equally misjudged the creator of the modern New York *Times*.

Ten years after his death men were still disputing over the significance of what he did. Many hold that it was magnificent, a few that it was sinister; but none denies that it had and still has significance. The institution that he created remains powerful in itself, but that is not all. It is possible that its chief importance may lie in the influence it has exerted on other newspapers and, indeed, on all forms of journalism; which would mean that its creator established more than a successful newspaper. As an eminent publisher Ochs is of interest primarily to the craft and there is every reason to believe that an eminent

[1]

publisher is all he aspired or intended to be; but, like every exceptionally strong man, he was and did much that he never contemplated being or doing.

Many of the charges that his detractors brought against him are obviously false; but many of the merits his friends ascribed to him he denied as vigorously and as sincerely as he denied the accusations; yet in some instances both praise and criticism were well founded. Although he might have repudiated both, the mayor's proclamation and the printer's remark about the lights were both justified, and their relative importance depends upon the point of view.

Adolph Ochs's active career extended from 1879 to about 1933. He lived until 1935 but for the last two years was comparatively inactive. The period of his vigor corresponds closely to the period of our national history in which the system of free competitive enterprise achieved its most spectacular results. The panic of 1873 swept away most of the wreckage of the Civil War period except in the South. It was a violent, unjust and, in many individual cases, disastrous means of clearing up the rubbish, but it was effective. After that convulsion the ground was unencumbered and the builders set to work with a will.

They achieved magnificently in the physical world, but they built more than material things. They built prestige and moral, as well as physical and financial, power. In the period between 1875 and 1929 the American businessman attained a lordlier status than businessmen have held anywhere else in the world with the possible exception of Renaissance Italy.

The Fuggers, who were not Italians, were feared and the Rothschilds, who were not Italians, were courted, but both were despised at the same time. Clive and Warren Hastings, Englishmen, were mighty potentates in India, but at home they were regarded with a supercilious eye. Roman Crassus' wealth made him the colleague of Caesar, but the methods by which Crassus obtained his wealth hardly qualify him to rate as a businessman. But the Venetian Doges were merchants and Cosimo de' Medici was a banker, yet the reverential awe with which they were regarded by their countrymen probably exceeded—albeit not by too much—the reverential awe with which the first J. Pierpont Morgan was regarded by his countrymen.

Furthermore, the stage on which the Florentines and the Venetians played their parts was far narrower than the continent-wide proscenium that framed the drama of the Rockefellers, the Vanderbilts, the Carnegies, the Harrimans and Hills, the Schwabs and Fricks and Huntingtons, the Dodges, Raskobs and Fords.

It was not primarily a matter of money. Great fortunes had been accumulated earlier—by the Astors, for example, and Peter Cooper and Stephen Girard—without the accretion of any such prestige as was acquired by the leaders of American business between the panic of '73 and that of '29. True, they accumulated hatred, as well, but a certain amount of hatred is the inevitable accompaniment of prestige and power. It does not appear that the sum total of detestation vented upon the Americans was disproportionate to the lordliness of their estate. They were denounced by muckrakers and fought by Populists and Bryanites, but they were rarely seriously threatened either in person or in property. Practically without exception they died in bed, attended by learned doctors, both of medicine and theology, and their children inherited without incident.

The Italian businessmen fared worse. Doges and Medici were frequently assassinated, sometimes to the accompaniment of loud applause, and it was not unknown for them to end on the block, with sequestration of their estates to follow. Yet others had conferred upon them the title of *Pater patriae*, by popular acclaim. To point out that American businessmen of the Imperial Age of business were hated therefore does not mean that they failed to dominate the imagination of the country. A scattered few fell afoul of the law and suffered penalties—although not the gallows—but others had conferred on them the title of Captain of Industry by popular acclaim. A vast number of Americans—in effect, indeed, a majority—firmly believed that the prosperity of the country rested in the hands of the great magnates and as sturdy a President as Grover Cleveland thought it quite in order to call on them to rescue the nation in time of trouble.

AN HONORABLE TITAN

Woebegone writing gentlemen, by no means all radicals, have fixed upon this period of our national history as singularly inglorious. Its opening phase Bowers described as "The Tragic Era." Mark Twain called it "The Gilded Age," in sour contradistinction to the golden age. Thomas Beer labeled its middle period "The Mauve Decade," alluding to a famous description of mauve as "pink trying to be purple" and thus throwing a cast of fraud over the time. Henry Adams educated himself to see in it the beginning of the process that was bound to result in the moral and political disintegration of the republic. Henry James found the United States of the period intolerable and indignantly shook its dust from his feet. None of these was a muckraker, and few among them rest under any imputation of harboring leftist tendencies. The genuine radicals, of course, were far more violent in their opinions.

Altogether the consensus seems to be that for half a century America worshiped in the temple of Mammon, nor can the most ardent patriot brush aside the mass of evidence supporting the theory. Stealing is common to every age and to all nations; but there is reason to consider the stealing that went on in this period in this country grandiose beyond all precedent. The fleet from Acapulco, for which Drake scoured the Spanish Main, carried only small change by comparison with the loot that various American buccaneers seized on dry land. Cynicism is as old as history, but it may be argued with some plausibility that it was unprecedentedly widespread in America at this time. It was exhibited more spectacularly when Caligula made his horse consul and when the Praetorians put up the empire at auction, but in those cases the populace was helpless in the iron grip of militarism and the cynics belonged to a tiny ruling class. Grant and Harding were the deliberate choices of the American people, designated by the votes of millions in free elections. Denial of the dignity of the individual is generally conceded to have reached its climax in French Louis's "*L'état, c'est moi,*" but is that any more complete than W. H. Vanderbilt's "The public be damned"?

Dishonesty, cynicism and arrogance add up to vulgarity; and when woebegone gentlemen denounce the Imperial Age of business as vulgar they are not to be gainsaid. Even were the voices of history silent, the architecture, painting, sculpture and domestic furnishings of the period bear eloquent testimony to the fact that it had its quota of shoddiness and fraud. It is futile to attempt to deny the accusations, for they are supported by sufficient proof; but it does not necessarily follow that the case is closed. Judgment should not be entered without a thorough examination of any mitigating and extenuating circumstances that may exist.

The American people are constantly referred to as conspicuously idealistic, but idealists are not commonly found as worshipers in the temple of Mammon. The American people would not have stayed there so long had there not been something about it other than the crudities that so offended the Henrys, Adams and James, and that aroused the fierce indignation of Mark Twain. Without questioning the existence of the crudities and without attempting to palliate their objectionable nature, one may yet inquire, what else?

It was an era of commercial and industrial giantism. The scale of operations in those days was so vast that the sheer scale affected the thought of the time. It applied to vices as well as virtues. In morals, perhaps, there is no essential difference between stealing a milk bottle and stealing a railroad, but the impact of the two operations on men's minds is widely different. No weakling can carry off a railroad and nothing can prevent humanity from admiring strength.

The strength of the nation increased prodigiously in the half century following the Civil War. Nothing like it had ever been seen in the world up to that time and it was confusing. None were more utterly confused than the men who were themselves performing the miracles. Andrew Carnegie has left a naïve and sincere record of his astonishment at his own achievement. Adolph Ochs was amazed by the New York *Times*. He was confident of success from the day he first came to New York, for he was aware of his own powers; but, like the Arabian fisherman who released the djinni from the bottle, he got enormously more than he had bargained for and to a certain extent it disconcerted him. In letters, in conversation with friends, occasionally in public statements, he repeatedly betrayed a very real anxiety over what he was going to do with this giant he had turned loose upon the world.

In that anxiety there is perhaps a hint of what it was about the men of the Imperial Age that enabled them to hold the imagination of the country in thrall for decades. Some of them were responsible. If all, if even a majority, had been so, perhaps the spell would not have been broken to this day. The tremendous shock of the last quarter of a century was not the crash of 1929, but the discovery, after the crash, that the then current giants of the business world had not the glimmer of an idea of what to do about it. They would not, or could not, assume responsibility and that finished their moral dominance.

It had not always been so. In 1869 there were business leaders sturdy enough to stiffen the wavering Grant, advising him to release the Treasury gold and smash Jim Fiske, and the market with him. In 1893 the elder Morgan, summoned to act by Cleveland, did act, throwing the resources of his banking house to the support of the Treasury at risk of heavy loss, but stopping the run on gold. People of such quality deserved confidence. Doubtless they received too much, more than was good for them or for the country; but they deserved some confidence.

The period produced all too many men who created nothing and flourished by snatching what others had created. They were so conspicuous that their lurid record tends to blind us to everything else and we are inclined to wonder at the quiescence of our fathers in an era of pillage. But it was not the pillage that fascinated our fathers, it was the production. The very name of Erie, for example, has come to stand for a long chronicle of crooked finance. Connoisseurs of sharp practice have found in its records almost perfect examples of nearly every variety of thimblerigging known to the market, and they have exploited those records endlessly. The result is that while everyone knows of the scandal of Erie, hardly anyone thinks of the great constructive labor that made the railroad worth looting.

The fact is that the giants were respected because they really were gigantic. It is interesting, perhaps ironical, that one of the clearest appreciations of this quality of the men of the Imperial Age was voiced by a public figure whom no one has ever accused of excessive admiration of Big Business. In an address at San Francisco in 1932 Franklin D. Roosevelt said:

The United States fearlessly, cheerfully, and, I think, rightly accepted the bitter with the sweet. It was thought that no price was too high to pay for the advantages which we could draw from the industrial system. The history of the last half century is accordingly in large measure a history of a group of financial Titans, whose methods were not scrutinized with too much care, and who were honored in proportion as they produced the results, irrespective of the means they used.[1]

If Adolph Ochs had been given to rhetorical flourishes, "All of this I saw and much of it I was" would have been a true comment from him on the Imperial Age of business. From 1896, when he acquired his New York newspaper, until his death he stood at the very center of things, occupying a post of observation superior, perhaps, to that held by any other American. He was constantly consulted and frequently deferred to by the nation's economic, political and intellectual leaders. His business was dealing in information and at that business he had no superior.

But he was a detached observer only in a special and limited sense. He sedulously avoided involvement in any business enterprises not directly connected with the production of his newspaper. Financially, he was detached, carefully detached in order to preserve his independence; but in every other sense he was thoroughly a man of his time. He had his niche along with the others. If Morgan is an acceptable symbol of the finance of the period, if Rockefeller typifies its merchants and Carnegie its industrialists, Ochs may be said to represent its traffic in ideas. He was, of course, a manufacturer, too; as Carnegie applied labor to iron ore to increase the value of the raw material, so Ochs applied it to paper and ink for the same purpose. But the paper and ink in a newspaper bear somewhat the same relation to the real product that the package does to other manufactured articles. The real

---

[1] *The Public Papers and Addresses of Franklin D. Roosevelt*, address at the Commonwealth Club of San Francisco, Vol. 1.

product is information, which the paper and ink carry to the purchaser. It is for this reason that a newspaper publisher may aptly be described as a merchant of ideas.

It is not necessarily a flattering designation. A conscienceless or incompetent merchant of ideas distributes goods every whit as poisonous as any dispensed by a dealer in adulterated food products. But this one was conspicuously conscientious and highly competent; it is a fair assumption, therefore, that the nature of his trade makes him a better, or at any rate a clearer, exponent of the spirit of his time than a man who dealt primarily in steel, or oil, or any other material thing.

Say this for the Imperial Age—whether impartial history finally writes it down as good or bad, it was interesting. It is difficult to believe that in any other period of equal length so many men so far overshot the marks they had set for themselves. It was a time of ambition realized and vastly over-realized; almost the only such time of which we know anything. The records of the race hold much material showing the effect upon populations of unexpected adversity, but there is little to show how men are shaped by the impact of equally undreamed-of success. That is one reason why the period from 1873 to 1929 in American history is puzzling. We have no adequate standards of comparison.

In some respects Adolph Ochs is not altogether a satisfactory archetype of his time. For one thing, he exhibited better taste in his private life than was shown by some of the conspicuously successful men among his contemporaries. He was never either swinish or gaudy, which is to his credit as a man, but does nothing to assist the biographer in writing an interesting narrative. Indeed, by comparison with the more lurid figures of the time a quiet, hard-working, family man is downright drab.

Again, his thought was somewhat in advance of that of most of his contemporaries. He fell into some of the errors of his time, but the more blatant he avoided, because he usually saw a little further ahead than did most of the leaders. He was a conservative, but only in the sense that he believed it wise to make haste slowly; he never believed in standing still, or in trying to go backward. But all this was essential to his position. A man cannot trade in ideas successfully unless he knows his stock in trade and is able to estimate pretty shrewdly the relative value of the ideas in which he deals. He was incessantly denounced by radicals and that is well known, for they did it publicly and as loudly as they could; what is not so well known is the frequency with which he was denounced by reactionaries, for they usually did it privately, although not less violently.

It would be a grossly false commentary on the time, however, to assume that, because a man was respectable personally and alert intellectually, therefore he was unrepresentative. It is true enough that some of the giants were neither and their spectacular doings have received a disproportionate share of attention; but more frequently the representative men of the period were correct in their private conduct and far from unaware of the world around them.

In one of his aspects, however, Ochs was the perfect exemplar of his time, at one with the greatest of the Titans who walked the earth in those days. This is his aspect as an idealist.

This is not a feeble attempt at paradox, although it must be granted that the statement, standing without a careful definition of terms, is misleading. The word "idealist" is used here in its original sense as meaning one who believes that the idea is greater and more important than its expression. The word is so commonly misused today that one hesitates to apply it, yet there is no adequate synonym. We have fallen into the habit of calling every humanitarian an idealist; we frequently refer to romantics as idealists; and in the minds of many the word has already come to mean merely a sentimentalist. But the man who believes in the idea, more than in its manifestation, is clearly an idealist; yet he is not necessarily either humanitarian, romantic or sentimental.

Nothing is more certain than that among the colossal figures of the Imperial Age of business most of the really huge ones were idealists in this sense. Even the most skeptical will grant it in the case of Andrew Carnegie, who left the proof not merely in his philanthropies but even more vividly in his writings; although the Laird of Skibo was pronouncedly humanitarian, romantic and sentimental. But what of the others, who built no libraries, mooned over no ancestral ruins and frankly found no sweet savor in the uses of adversity? What about Ochs, for example, or Morgan, the banker, Hill, the railroad builder, Wanamaker, the merchant, Ford, the manufacturer?

The term applies to every man of them and to many of their contemporaries. Perhaps one may exclude such persons as Daniel Drew, the speculator, and "Bet-You-a-Million" Gates, neither of whom built anything perceptible except reputations for sharp practice. For a long time Morgan was the ogre of the liberal and radical press and his physical appearance became the cartoonists' symbol for the embodiment of materialism and ruthless greed; yet Morgan once appeared before a Congressional investigating committee and argued, with patent sincerity and with an eloquence that took his critics aback, that his bank was less important as a financial institution than as visible, tangible proof of the idea that character is the only real security in the money market. Certainly he may have deceived himself; but there is no reason to doubt that he set the idea above the business.

John Wanamaker unquestionably believed that his millions were most significant as a measure of the soundness of his idea that fair dealing is the only basis of sound merchandising. Skeptical posterity may point out a number of other reasons for his success, but we are considering here only the man's own belief.

James J. Hill thought himself not altogether unworthy of his title of "the empire builder," for an empire, not merely a railroad, was what he set out to build and what, to do him justice, he did build. If the dust storms made his efforts disastrous in the end, that doesn't alter the fact that the man regarded his profit as the measure of the soundness of his idea.

One of the Rockefellers brought down a storm of objurgation and ribaldry upon his head by comparing the building of the Standard Oil Company to the cultivation of an American Beauty rose, brought to perfection by pinching off superfluous buds. The simile may have been ill chosen, but there was no affectation in his adoption of a poetic attitude toward a business enterprise. It was common enough at the time.

A DISCOURSE ON TITANS

Of course such claims, especially toward the end of the period, were sometimes advanced without a shred of sincerity, but that is no sufficient reason for assuming that they are always mere cant phrases, mouthed by men intent only on covering up their evil doings. Frequently they were nothing of the sort, but expressions of a man's profound belief, a belief profound enough to impel him to sacrifice profits rather than betray the idea. This is conspicuously true of Adolph Ochs. He made a large fortune out of his newspapers; but he repeatedly ignored opportunities to increase it, not because the opportunities were illegitimate, but because preoccupation with money-making outside the newspaper business would have interfered with his development of the idea of which the newspaper was the representation. In this he was unusual, but by no means in opposition to the spirit of his time. Money-grabbing characterized it, but money-grabbing has characterized all times; if it is unusually conspicuous in the age of the business Titans, one explanation is that there was more to grab. Emphatically, it was not the sole characteristic.

The difficulty is not in perceiving either the spaciousness or the villainy of the period. Both are clear and plain. The difficulty is in distinguishing between mere size and genuine power. Observers have pointed out, somewhat sardonically, that of the business enterprises that loomed gigantically in 1900 very few were still in existence in 1945, and have cited that as an argument against bigness, but it is a partial, not to say superficial, view. Size is no guarantee of permanence, but neither is it necessarily proof of impermanence. Size depends upon many factors, upon time, which flies, and upon extraneous circumstances, which may be irrelevant. Permanence depends upon the soundness of the idea, not upon the size of the institution.

Emerson's dictum that an institution is but the lengthened shadow of a man is capable of some interpretations that may not have occurred to the Sage of Concord. For instance, there is Daudet's picture of Tartarin, the absurd little Gascon. He climbed the Alps and stood upon the highest peak at dawn. Before him, to the west, a vast cloud bank filled the valley and as the sun behind him rose slowly it projected his silhouette upon the cloud bank so that for a moment the shadow of Tartarin hung portentously over half of Savoy.

It is beyond debate that among the apparent Titans of the Imperial Age of business were not a few who were in point of fact no Titans, but Tartarins, monstrously exaggerated by the time, which they had not calculated, and by circumstances, which they had not controlled. There were, however, some among them whose shadows did not vanish with the first change of the wind, because their size was not a trick of light and cloud; and these, in their respective fields of action, are still powerful influences. These were idealists in the real sense, men faithful to ideas that were not merely expedient at the moment, but profoundly true and therefore immutable.

The excuse for this book is the belief that Adolph Ochs was one of these; but no such belief is established by mere assertion. It must be supported by evidence; and that evidence, if you please, is the story that follows.

CHAPTER I

In Which a Soldier Comes Home from the Wars and a Boy Goes Out into the World.

WHEN the long bloodletting was plainly coming to an end in 1864 Captain Julius Ochs, late of the 52nd Ohio Volunteers, returned to his home and family in Cincinnati under the impression that the war was over. It was a delusion, of course, but it was nothing singular; it was shared by many of the men who had done the fighting, even up to some of the highest rank. For example, General William T. Sherman was as completely deluded as Captain Ochs. In a now famous letter written at this time he advised young men to go South, for since the sole issue that had divided the country had been abolished by force of arms, the region offered wonderful opportunities to young men with intelligence and willingness to work.

So it seemed to Captain Ochs, and he acted on the theory although, as a matter of fact, he was no longer a young man. On the contrary, he was verging into middle age and he had a wife and five children. But he needed opportunity, for the war had certainly not afforded it. He was no conquistador. All he brought from the battlefield was a magnificent set of whiskers and the consciousness of duty faithfully, if not especially brilliantly, performed. It was precisely what a million other men, in blue and in gray, carried with them as they trudged wearily back to pick up their shattered lives and try to make something comprehensible out of them again.

In point of fact, Captain Ochs had no business in the army in the first place. He was no more cut out to be a soldier than was Private Sidney Lanier, who had fought on the other side. They were mystics and dreamers, both, to whom the stern realities of military life were

[13]

harsh interruptions of the life of the spirit, the only true reality that either knew.

Yet in Julius Ochs there was certainly something that responded to the bugles, a fascination much more deep-rooted than the impulse that sets the street crowds cheering as a steel-tipped column swings by. It is shown not merely by the fact that twice he volunteered his services in time of war, but also, and more conclusively, by the fact that he sired a long line of soldiers. All the rest of the man's life militates against the notion that he was dazzled by military glamor; but he left to his descendants a quality that has carried them into uniform again and again to serve in every war the country has fought since 1846.

Basically, no doubt, it was a rigid sense of duty, inherited from generations of forebears whose characters were bent to the austere standards of the Old Testament. All available records indicate that Julius Ochs was gentle in the ordinary relations of life; but the testimony is unanimous that his probity was beyond question. A man cannot be completely honest if he is soft at the center; he may be tenderhearted, but there must be iron in his spine if he is to maintain his integrity through a long life.

In 1865, however, he assumed with General Sherman and Private Lanier as well as countless others who had borne arms that when the guns ceased firing the war ended. In that case, the South ought to be an excellent place for men of good will. Only by long and bitter experience were the soldiers to learn that when their war ended the politicians' war began, to last ten times as long and to engender ten times as much bitterness as the war fought with arms. When Julius Ochs took his family to Knoxville, Tennessee, he was moving back into the area of conflict where his qualities of mind and heart—his learning, his respect for rightful authority, and his profound faith in the reality of spirit surpassing that of matter—were least advantageous to their possessor. Tennessee, like the rest of the South immediately after the Civil War, needed the virtues of the frontiersman; Ochs offered those of the sage and found his offer neglected.

Born at Furth, in Bavaria, in 1826, he was educated in the Gymnasium in Cologne at the time when German education was establishing those standards of thoroughness which the rest of the world was to find hard to meet for the next century. He did not proceed to the University. Family tradition has it that he was denied admission because he was a Jew, although at that time anti-Semitism in Germany had reached nothing like the crazy intensity of later years. Perhaps it was this experience, or perhaps it was a touch of the revolutionary fever that was to flame up throughout Germany two years later; but something made him dissatisfied with Bavarian life and he turned to the New World.

He brought no money into America, but he did bring equipment that should have made him highly valuable to a new community. He was well grounded in French, Italian, Spanish and Hebrew, as well as German and English. He knew the classics and some mathematics. He had served his time in the army and was a competent drillmaster, presumably knowing something also of tactics and strategy. It was his military training that he first found of service, for hardly had he reached this country when the Mexican War began. Ochs promptly volunteered and before the end of the conflict was adjutant of his regiment, but the unit saw no service at the front.

Afterward he taught French in a girls' school at Mount Sterling, Kentucky, and disliked it. Why, it is now impossible to say, for in later years he showed marked talent as a teacher; but he remained only a short time, and then yielded to an impulse that was to betray him again and again—he went into business as a merchant. As will appear later, he actually had a marked talent for business of a certain type, but it was not the type of the independent enterprise. Every time he tried to set up his own establishment he failed, or achieved only a starveling success; not until many years later, when he came under competent administrative direction, did he show what he really could do in a business office.

The fact seems to be that Julius Ochs at this time was something of a wanderer, but his drifting had one fortunate result, when it carried him to New Orleans and brought into contact with a young countrywoman She was Bertha Levy, born at Landau, Rhenish Bavaria, and evidently a vigorous personality. She had become so heavily involved in the revolutionary movement of '48—when a student martyr of the movement was shot down in the street, she and some other schoolgirls ostentatiously dipped their handkerchiefs in his blood and preserved them as precious relics—that the police became too much interested in her and her family were advised to get her away before serious trouble followed. So she came to an uncle in Natchez, Mississippi, where she remained until the whole family came to America after the rising of '48 had been stamped out.

There is interest and possibly a significant sidelight on later history in noting the attitude of these young people. They were no halfhearted immigrants. When they came to America, they left Bavaria behind. It was not that they forgot the old country; on the contrary, they cherished its traditions and bequeathed a sentimental delight in them to their children; but from the moment they landed in the United States Bavaria was to them merely a land bathed in the golden glow of memory, not an earthly paradise to be regained as soon as possible. America was the homeland, the land of stern reality, the land commanding allegiance. This seems to have been the attitude of most newcomers at the time; not until long afterward did America come to be regarded by Europeans as a place in which to make a great deal of money rapidly and then to be deserted for a leisurely life in the old country.

Proof of a different attitude on the part of Julius Ochs and Bertha Levy is the intensity with which each adopted the local social and political coloration. Finding his adopted country engaged in war almost immediately after his arrival, Ochs assumed as a matter of course that his duty was to defend it. Finding her adopted country—which was Mississippi, not the United States—considering itself oppressed and threatened, Bertha Levy became as fiery a defender of its rights as any native. So deeply was she imbued with southern doctrine, indeed, that even marriage to a man whose sense of duty led him into the Union army could not change her. On one occasion she became embroiled with the Federal authorities by an attempt to run quinine across the Ohio River bridge at Cincinnati for delivery to the Confederates.

Perhaps this was not purely an expression of southern sympathies.

There may have been an element of mere humanitarianism in it, for in those days of relatively civilized warfare the act of the Federal authorities in making medical supplies contraband of war was regarded as pretty ghastly, even in the North. In any event, the fact remains that on one occasion the wife of Captain Julius Ochs placed a considerable quantity of quinine in a baby carriage, placed the current baby on top, and endeavored to cross the bridge. She was stopped; but warfare really was pretty civilized then, and her relation to a loyal officer, instead of ruining the officer, saved her, certainly from considerably difficulty and possibly from deportation across the lines.

Incidentally, the story was the occasion of a genial but stubbornly contested debate carried on by two of her sons for a lifetime. Who was the baby? Adolph persistently claimed the honor, much to the annoyance of George, who maintained that it was he who rode on the quinine. Chronology sets against Adolph in this case, for George was the younger and the presumption is that the smaller baby would have been chosen for the purpose.[1]

But in 1865 this was all over, and the hearts of men of good will overflowed with delight at the prospect of enduring peace. No one responded more fervently than Julius Ochs, a born wanderer, cherishing always the illusion that greener fields and fairer skies were around the next turn of the road, never wavering from the faith that men are essentially reasonable and that war is a betrayal, not the expression, of their true nature. To go back into the shattered land and assist in its rebuilding seemed to him therefore both morally right and practically reasonable.

Knoxville he had known before the war, and it was consistent with his idealistic spirit to wish to return there, not as an invading soldier, but as a peaceful merchant, to throw in his lot with the vanquished and to help them restore their shattered civilization. To Knoxville, therefore, he went, a mild man venturing into a bitter land, a reasonable man in a region recently torn by a hurricane of unreason and strewn with wreckage not of material things only, but also of ideals, of hope and of faith, a highly civilized man in a place where civiliza-

---

[1] The third brother, Colonel Milton B. Ochs, to the writer.

[17]

tion had to be rebuilt from the bottom up. It was gallant, in some respects it was superb; but the flat truth is that it was at the same time absurd. A greater misfit can hardly be imagined unless, indeed, it may be found in Sidney Lanier about the same time trying to make a living by playing the flute in Brooklyn.

Such casualties always follow a great war, and sometimes they are as heroic as anything done on the battlefield; but they gain no glory for their victims. On the contrary, derision is their lot more often than acclaim. Failure is failure, and an unsentimental world has no time to lose looking beyond the fact and seeking understanding in its causes. In the harsh, postwar world of Knoxville Julius Ochs was a failure, and if his failure was attributable in part to the loftiness of his ideals and the guilelessness of his character, such considerations did not alter the fact. By his own unaided efforts he could not support his family; and that was that.

There was one department of his life, however, in which the judgment of the world did not hold good. This undeniable failure as a merchant and businessman scored an equally undeniable success within the walls of his home. Proof of it is written across the life of his oldest son—in the lives of all his children, for that matter, but more impressive in this instance because of the character of that son. Adolph Ochs was to be brilliantly successful precisely in those ways in which Julius Ochs had failed most lamentably, but the younger man never despised his father. It was not mere filial piety. There was that in the old soldier which any intelligent man—and the son was one of the most intelligent men of his time—could not fail to recognize with respect, an element unrelated to business acumen, hence not affected by its presence or absence. Julius Ochs had character.

Within certain well-defined limits he was a tolerant man. In ordinary affairs he made no attempt to impose his ideas and opinions on his family. Strongly religious himself—he served for a time as an acting Rabbi for a leaderless congregation—he brought up his children in a religious atmosphere, but he did not interfere with the battle of ideas that raged constantly in his home.

her duty and she did it; but she also knew her mind and she spoke it. So did her children, and as long as it was a question of practicality or expediency no restraint was laid upon them.

But there was a limit. When the question was one involving what Julius Ochs considered right or wrong, the ordinarily mild and tolerant father could and would crash down with a "No!" that had the weight and effectiveness of the car of Juggernaut. Some of his notions of right and wrong seem rather outmoded today. For example, he would never have a playing card in the house, and the code of decorum prescribed for his daughters and the young men who attended them was austere by modern standards.[2] But a great deal of what he rigidly imposed upon his children has been sustained by the wisdom of all generations. Honor he demanded. Scrupulous financial integrity, truthfulness, courage—on these matters there was no debate and no tolerance of the slightest deviation from them. When right and wrong were involved, he was not merely to be respected, he was to be dreaded; and on such matters his word was law.

If Julius Ochs had been a succesful businessman would the distinction between moral worth and financial worth have been impressed so clearly upon the mind of his son? It is possible that the merchant's failure was not the loss that it seemed to the rest of the world; for that very failure, coupled with the man's rigid adherence to a high moral code, must have made the child familiar with a truth that many men acquire late in life and some never—that money is a poor measure of intrinsic worth. Julius Ochs was almost devoid of the acquisitive instinct; but his son lived and died knowing him for an honorable man. Therefore the son never fell into the error of confusing the acquisitive instinct with the thing that makes a man worthy of honor and trust.

In later years Adolph Ochs presented what many people regarded as an anomaly—a born money-maker with small respect for money. To say that he did not love money is going rather far. Certainly he liked it. He liked to have it, he liked to spend it, he had a keen appreciation of its power, he enjoyed accumulating it and he knew how.

[2] Colonel Milton Ochs, son, and Mrs. Iphigene Ochs Sulzberger, granddaughter, of Julius Ochs to the writer.

All these traits are characteristic of a money-lover. But his attitude toward money seems to be pretty well summed up in Lord Melbourne's comment on the Order of the Garter: "I like the Garter; there is no damned merit in it." Perhaps the reason is that he had had before his eyes from his youth up an example of merit not connected with money.

The influence of the mother on her son is more difficult to assess. There is no doubt whatever that it was important, but it was exercised so smoothly and unobtrusively that it can be isolated and identified only rarely.

The life of Bertha Levy Ochs is, in fact, curiously contradictory. The episode of the handkerchief dipped in blood and the episode of the quinine-running are separated widely in time and space. They would seem, therefore, to indicate certain consistent and persistent traits of character, a temperament fiery, impulsive, rash. Yet a long life after the Civil War—she died in 1908—flatly contradicts this impression. Far from being a firebrand, she was for decades a refuge and sanctuary for her son. From her he could always get calm and well-considered counsel in times of stress.

She regarded him somewhat doubtfully. The boldness and enormous size of his projects occasionally appalled her, and there was at least one moment when she was half convinced that he was mad.[3] But there was never any question of her complete devotion to him, or of her pride in his achievements. She was born with courage and as the years passed she acquired wisdom. Adolph Ochs was not the man to be easily guided by anyone's advice, but he valued a disinterested opinion; and from his mother he could always get a frank one, untainted by any ulterior motive and not weakened by a faint heart.

Nor is there much reason to doubt that she transmitted to him a share of her own temperament. Julius Ochs, with all his virtues, was not the man to go skating delicately and joyously over thin ice. The opinion of the newspaper world to the contrary notwithstanding, his son liked nothing better. Later on in this story the point will be em-

[3] It was when, already overwhelmed with debt, he proposed to take on half a million more to secure the New York *Times*. Mrs. Ochs actually consulted a trusted friend as to the advisability of taking legal steps to restrain him; but fortunately she was dissuaded.

phasized and supported by an impressive array of evidence; but for the moment let it go as a mere assertion. The girl who was fired by the revolt of '48, the girl who got a thrill out of defying the military power of the United States, bore a son who had something of her lordly contempt for appalling odds—a man who could see a roseate future in a devastated region, a man who could see fortunes in bankrupt newspapers, a man who could see a superb newspaper staff in a group of men who had failed, and a man who always dared back his own judgment against the opinion of the world.

All this, however, was far in the future in those early Knoxville days. At the time, all the evidence seemed to support the view of a cynical world that believed Bertha Levy, in the expressive southern phrase, "had driven her ducks to the wrong market" in marrying Julius Ochs. He was not a successful merchant. He was not, apparently, a competent businessman of any kind. If Bertha Levy had been endowed with no wisdom other than that of a smart sophistication she might have had every reason for despair. But somewhere, somehow, she had acquired the capacity to understand that an honorable man and a kindly man has a value that is not apparent to a cynical world. Her devotion to her superficially incompetent husband never wavered.

It is not unreasonable to assume that this, too, had its effect on the boy. It is beyond belief that he reasoned it out in childhood. It is possible that he never reasoned it out at all. But from the cradle he had before him the example of a human being who looked beyond superficialities and managed to understand the basic essentials of character. In after life Adolph Ochs proved himself conspicuously good at exactly that sort of penetration. It is easy to believe that one reason for his capacity was the example of a mother who had an extraordinary appreciation of the meaning of the Scriptural text, "Man looketh upon the outward appearance, but the Lord looketh upon the heart."

Julius and Bertha Ochs both died long ago, and not many who knew them survive. Even those must look back through the mists of memory that refract and distort the truth. It is hard, now, to obtain anything like a realistic appraisal of their characters. But it is not inconsistent with such facts as are established to infer that one gave to their son honor and the other gave him understanding. If that is true, the boy inherited a great legacy, even though he went out into the world without a penny and without an influential friend.

Men who have served through one or both of the total wars of the twentieth century find it difficult to focus their minds to the scale of the American Civil War. To say to them, whose eyes have seen the occupied countries and Germany in 1945, that Tennessee was devastated in 1865, is to risk rousing their incredulous amusement. When the war was over most of the houses in Tennessee were still standing. There had been no mass executions, no death marches, no deportations of slave labor. As compared with, say, Poland when the Germans were expelled, Tennessee was hardly scarred.

But the effect of a catastrophe is measured by relative values. The Civil War was by far the bloodiest and most ferocious we had experienced up to that time and the shock it administered to its victims was proportionately great. A whole way of life had collapsed and the soft illusions with which men are accustomed to pad the sharp edges of reality had been ruthlessly stripped away. Tennessee was facing life in the raw and the bitterness of disillusionment depends not at all upon the size of the disaster that brought it about.

Not merely the economy of the South but its whole social organization had been dislocated, and for the first year or two the competition among men was not for wealth and power, but for bare survival. In such a situation people's point of view changes. The soft amenities lose importance and what is necessary is accepted—matter-of-factly by the sturdy, with lamentations by the weak, but accepted by all because there is no escape.

Today, in a more stabilized environment, the statement that Adolph Ochs went to work to earn his own living at eleven may give a somewhat false impression. He had been born March 12, 1858, which means that he went to work in 1869. In the year 1869 in Tennessee attitudes were different. Even then public opinion did not exactly approve of child labor, but if necessity forced a boy to go to work, he got more praise than pity. Young Adolph was not especially articulate and it is doubtful that he thought things over very much or very clearly—what boy of eleven does? But there is every reason to believe that he never for a moment regarded himself as the pitiable victim of malignant fate.

Why should he? Nearly everybody around him was poor, nearly everybody worked hard, and if things were a little worse for the Ochs family than for the average household they were not much worse. The whole region was a victim of the war and only the weak whined about it. The strong accepted it and did what they could; and Adolph Ochs was among the strong.

The best evidence of this is the nature of the memories he preserved from those years. There is no record that any slight or insult clung to his mind although he must have encountered some; yet he did not forget them because he was imperceptive for he remembered clearly innumerable jests and absurdities and apparently he never forgot one single act of kindness that came his way. The tale of the breeches is a case in point. At some time during this period the state of Adolph's trousers, his only pair, became lamentable, but with six healthy children—another had arrived since the family left Ohio—to be clothed there was not much that his mother could do about it. A kindly neighbor, observing the situation, took a pair that her husband had discarded and cut them down to the boy's size, to his immense satisfaction.

The passing years brought wealth and power to the boy, but misfortune to the neighbor. Her husband died, and word came to Adolph Ochs in New York that she was having a hard struggle. At once the cashier of the New York *Times* received orders to mail a handsome check to her monthly and charge it to Ochs's account. The woman outlived him, but by his specific command to his heirs that pension remained a charge on his estate until her death. "That account ran for the better part of half a century," one of them said later. "It was probably the most expensive pair of pants in history."

The job he took was that of a carrier boy on the Knoxville *Chronicle*, and it is possible to speak with certainty about its effect on him because he has left a written record of it. Sixty-five years later he sent a message of greetings and salutations to the carrier boys of the Chattanooga *Times* and, after expressing pride that he had begun his newspaper career as a member of their guild, he continued,

"I had to appear at the office at five o'clock in the morning. The paper came from the press unfolded and the carrier boys had to fold the papers by hand. There were fifty papers to be delivered on my route, and I had to walk nearly four miles to deliver them—then home to breakfast, and thence to school. For this task I received twenty-five cents a day ($1.50 per week)."

During much of the school year it is dark and cold at five o'clock in the morning. For a small boy to crawl out of bed and go shivering into the blackness, with a four-mile tramp ahead and then the school day to follow was formidable. His fingers and toes must have been numb many a morning; but frost-nipped ears and weary legs were not what he remembered. What he called the "notable recollection" of that time was "that Father Ryan, a Catholic priest at Knoxville, who, perhaps, had been a carrier boy in his youth, gave me two dollars as a Christmas present." The pain and fatigue slid off his mind, but the kindness stuck.

Like everyone else, Adolph Ochs had his ups and downs. More than once he came close to despair, but his life, taken as a whole, seemed to him in his old age an exceptionally good one. As humanity goes, he was a happy man; and perhaps this letter to the carrier boys explains why. With curiously few exceptions, the disappointing and disagreeable he could forget, but a kindness never. If an old man, looking back over the years, sees his life mainly as a list of remembered kindnesses, why should he repine? No matter how full of trouble that life may have been, if he recalls the bright spots vividly and the bad ones dimly, if at all, he will certainly develop a mellow serenity, as this one did until great trouble and physical illness descended upon him together and almost extinguished his bright spirit.

Six years the boy worked in Knoxville, first as carrier boy, then as office boy, then as printer's devil, apprentice and finally journeyman. This service was interrupted once, briefly, by a job as clerk in a drugstore and once for a period of nearly a year which he spent in Providence, Rhode Island, where a relative kept a grocery in which Adolph worked as "cash boy" by day and by night attended a business college. There is singularly little in the records about this experience. It is a reasonable inference, however, that he learned at least the rudiments of accounting and perhaps something of business practice in general.

Much more vivid was his recollection of learning the printer's trade. This, he used to say, he acquired rather by accident than by resolution. At fourteen Adolph definitely abandoned school and took a full-time job in the *Chronicle* office, where his duties had to do with running errands and sweeping up rather than with the mysteries of the craft. According to his own account, he was free to leave around midnight, but his way home lay alongside a cemetery and the prospect of passing a cemetery at midnight so terrified him that he preferred to hang around the office a couple of hours longer until one of the printers, who lived in the same direction, came off duty and could walk along with him.

During this idle period, more to kill time than for any other reason, he began to practice setting type, working from the case, of course, for this was long before the day of the typesetting machine. One may doubt that this was the primary reason, for the boy was already ambitious, but perhaps the cemetery had something to do with it, and it is an entertaining yarn. After all, if ghosts could inspire resolution in a fainthearted Prince of Denmark, why not in a stouthearted proletarian of Tennessee? At any rate, Adolph's left hand soon learned the art of holding the stick lightly, but firmly, while his right hand darted over the boxes with increasing speed and accuracy. At seventeen he was regarded as a competent printer capable of holding down a man's job and worth a man's pay. He worked briefly in Louisville as an apprentice and came back to Knoxville as a full-fledged printer.

A printer, in 1875, may have been no more adept but he certainly was more versatile than are many holders of Typographical Union cards today. Printing, like everything else, has undergone a high degree of specialization. Many a modern linotype operator, skillful at the keyboard, couldn't make up a form to save his life. But in 1875 in

[25]

a small-town newspaper shop a good printer had to be able to turn his hand to anything. By current standards equipment, even in the best shops, was crude. To make up a page with hand-set type, brass rules and electrotypes backed with wood which swelled and shrank with every change in the weather; to transfer the forms successfully to a flat-bed press; to build up the cylinder carrying the paper to meet the inequalities in the form so as to secure an even impression; to adjust the rollers—frequently molded in the shop of a mixture of molasses and glue—so as to distribute the ink evenly, a man had to to be a great deal more than a typesetter. Indeed, he had to be a sort of merger of the best features of a juggler, a tinker and plastic surgeon; and when the machinery jammed in spite of his best efforts, it was regarded as a help if he had the arms of a wrestler and the vocabulary of a mule skinner as well.

Physically, Adolph Ochs was not large—he stood five feet seven and in youth was slender—and his facility in objurgation was never conspicuous, but in all other respects he was a good printer.[4] His hands, of course, soon lost their cunning after he left the case for an office desk. For fifty years if he had tried to dump a stickful of hand-set type he would almost certainly have pied it. But a good printer's eye is as important as his hand, and Ochs's eye never lost its skill. To the end of his life he could stand over an imposing stone—"make-up table" to the modern generation—and tell at a glance whether or not the page was right.

This seems a small matter in a giant newspaper organization, but it may have contributed more to Ochs's success than is generally recognized. Both his papers, the one in Chattanooga as well as the one in New York, were known in the craft for their handsome dress—always conservative, but always smart. Efforts to maintain typographical ex-

[4] This is not mere inference, but the unanimous testimony of four practical printers, Charles F. Hart, for many years mechanical superintendent of the *Times*, William A. Penney, long foreman of its composing room, and the two men occupying corresponding positions on the Chattanooga *Times*, I. G. Gardner and J. Harry Street. As anyone who knows the craft will agree, old printers may stray from strict veracity on other things, but they will not call a man a good printer unless he is good.

A SOLDIER COMES HOME

cellence certainly were not discouraged by knowledge in the composing and press rooms that the big boss was himself a practical printer. There was no need to tell him—if a page was right, he knew it, and if it was not right he knew it twice as well.

Once in his latter years, when the *Times* was an enormous organization with a thousand problems pressing upon its head—this, let the lay reader understand, is a tale primarily for printers—he spent hours with his composing-room foreman experimentally filing off the serifs on certain head type, to the end of picking up half a character to the line without destroying the beauty of the type. They did it, too, and had mats cut to their special order.[5] For the benefit of the layman it may be explained that the serif is the tiny projection at the top and bottom of printer's type; and the point of the story is that a man who paid attention to the serifs had an extraordinary eye for detail.

In the small world of Knoxville newspaperdom everyone knew everyone else. By the time he had become a full-fledged journeyman printer Adolph Ochs was personally acquainted with everyone in any way connected with a newspaper in the town, including one remarkable character destined to play an important part in his life. This was a tall, rawboned Scot with a beard rivaling Julius Ochs's own, and with a war record more imposing. J. E. MacGowan had seen plenty of hard service and had risen to the rank of colonel before the end of hostilities. In the post-Civil War South many an editor was called "colonel" although he had never smelled powder; but MacGowan won his title in the service of the Union.

Like many newspaper men he was something of a rolling stone, having worked all over the country, and in the late seventies he found himself in Knoxville as an editorial writer for the able but bitter and vindictive "Parson" Brownlow, stormy petrel of Tennessee politics in the Reconstruction period. MacGowan was already in middle age and Ochs was only seventeen, but in spite of the disparity in years a strong liking, based on mutual respect, grew up between them.

To this pair in 1878 came a third Knoxville newspaper character,

---

[5] William A. Penney to the writer.

one Franc S. Paul, with a scheme for starting a new venture in Chattanooga. By one account Paul went ahead and brought the other two in as employees; by another, they went together in partnership. Be that as it may, the year found them all in Chattanooga, working on a paper called the *Dispatch*, which wavered along for a few months and then folded under them, leaving MacGowan and Ochs stranded.

So stated, the incident seems of small importance, and measured on a scale no larger than that of the history of Chattanooga it was microscopic; but in the life of Adolph Ochs it bulked tremendously. He was not quite nineteen. It was his first venture into business on his own. It was a smash. There are all the elements of tragedy utterly black. Ten years later he could laugh in the face of worse crises, but at nineteen every setback is disaster and a real disaster is horrible beyond utterance.

Perhaps it was worse on young Ochs than it would have been on the average youth, simply because he was so supremely confident when he set out. He was certain that he would make the fortune of the whole family, for whom he felt responsible. He wrote home a letter on the stationery of the *Dispatch* which expresses his attitude with singular clarity. After congratulating his mother on her birthday, he continued, "May God spare you to see Nannie married to a millionaire; George President of the U.S.; Milton a Senator; Ada a famous authoress and Mattie a successful merchant or large salaried Rabbi's daughter [wife?]. As to myself my prayer is that I may soon be able to make for you all a comfortable home where want is unknown and send my brothers and sisters on their different roads rejoicing."[6]

Instead of accomplishing that, he didn't even have a job himself and all his generous hopes were turned into mockery. A generous man's own losses may not bother him much, but a sudden realization that he can do nothing at all for those he loves is different. It hurts damnably. Chattanooga soon forgot that there had ever been such a paper as the *Dispatch*; but its collapse was vivid in Adolph Ochs's memory for more than fifty years.

[6] Ochs to his mother, December 3, 1877. Ochs MSS.

A SOLDIER COMES HOME

There is a tradition that he would have returned to Knoxville, but didn't have money enough to buy a ticket and was ashamed to ask the family for it. So he turned his hand to whatever work he could find, and by the time he had money for transportation he had fallen in love with the place and didn't want to leave.

CHAPTER II

Interlude Devoted to the Chaos That Was Tennessee in the Postwar Period.

PETERSBURG, in Virginia, was the Civil War equivalent of Stalingrad, but Chattanooga occupied a position fairly comparable to that of Cologne eighty years later. It was a city of strategic importance, captured early, held bitterly, wrecked in turn by the great guns of both armies. If the city was much less thoroughly smashed than Cologne it was because the artillery of the time was relatively weak, not because any effort had been spared to reduce it.

But from the economic, as well as from the military, standpoint Chattanooga's position was strategically important. It is located at the extreme southeastern point reached by the Tennessee River. The suburbs of the modern city stretch across the Georgia line and both North Carolina and Alabama are near it. Chattanooga lies in a roughly circular valley surrounded by a ring of mountains broken at three important points only—where the river enters and leaves the valley and at the Rossville Gap. Two railroads enter Chattanooga along the banks of the river; all the others come in through tunnels.

Water transportation has been so largely superseded by railroads in this country that it is now hard to comprehend the importance once attached to such a river as the Tennessee. In the beginning railroads were not regarded as systems of transportation in themselves, but as adjuncts to the much more important waterways. They were rather in the nature of portages. The very name of the first important railroad in the country reflects this view. It is the Baltimore and Ohio and it was built to compete with the Erie canal in carrying goods and passengers between the inland river system and tidewater. The builders were aiming, not for the state, but for the river Ohio; once they could tap that river, they thought there would be no need to go farther, for they would be over the mountain barrier and waterways would take care of the rest.

What the Ohio was to middle Atlantic ports, the Tennessee was to southern ports. Both Charleston and Savannah regarded rail connection with some point on the Tennessee as access to the vast Mississippi system, and the river came closest to those ports at the huge, irregular curve called Moccasin Bend. Before the Civil War, therefore, a line had been driven across the mountains from Atlanta to reach the river "at the point nearest Rossville, Georgia," which point was the present site of Chattanooga. By the time it was completed, another line was being built from the west, traversing the length of the state of Tennessee from Memphis, and a fourth from the north. Naturally, they aimed to link their termini with that of the line from the coast, and thus Chattanooga became a railroad center.

But geography was not its only natural advantage. In the immediate neighborhood were coal, limestone and huge beds of iron ore. It was still the age of iron, for steel for only beginning to come into the dominant place. The Chattanooga ore was excellent for the production of iron and at the time few paid much attention to the fact that its high sulphur content made it less desirable for the production of steel than the ores around Birmingham and those near Lake Superior. At the close of the Civil War men with foresight saw here a great deal more than merely a shattered village once inhabited by three thousand souls. At the time "manifest destiny" was a term still in good repute and it seemed the manifest destiny of Chattanooga to be a great manufacturing city, probably the greatest in the South.

These factors combined to bring to the place in the decade following the close of the war a population of a special type. The advantages of Chattanooga were real, but they required exploitation and development. Rewards were within sight, but only for the energetic and skillful. It was not a place in which a man might take his ease, not a comfortable environment for the slothful. It was a city *in posse*, not *in esse*, and the irresolute, the pessimistic, the fearful were not merely useless, they were handicaps upon the driving force that alone could realize the possibilities of the region.

Chattanooga was in the South, but hardly of it. The plantation system had never extended into the mountainous regions between the Potomac and Alabama and the Negro population was comparatively small. The disagreement with the Secessionists that caused West Virginia to break away entirely prevailed to some extent throughout the Appalachian massif and East Tennessee furnished many troops to the Union armies. Chattanooga for some years before 1861 had had at least one frankly Abolitionist newspaper. Once hostilities began the city became a prime Federal objective, falling in 1863 and although the Confederates held the ring of mountains around it and for a time had it cut off, they never actually regained the town. Throughout the long series of desperate and bloody engagements that made every foot of the surrounding country a battleground, most of the Union attacks were launched from Chattanooga.

Thus it was familiar to more northern than southern soldiers and when the war was over many of them, attracted by the resources of the country, came back—witness MacGowan. In 1878 a local census showed that of the 11,500 inhabitants of the town less than 800 were natives. The others represented all of the states save four and nineteen foreign countries.[1] The intellectual climate of the place therefore was distinctly not that of a typical southern town.

It had, indeed, much of the aspect of the frontier. For one thing, the number of young men, such as Ochs, come to seek their fortunes was probably disproportionately large. For another, the place was growing with great rapidity—nearly 400 per-cent increase in thirteen years is eloquent of that. If it was not as uproarious as some of the western cow towns twenty years later, it was yet very distinctly on the lively side. The code duello had long been repudiated by law and, in principle, by public opinion, but in practice resort to gun- or knife-play to settle private disputes was commonplace. At least twice Adolph

[1] The information regarding Chattanooga in this and the succeeding chapter comes largely from the researches of G. E. Govan and J. W. Livingood, especially from "Adolph S. Ochs: The Boy Publisher," a paper published by them in the East Tennessee Historical Society Publications, No. 17, 1945.

Ochs's ebullient brother, George, became involved in a fracas of the sort,[2] and it was not uncommon for citizens of weight and dignity, as well as young bloods, to go armed.

The distinctive characteristic of the Chattanooga of the time was, however, its vitality. It was alive to the fingertips. Crowded, unsanitary, ugly and lawless, it was nevertheless endowed with a lusty life that tingled in every fiber. Men believed in themselves and in the future. They had implicit faith in their own strength and skill to accomplish pretty much anything they chose to accomplish.

In this the city reflected the spirit of the time in the North and West, rather than in the South. The triumphal march of the tobacco and textile barons was not to begin for twenty years. Birmingham as yet was no more than a country village. Atlanta, even more completely ruined than Chattanooga, was just beginning to pull itself together. The Tennessee city had a long lead over most of its neighbors, Atlanta excepted, and few of its citizens doubted that it was destined to maintain and increase that lead.

It was both a bad and a good environment in which to spend one's youth. To a boy conscious of maturing powers it was tremendously stimulating. All the world seemed to lie open to conquest by strong men. Hardened and toughened by war, they were not to be daunted by physical obstacles. Spanning rivers, rending mountains, and heaving huge masses of masonry into the sky for great buildings were tasks precisely to their liking. Energy, skill and determination applied to the natural riches around them were producing wonderful results and few doubted that they would produce every desirable thing.

If there was little reflection and less caution in the period, what of it? There was a continent to be subdued and subjugators are not often cautious, reflective men. There was more than a touch of barbarity in it all, but no philosopher, dismayed by the ruthlessness, the waste, both human and material, the crass materialism, the contempt for beauty and the ignorance of all the more subtle values of existence, has as yet demonstrated that this particular sort of job can be done in any other way. The conquest of a continent is accomplished by sweat-

---

[2] He describes them with gusto in his account of the family history.

ing men, not by perfumed men, nor even by sedentary thinkers, wrapping their meager frames in hooded gowns against the cold.

America was on the march. That part of it that took place in geographical space has received so much attention from historians, novelists, poets and playwrights that every literate American knows something of the vast surge across the plains, over the Rockies and down to the Pacific beaches. But part of it was not geographical. Even the people who stayed in a place like Chattanooga were on the march, sharing an advance in technology no less spectacular than the trek of the western pioneers.

Iron was the basis of an industrialism that soon began to proliferate amazingly. By 1878 there were nineteen concerns engaged in the metal trades; but there were also sixteen woodworking outfits and two carriage and wagon makers, using both wood and metal. There were three brick kilns, an ice manufacturer, three "flouring mills," two textile mills and two cotton compresses.[3] Ten steamboats of from 150 to 300 tons' burden operated on the river, as well as countless barges and flatboats. Much of the lumber that supplied the woodworking factories, however, was floated down the river in rafts.

The river was still the great transportation factor, the railroads as yet being merely supplementary to it. Freight was already moving to the rail lines, but for a dozen years yet the river was to dominate the imaginations of Chattanoogans. It was—and is—a majestic stream, swinging, just above the city, in a mighty curve southwest and then southward to the very foot of Lookout Mountain, then turning northward again on its long journey to the Ohio and so to the Mississippi, inclosing a peninsula shaped like an Indian moccasin, from which comes the name, Moccasin Bend. But it was an unreliable river, given to sudden rages, especially in the spring when snows were melting and rains were heavy in the Appalachian mountains where it rose. At such times it would inundate the country for miles and Chattanooga, perched on rising ground somewhat above the general level of the valley, would become an island, except, indeed, for the lower part of the town, which would be submerged.

[3] Govan and Livingood, op. cit.

Below Chattanooga there were rapids which at low water closed navigation except for the lightest craft. For nearly a century a perennial political issue was the city's struggle to procure government aid to improve navigation on the Tennessee, a struggle won only many years after Och's departure from the town, when the Tennessee Valley Authority undertook its vast project. But in 1878 effective aid was far in the future, a roseate dream, whose realization was the aspiration of all patriotic citizens.

Thus from the standpoint of an active and vigorous young man the Chattanooga to which Adolph Ochs came had nearly everything. For the present there was great and rapidly increasing business activity, which meant opportunity for the skillful and energetic; for the near future, there were deposits of iron ore and coal as yet hardly touched and vast forests close by; finally, in the more distant future there was the great dream of the opening of the river which optimists were convinced would eventually make Chattanooga a port attainable by ocean-going vessels. Present opportunity and an apparently unlimited future —what more can a young man ask?

In the case of this particular city, however, there was an additional appeal to men sensitive to anything beyond material interests. The country surrounding the town is extraordinarily impressive, both for its scenic beauty and for its historical interest. Lookout Mountain looms above the city on one side, Missionary Ridge on the other. Each was the scene of desperate struggles during the Civil War, while across the river is Walden's Ridge, also fought over. Modern Chattanooga is far better groomed than the little town of 1878, but even today what clings to the memory of the ordinary visitor is not the city itself but the superb outlook from the mountains around it. Hardly anywhere else in America can the spectator stand with so much and such dramatic history unrolled like a map before him. Chattanooga was capable of arousing in its young men a pride not connected with material things.

As a matter of fact, however, it is arguable that Chattanooga's interest in material things, that is to say, in commerce and industry, may have contributed to its spiritual health at this period. So stereotyped

is our way of thinking that an accusation of materialism against a city
—or a man—is condemnation out of hand. We do not stop to consider
how many immaterial forces there are quite as destructive as love of
fine raiment and sumptuous fare. Hate, for example, is immaterial.
Vindictiveness, spite, suspicion and intolerance belong to the realm of
spiritual things—at least they are not material. To sink into materialism when one might do better is deplorable; but to cling to materialism when one might do worse is a very different matter.

Time is indeed of the essence in this case. It was a dozen years after
the close of the Civil War, and those years had written in the South
one of the blackest chapters in the history of American government.
The initial mistake was made in Washington, when all the hatreds
that four years of war had impounded against Abraham Lincoln burst
upon the head of his luckless successor, and a peace of vengeance, not
of reason, was imposed upon the defeated. But that was merely the
initial error. Ruthlessness had its usual effect. It brought to light and
developed prodigiously every evil quality southerners possessed, and
for ten years the unfortunate country was racked by a second war,
not of Federals against Confederates, but of brutality against vicious-
ness, a war in which all concerned were defeated from the start.

Tennessee, on the northern fringe of the Confederacy, did not suffer
the extreme debauchery of government to which some of the states
were subjected, but it had trouble enough, at that. Parson Brownlow,
a man of wrath, provoked a reaction in which respect for legal forms
and orderly procedure suffered heavy damage; and the state was visited
by its quota of the carrion birds who follow the battle to despoil the
dead and wounded. Over most of the South, and over a large part of
Tennessee, politics absorbed a disproportionate part of all attention
and all energies; and politics had largely degenerated from the science
of the conduct of public affairs into a contest of spites and animosities,
based in part upon personalities and in part upon certain notions which
the heat of passion had solidified into dogma. Political discussion in
the South was no longer a battle of ideas but, at best, an intellectually
sterile threshing over of old straw and, at worst, a contest among crooks
over the division of the swag.

Chattanooga did not escape all of this; but Chattanooga could not devote all its time and energy to the sort of thing with which much of the South including much of Tennessee was preoccupied. After all, Chattanooga had coal to mine, had iron to extract, had plows and boilers and steel rail to fabricate, had timber to saw into lumber, and lumber to convert into doors and sashes, furniture, wagons and carriages. Chattanooga, busy with material things, had less time to spend hating the man next door and contriving his ruin.

In Chattanooga, if a man was a good wheelwright he was valuable, and it was not practical to cast him out because he came from Pennsylvania, or, perhaps, from Bohemia. Tailors were too badly needed in Chattanooga to reject a good one because he happened to be a Jew. If a brickmason came from Alabama, or a carpenter voted the Republican ticket, the need for artisans was too great to permit such considerations to be dominant.

This, without doubt, was one of the good effects of materialism. The inhabitants of the town brought with them all their old prejudices and they did not suddenly turn into liberals; but they did turn into materialists and the prejudices had to be toned down far enough not to interfere with business. But the population was so cosmopolitan that the prejudices tended to cancel out and the net effect was toleration. Race and religious antagonisms were not obliterated, but they were diluted to the point at which they became relatively innocuous.

Anti-Semitism no doubt existed but it was more in the nature of an idiosyncrasy than a social poison. Chattanooga indubitably had people who regarded Catholics as idolaters and Episcopalians as pseudo-Catholics; while others looked upon Baptists as fetish-worshipers and Methodists as mere variants of Baptists. If there were some who deplored the existence of Jews, what of it? When Baptists and Episcopalians, Catholics and Methodists, were likewise deplored in one quarter or another, the Jews had no reason to feel that they were singled out for any special dislike. It was a case reinforcing Voltaire's observation that England, with only two religions, would have been rent by civil war, but with forty everybody hated so many others that they all got along quite amicably together.

In this, Chattanooga was a microcosm of the nation. America was going through the same experience. The wave of materialism that inundated the country in the half century following the Civil War doubtless justified all the lamentation it has occasioned for it did produce many ghastly effects, not all of which have been eliminated from American life even yet. But there is a possibility, indeed a strong probability, that in some ways it had a prophylactic effect. If it discouraged the development of philosophy, it also discouraged the development of fanaticism. If it rendered American culture somewhat meager and barren, it made it at the same time an unfavorable field for the development of the more extreme forms of racial and religious hatreds. To refuse to hate one's neighbor merely because the fellow happens to be useful is, it must be granted, a low motive; but if it stops one from cutting his throat, why, his throat remains uncut, and as regards the maintenance of public order that is the great objective.

The materialism of the last third of the nineteenth century did do something toward pulling together a nation rent by civil war. It did do something toward reinforcing the old American doctrine that a man's value to society is to be measured by his work and not by his race or creed. All this was clearly understood by the men of the time. What they did not understand was that this same materialism was also setting up false standards that would lead to collapse half a century later. We, on the other hand, having witnessed the collapse, find it hard to remember the reverse side of the shield, the only side that the men of 1878 could see.

Thus we find it difficult to comprehend the almost religious enthusiasm of men engaged in setting up an iron foundry or a textile mill in Chattanooga, or, on a larger scale, a John D. Rockefeller engaged in organizing the oil business. For many years, at least in radical and liberal circles, Rockefeller was the national symbol of hypocrisy because he did not hesitate to assert publicly his belief that the hand of God had led him to the accumulation of the largest private fortune ever known up to that time. Yet he believed because he had evidence —not as conclusive as he thought it, but yet evidence—that his activi-

ties tended to contribute to the moral as well as the material betterment of mankind.

So it was in Chattanooga when Adolph Ochs came to town. Men
worked hard because they worked happily. They were making money,
but they believed in all sincerity that they were making a great deal
more than money. They were finding a way out from the despair that
had lately overwhelmed the country. They were building a city, but
they were also rebuilding a way of life based, as they thought, on
broader and firmer foundations than had underlain the old one. It
was profitable work but it was also, as they saw it, honorable work, a
contribution to the general welfare as well as their own. This inevitably
gave them an uplift that sometimes ran into moral arrogance; but it
also sustained them through herculean labors and it was the best possible inoculation against despair.

All the remainder of his life Adolph Ochs looked back upon these
years in Chattanooga as among his best and the city itself he held in
an affectionate memory that the passage of time merely mellowed and
never dimmed. He had had plenty of misery in these years. They
brought him closer to total ruin than he ever was again. They had
brought him much personal sorrow, as well as happiness. They were
laborious years. But they were youth. He was a young man in a young
city in a young era, and any man who has had that experience can say
Et ego in Arcadia, even though to the skeptical a smoky, noisy industrial town may seem a strange representation of meads of asphodel.
But when life is buoyant, when the future is bright, when one's task
is not merely to one's liking but also definitely service to the public
good, why, noise and smoke are trifles to be laughed off and the grimi-
est city can be as fair as any meadow conjured up in a poet's dream.

CHAPTER III

In Which a Man, Too Soon Matured, Masters His Environment but Succumbs to His Own Enthusiasm.

I

IT MAY not be literally true that he lacked money to get out of town, but the collapse of the *Dispatch* unquestionably left Adolph Ochs in a tight place. It is by no means beyond belief that he literally couldn't get away, for the monetary system of the United States was still extremely rigid, and in such a place as Chattanooga, with a rapidly growing population and a rapidly expanding business, currency was always at a premium. Men of considerable wealth frequently found themselves pressed for cash; for that matter, the whole country suffered recurring "bank panics" until means were devised for introducing elasticity into the currency. There is nothing inherently incredible, then, in the story that when the paper went down Ochs, and probably MacGowan too, was left literally without the price of a ticket to Knoxville.

But even if it is true, the story carries not quite the significance that would attach to it today. Lack of cash was not then the evidence of careless improvidence it has since become; it was more annoying than embarrassing, because it happened constantly to all kinds of people. Young Ochs doubtless was irritated and disgusted by the unfortunate end of his adventure, but there is no indication that he was really cast down. All the incident meant was that he had to find something to do and find it quickly.

The immediate problem was solved in a way that is not quite clear— Ochs became "receiver" for Paul's share in the *Dispatch*.[1] Apparently

[1] Govan and Livingood, *op. cit.*, also an unpublished manuscript by Edward H. Edwards, "Adolph S. Ochs as I Know Him," hereinafter referred to as Edwards MS.

this was an informal arrangement as the paper did not go through bankruptcy proceedings and, if it had, a minor could not have been appointed receiver. Probably it was simply an agreement that Ochs was to collect any money that was due Paul while the latter was busy elsewhere. At any rate, the work was merely a stopgap and did not last very long; but it is worthy of mention as illustrating the confidence that older men had in this boy of nineteen. It was confidence in his integrity, of course, but it was also confidence in his common sense; Paul was certain that Adolph would not steal the money but he was also certain—and this is uncommon—that here was a lad of nineteen who wouldn't lose it, or mix up the accounts, or permit anything collectible to escape him.

A more impressive evidence of his standing in the community came shortly afterward, when Ochs and another young printer, David B. Harris, persuaded the city council to give them a contract for publication of a new city directory. The amount involved was only $50,[2] but in the Chattanooga of 1878 that was a much more considerable sum than it is today; and certainly the preparation of a new directory was not a job to be intrusted to contractors whom the city council regarded as mere schoolboys. At nineteen Adolph Ochs was accepted as a man of business.

This view was justified by the appearance of the Chattanooga *Directory and Business Gazetteer* in April, 1878. Ochs and Harris had done a competent and thorough job laboring against great difficulties. They had no staff, no plant or equipment. They gathered the information themselves and put it together in the "Commercial Book and Job Office," belonging to Harry F. Griscom, who lent it to them for the purpose. Griscom's younger brother, William Griscom, just over ten, came along with the shop as the only assistant.

Compiling the information involved a house-to-house canvass of the entire town, but when enough material had been gathered to make

---

[2] Govan and Livingood were unable to find evidence to substantiate the tradition that the council actually remitted $300 for the job. Possibly total income from the directory, including sales of advertising space, etc., amounted to that sum. In any event, it is certain, as will appear in the narrative, that shortly after completion of the directory Ochs did not have $300 or anything like it.

a start Ochs left the leg work to Harris and himself began setting type and making up forms. Although the Commercial described itself as a "book" as well as a job office, it had no bindery and the sheets had to be transported to Nashville for binding. Every printer knows that a book job is tricky, not so much on account of its typographical difficulty as on account of the disastrous effects of even momentary carelessness or lapse of attention. It is emphatically a job for a careful man, and the fact that Adolph Ochs was successful in his first effort of the kind is evidence that before he reached his majority he had developed something of that close, unremitting attention to detail which was to be conspicuous in his later life.

From the job, however, he collected a great deal more than the sum, whether $50 or $300, that the partners took in. Before it was over he had an intimate, detailed knowledge of the town such as he could hardly have amassed in any other way. Knowledge of his town is one of the prime qualifications of a newspaper man and especially of a newspaper executive. In putting together that directory Ochs had been compelled not only to learn every commercial and industrial resource of the town but to check, recheck and verify all figures, names and addresses connected with them. It is probable, incidentally, that he extended widely his personal acquaintance with the townspeople, although, in view of his gregarious instinct, it may be that he already knew by name every man, woman, child and dog in Chattanooga.

There is never a doubt that he emerged from the experience much better equipped to manage a newspaper than he had been before.

But neither is there any doubt that this early maturity was bought at a price. Adolph Ochs paid for it with his youth. Decades afterward associates of the millionaire publisher, who then had whatever money could buy at his command, noted with astonishment his delight in simple pleasures that most of them had long outgrown. Picnics and impromptu dances, old-fashioned songs, long hikes on trails and footpaths, a two-dollar bet on a horse race enraptured him; but the opera, the more sophisticated theater and the subtler arts interested him only mildly. In some measure this is doubtless attributable to an innate simplicity that no circumstances could have affected; but it is highly probable that in part it was due to the fact that in his youth he had been denied opportunity to exhaust the delights appropriate to youth, so in age he found them still fresh and vivid.

There is no occasion to sentimentalize the man. He made a good bargain. At the price of gaiety he purchased responsibility, dignity and honor. It was a trade that rational men must approve; but it is simple justice to recognize that what he got he paid for and at no trifling rate. He realized at least part of the cost himself; formal education he always missed and he saw to it that his younger brothers did not have to pay that price. Both George and Milton got better schooling than Adolph —not entirely to their satisfaction when they were young and would have preferred life in the great world to books, but to their great advantage later as they readily acknowledged.

On the other hand it would be a mistake to dehumanize Adolph entirely and erect him into a monster of filial piety, industry and resolution. The records of those early days are fragmentary and even the fragments are usually vague and uncertain; but there are a few indications authentic enough to dispel any suspicions of a youth "grand, gloomy and peculiar."

In the first place, Adolph Ochs was popular with his fellow printers and no little tin god was ever popular with printers. When he left Knoxville to go to Louisville the rest of the office force chipped in to buy a copy of Hood's poems on the flyleaf of which they wrote a flattering inscription signed with sixteen names—a book, incidentally, that fifty years later the eminent publisher of the New York *Times* cherished as another might have cherished a first-folio Shakespeare.

In the second place there is extant[3] a facetious and doubtless exaggerated sketch by a printer associated with him a little later, William F. Stone, of Chattanooga, which despite its extravagance lays to rest any delusion that the boy was regarded by his companions as misanthropic. Stone's memory is of the days before the chatter of the linotype had broken the silence of the composing room. Setting type by hand was a quiet process with men intent on following copy; but when type was being distributed, a task that with the experts became almost

[3] In the Edwards MS.

automatic, conversation, song and laughter were possible. The jesting that flew back and forth, from alley to alley, became extremely pointed at times, for the old-fashioned printer was never famous for his delicate consideration of sensibilities. The thin-skinned did not often last long in a printing office; but Ochs did last. He was no Caruso, but he joined in the singing. He had no barbed wit of his own, but when he was the victim of the wags he could take it.

Nor was his life one unending round of labor. There were interludes, few and brief it is true, but still breaks in the monotony of toil. There are references to occasional picnics, to a few trips, sometimes by buggy over the incredibly bad roads into the country, more often by train to some near-by town. There was some social life—at least enough to convince Stone that young Ochs had an unerring eye for a pretty girl and a very effective line of talk to support his judgment. He was not what they then called a lady-killer, perhaps because he lacked time for serious pursuit; but he most certainly wasn't a failure with women, either.

At least one source of entertainment in these days had a lasting effect upon him. He secured a job—as did his brothers, George and Milton —as usher in the local theater. The pay was little, if anything, but the position offered an opportunity to see all the shows, and that meant much, far more than it would mean today, for these were the great days of "the road." Even as small and remote a town as Knoxville was visited by the mighty, and in the democracy of the theater it was possible for an usher, especially if he were polite and obliging, to make at least a speaking acquaintance with great stars. For example, it was here that Ochs met Julia Marlowe in her youth. Here he encountered many others, forming acquaintances that in some cases developed into lifelong friendships.

There is, in fact, a family tradition that in at least one instance the glamor of the theater quite overwhelmed the young man.[4] There was one leading lady so fascinating that Ochs went to the theater resolved to propose marriage, but when he got there his nerve failed him and he backed out without saying anything. Perhaps this tale should be

4 His daughter to the author.

[44]

taken with a grain of salt; fifty years later he renewed the acquaintance, and it would have been quite in character for him to have invented the fable out of gallantry.

Be that as it may, there is no doubt that these years gave him an interest in the theater that lasted as long as his life. It was not that he became a dramaturgist. His interest was never that of the specialist, fascinated by subtleties and experimentation, but merely that of a normal man with an alert intelligence interested to some extent in every form of human activity, and especially interested in a form that while appealing to the intelligence also afforded a pleasant method of relaxation.

He was not, however, universally competent. There were some things that even Adolph Ochs couldn't do. Stone narrates with gusto one of his failures, and it is worth recording because, after all, a man who could do everything would hardly be human. Ochs came to Chattanooga, Stone says, with a little tin trunk in the tray of which lay a piccolo—lay untouched for months until a printer who was something of a musician espied it and negotiated its purchase.

Shortly thereafter at some local festivity a casual assemblage of amateur players—the sort of ensemble severely, if vividly, described in the parlance of the day as a "spasm band"—began playing military marches and the new owner of the piccolo starred, throwing off trills, runs and brilliant staccatos with apparent ease.

"That's your old piccolo, Adolph," remarked a bystander.

"I don't believe it," was the grim reply. "It never would do anything like that when I had it."

II

Nearly seventy years after the event the causes of the decline and fall of the *Dispatch* are not altogether clear. What is clear is that Adolph Ochs understood them and felt that he could have remedied them if he had been in power and not in a subordinate position. From this time on he would never be associated with any newspaper enterprise in which he was not assured of a free hand.

Later this insistence on control cost him large sums of money and prevented completion of many deals he would have liked to make; but he never hesitated to pay whatever was necessary to assure control or to withdraw from any negotiation when it became clear that control was not to be obtained.

The wisdom of this course is acknowledged by newspapermen generally and many of them have assumed that Adolph Ochs was born with it. He appeared in New York equipped with so much understanding of obscure matters that the tendency has been to assume that he was endowed by nature with all his extraordinary qualities. But this assumption is highly questionable. Certainly a great deal of what he had was no natural endowment, but an acquisition obtained by painful experience. The necessity of having control, for example, he learned the hard way. He did not have it on the *Dispatch*, and the result of not having it was that presently he was on the street, jobless and moneyless.

The really extraordinary thing about the man was that he had to be hit over the head only once to be convinced of the error of his way. Most of us have to be pounded again and again before we get the idea, if we ever do. In later years all New York newspaperdom marveled at the way in which this "inexperienced" Tennessee publisher neatly side-stepped mistake after mistake into which others fell; but examination of the record proves that there was no wizardry about it, except as vivid memory and keen understanding are magical qualities. In nearly every case the mistake that Ochs avoided in New York he had made at one time or another in Tennessee; or if he had not made it himself, he had suffered from it when others made it. His necromancy was not that he never made mistakes, but the fact that he rarely, if ever, made the same mistake twice.

When the *Dispatch* went down, he felt that it was a mistake not to have had control, and he never made that mistake again. It may be argued plausibly that the newspaper's failure was to him a blessing in disguise for it taught him before he reached his majority and at trifling cost a lesson tremendously important to a man of his type.

Twenty years later a similar collapse might easily have broken him once for all; but at nineteen it was merely an annoyance, not a catastrophe.

He was unshaken in his determination to run a newspaper in Chattanooga, a determination that was based on something more than ambition. It rested also on a clear perception that the field was open. True, the harvesters were many, but they were working with poor implements and in the wrong way. Chattanooga was a newspaper graveyard. Although it was only forty years old, the city had had at one time or another at least sixteen newspapers of which thirteen had given up the ghost by 1879. The survivors were two weeklies and the Chattanooga *Daily Times*, which had recently absorbed the remains of the ill-starred *Dispatch*.

The history of the *Times* was not one to encourage faith in the commercial soundness of daily newspaper publishing in Chattanooga.[5] Appearing first on December 15, 1869, it challenged the *Republican*, for the past two years the dominant newspaper in the town. The *Republican* was Chattanooga's third daily; it had absorbed the *American Union*, which, in turn, had succeeded the city's short-lived, but celebrated, first daily newspaper. This was the Chattanooga *Rebel*, Franc M. Paul, publisher, and Henry Watterson, editor, which was neither absorbed nor put into bankruptcy but, if its editor's account may be accepted, attained the most spectacular end in the history of American journalism. The paper, said Watterson years later, was just ready to go to press with a fiery editorial denunciation of the Yankees and the Yankee army, when a squadron of Federal cavalry and a battery of artillery burst into one end of the town, whereupon the newspaper staff prudently departed by the other. Their speed exceeded that of the cavalry, so the artillerymen crammed the lead type into a field piece and shot it after the fleeing editor. Thus the Chattanooga *Rebel*, like the Prophet Elijah, departed this life in a chariot of fire.

Its successors ended less noisily, but not less certainly. The *American Union* was absorbed by the *Republican*, the *Republican* failed, the *Evening Mail* failed, the *Daily Enterprise* failed, the *Commercial*

---

[5] Cf. Govan and Livingood, *op. cit.*, and Edwards MS.

changed to a weekly, the *Daily Herald* failed, and the *Dispatch* was taken over by the *Times*. Counting the innumerable weeklies that struggled along anywhere from a few weeks to a few years, the journalistic history of Chattanooga was marked by more tombstones than milestones. Even the *Times*, although it still panted, was experiencing a living death, rather than triumphant life. Its circulation was approximately two hundred and fifty copies a day, it had a debt of fifteen hundred dollars and its income was less than the expense of production. The competition of the *Dispatch* had been very nearly the finishing blow for although the *Dispatch* had succumbed the *Times* could not recover the loss of revenue that its competition entailed.

III

Into this charnel house blithely stepped young Adolph Ochs. He had finished his directory job and sought new worlds to conquer. The grisly skeletons of dead newspapers all over the place were not warnings to him, but merely so many obstacles out of the way. He was a gambler to the fingertips, but of the type of the poker player, not that of the crapshooter who depends altogether upon his luck. When Ochs held the cards he knew how to play them; and the more players he found betting against him, the better he was pleased for that meant that the stakes would be higher. He was certain he could avoid the errors that had caused the failure of the *Dispatch*; and that certainty was a strong hand that he was prepared to back to the limit.

He had no money and no financial backing; but he had one asset in the confidence of the men who had worked with him. He began to assemble the printers who had been thrown out of jobs when the *Dispatch* collapsed. He began to talk to them of an organization to put out a paper of their own; and the printers began to take fire.[6]

There are two things about this incident that throw a flood of light on the man's subsequent career. In the first place, he was not bluffing, he was betting on what he considered a good hand. He was not afraid

[6] Govan and Livingood; Edwards MS.; Colonel Milton B. Ochs and others to the author.

of being called; he wanted to be called, and that is exactly what happened.

In the second place, note what followed when Adolph Ochs talked business. The printers took fire and presently the whole town took notice. True enough, they were only country printers and it was a small town; but at this time the speaker was barely past his twentieth birthday. He seems to have made some effort to camouflage his youth; he was wearing a large and luxuriant black mustache that added somewhat to his years and he always signed his full name. Stone has a wicked suggestion[7] that this was due to an unfortunate experience during the year he spent as a boy in Providence, when he went to the general delivery window at the post office one day and asked if they had anything for "A. Ochs." The clerk, suspecting that he was being made the butt of a joke, fixed the inquirer with a cold and fishy eye, saying, "Nothing. And nothing for A. Cow, either." Thereafter, says Stone, Ochs was always Adolph.

Still, all Chattanooga was well aware that this was a very young man, hardly more than a boy; nevertheless, when he began to talk business, laying out his plans, painting his vision of the future, the citizens listened. They had to listen. Years later, in far more impressive surroundings, with a far more sophisticated audience, the thing will happen again. When Ochs talked business people always listened, as they will always listen to any man who is a supreme master of his subject.

In Chattanooga there was one man who heard, but did not take fire. He took fright. This was the unhappy nominal owner of the *Times*, one A. S. Cunningham, who had come from Nashville a couple of years earlier as full of steam and enthusiasm as Ochs himself. The *Times*, which had been under half a dozen ownerships in as many years, was at the moment in the hands of Z. C. Patten and T. B. Payne, proprietors of a book and stationery store, who had bought it under a court decree. Patten, who was a business genius, assumed the management and for something over a year did very well with it; but he had no great liking for newspaper work and when Cunningham showed up was content to sell to him, taking his note for $1500 in

[7] Edwards MS.

part payment. A short time later Patten and Payne dissolved their partnership, and in the division of the assets Patten took the Cunningham note.

Cunningham's experience was pretty dismal. If he had any original ideas about newspaper management they did not show up in the *Times*. He tried a long succession of partners[8] but the paper continued to drift steadily downward. The competition of the *Dispatch* so nearly finished it that when he heard rumors of Ochs's determination to start a new paper he threw up the sponge. He called in the young printer and offered him the *Times*, lock, stock and barrel, for $800 cash and assumption of the Patten lien.

It was a good offer, but unfortunately it was far beyond Adolph Ochs's means. Eight hundred dollars was as utterly out of his reach as eight millions. He didn't realize it at first. In his enthusiasm he assumed that, even though he didn't have the money, with a good indorser he could get it at a bank. But then he came into collision for the first time with cold business judgment. He found that while Chattanooga liked him and believed in him to some extent it didn't believe in him eight hundred dollars' worth. Ochs was a promising young fellow and certainly the *Times* ought to be continued; but eight hundred dollars was real money. Now, if he would come down somewhere within reason, say two-fifty. . . . In the end, E. A. James agreed to indorse for three hundred. Apparently James would have been content to go further, but that was all the bank would stand on his signature, and that was all Ochs could raise.

Then he produced one of those complicated financial schemes at which he was to prove adept in later years. The owner was anxious to sell and he was anxious to buy. There ought to be some way of building a bridge between them, and he found one.

It is worth examining in detail, for the situation was exactly the situation he faced eighteen years later when he was negotiating the purchase of a far greater paper. But the Ochs of 1878 was not as skillful as he was in 1896 and he trapped himself neatly.

[8] Govan and Livingood despair of even enumerating the entire list of men Cunningham took in and bought out in nineteen months.

The first obstacle was the lien, but that proved not too formidable. Patten was reasonable. He wanted his money, but he emphatically did not want the newspaper. He had just started the Chattanooga Medicine Company, which later was to bring him millions, and it absorbed his time and energy. He would agree to any scheme that promised him a fair chance to get out without having to take over the paper again. Ochs proposed monthly payments of $50 plus accrued interest —Cunningham had paid nothing for nearly two years. In the end, they agreed that monthly payments of $75 for thirty months would extinguish the lien, and that was that.

Then came the bargaining with Cunningham. His price of $800 meant cash, and if deferred payments were involved the whole situation was altered. Ochs proposed to buy a half interest, carrying control, for $250, with the right to buy the other half later. But Cunningham wasn't selling for $500 at all and certainly not on time. In the end, he agreed to sell control for $250 with the right to purchase the other half interest after two years at a price to be fixed by arbitrators at that time. This was the trap. Two years later a board of arbitrators, of whom Patten was one, awarded Cunningham $5500 for his remaining half interest. Thus he drew a total of $5750 for property he had offered at $800.

Failure to fix a price at the time of the sale cost Ochs approximately $5000. It was Lesson Number Two. Number One had been failure to secure control of the *Dispatch*, but Number Two was much harder, because it was his own fault. He had really had no chance to control the *Dispatch*, so when its failure threw him out of a job he was not compelled to blame himself severely. But he could have come to an agreement on the price of the *Times* and not to do so was carelessness for which he was to blame. He swallowed his bitterness and paid up, but he did not forget. He had not forgotten eighteen years later; and he didn't make that mistake again.

So on July 2, 1878, the Chattanooga *Daily Times* appeared for the first time with the superscription "Adolph S. Ochs, Publisher."

Thirty years later that name was to connote all that is sound, solid and conservative in journalism. On this occasion, indeed, it appeared upon a paper that to all outward appearance was sound, solid and conservative; but viewed in the light of what is usually accepted as plain common sense it was one of the most harebrained enterprises ever recorded, a gamble hardly surpassed since Jacob bought a birthright for a mess of pottage.

When Ochs had made his down payment he had fifty dollars of his three hundred left. Notary and other fees in connection with the filing of the papers cost him twelve and a half dollars more. The credit of the *Times* with the New York Associated Press was exhausted—as was its credit with everybody else, for that matter—and twenty-five dollars cash had to be paid to assure continuance of telegraphic news service. Adolph S. Ochs started his career as a daily newspaper publisher with a working capital amounting to twelve dollars and fifty cents!

True, it was in Tennessee in 1878, when everyone got along with remarkably little cash. True, Ochs was only twenty years old and may be supposed to have possessed his share of the adolescent's blithe disregard of risks. But even so, it was a hair-raising adventure, which no staid conservative, no one indeed but a born gambler, would have undertaken. More than that, it was thoroughly in character. We shall see this same man, no longer an adolescent but in his full maturity, undertaking another enterprise which, considering its vastly greater size, was an even dizzier gamble, and doing it with the same imperturbability and even greater success.

Nor was it characteristic of the individual only; it was characteristic of the period as well. In Chattanooga, for instance, Patten was launching on a shoestring the medicine business that was to make him immensely rich. Others were starting enterprises on no firmer foundations, most of which went to smash but some of which brought wealth and power to the adventurers. In the nation at large, now that the effects of the panic of 1873 were largely if not entirely effaced, tremendous energy was unleashed. John D. Rockefeller was slowly and carefully fitting together the elements that were to become his oil empire. Andrew Carnegie and his like were just beginning to comprehend the immense possibilities offered by the era of steel. James J. Hill, E. H.

Harriman, Collis P. Huntington, the railroad emperors, were making the whole continent available to workers and home builders. All of them were willing to run tremendous risks because the stakes were gigantic. If Ochs's deals now seem breath-taking in their audacity, in that he was a man of his time. It was a breath-taking period.

It is never to be forgotten, however, that most of these risk-takers were cleaned out in the end. It took audacity to accomplish much in those days, but audacity alone was not enough. The gamblers who survived to become captains of industry without exception had ideas as well as nerve; and the one among them who was to attain the summit in newspaper publishing was no exception.

IV

He needed ideas, for most certainly he had acquired little else. The *Times* was a four-page sheet, six columns wide. Its plant was a one-story shack—"building" is much too dignified a term—containing equipment scanty in amount and far-gone in disintegration. Most of the type had long been fit for the hellbox, and the flat-bed, hand-power press for the junk heap.[9] The front end of the single room was railed off for the business and editorial departments, and everything else was in the other end.

Nevertheless, this dilapidated plant could and did contrive to produce a newspaper which the townspeople contrived to read. It was a going concern and Adolph Ochs was in absolute control. It was a medium of expression for a man with ideas and there is every evidence that the proprietor was supremely happy when he surveyed his realm.

His first move was to hire MacGowan to write editorials for him at a dollar a day[10] and it is possible that MacGowan phrased the initial announcement of policy; but it is more probable that Ochs wrote it himself, first because he was unlikely to intrust that job to anyone else and, second, because its content unquestionably expresses his

[9] Edwards MS.

[10] Edwards MS. Others put the editor's stipend at $3 a week, which is not impossible as MacGowan at this time had other employment and wrote the editorials on the side. Within a few months, though, he was a full-time employee.

thought and that of no one else. It is an interesting document now, although there is no evidence that it fluttered Chattanooga at the time. Chattanooga had already seen sixteen newspapers started, almost always with a more or less grandiose declaration of policy. Chattanooga doubtless thought it was just another of those things and turned to the local items.

But after sixty-seven years it is easy to perceive in this pronouncement the basis of one of the greatest careers in journalism and the basis on which the New York *Times*, as well as the Chattanooga paper, was conducted to a huge success.

Ochs laid down four lines of policy. Each of them is significant; but he omitted one which was customarily included in those days, and the omission is fully as significant as any of the inclusions. "Without pledging the *Times* to any special course in detail," he thought it proper to say:

(1) It will be the foremost purpose of its manager to make it the indispensable organ of the business, commercial and productive, of Chattanooga, and of the mineral and agricultural districts of Tennessee, North Georgia and Alabama.

(2) The paper will contain the latest news by telegraph, markets from all the leading centers of trade, and the freshest news by mail. The local news department shall be as near perfect as hard work and vigilance can make it. In the items of general, commercial and local information, it is proposed to leave nothing to be desired, and no room for home or foreign competition.

(3) Politically, the paper will move in line with the Conservative Democracy of the South. In State affairs we shall take such course as will, in our judgment, best subserve the interests and protect and advance the credit and honor of Tennessee.

(4) In our efforts to reduce this brief programme to practice in these columns, we shall expect the aid and sympathy of the manufacturing, commercial, professional and working classes of our people. Being cognizant of the need of and the strongly expressed desire for such a newspaper in Chattanooga as the above outline indicates the *Times* is to be, we have taken the people at their word, and shall give them a chance to support that which they have been asking for—a paper primarily devoted to the material, educational and moral growth of our progressive city and its surrounding territory.

A MAN MASTERS HIS ENVIRONMENT

In this matter of patronage we shall make no "appeals," but rely upon that sense of propriety and justice which must teach every intelligent citizen that the obligation between himself and the paper is a mutual one, ours to print and circulate such a journal as we have described, his to see that he contributes his share, in proportion to the benefits such a paper confers on him as a citizen, the means to sustain it and promote its growth in material means and general journalistic value. In short, we shall conduct our business on business principles, neither seeking nor giving "sops" and "donations" except to or for legitimate objects of charity.

The conspicuous omission is that of any pledge to support any party or any cause through thick and thin.

Its significance is due to the fact that at this time in the South journalism had hardly attained to the status of a distinct business. Indeed, throughout the nation to a considerable extent the shadow of patronage still lay upon it. The collection and publication of information was considered as hardly a worthy object, in itself, for the dedication of an institution's whole energy and ability. It was customary, therefore, for newspapers to enter voluntarily into service, usually of a political party, sometimes of a political idea—one of the *Times's* local contemporaries was the weekly *Greenback Advocate*—sometimes of a religious sect or of a particular industry. All too frequently the service was not publicly avowed and a paper, professing to be free, was in reality the agent of a politician or an industrialist. But some sort of patronage was usually deemed essential.

The first unmistakable demonstration of Adolph Ochs's genius as a newspaperman was his realization that the time had come in Chattanooga when patronage was no longer essential, or even desirable.

Almost everything else he did can be explained in terms of logic and circumstance. Given the conditions under which he worked, any intelligent man would have done what he did. But it is impossible to explain how he knew the time had come to break away from the old methods. There were other newspapermen in Chattanooga not lacking in intelligence and knowing everything about the town that Ochs knew. MacGowan, for instance, was a man of first-rate ability, older than Ochs and with vastly more experience of the town, the section and the business. Yet MacGowan didn't see the point until Ochs explained it to him. Neither did anyone else but this boy of twenty.

Afterwards people, looking back upon this period, realized that it was obvious. Here was a rapidly growing community intensely interested in building up its industry and commerce. Such a community has great need of early and reliable information and can well afford to pay for it. Ochs supplied this need and profited. It was as simple as that. Thus the superficial sometimes convince themselves that it wasn't much of an accomplishment, after all, and blandly assume that the man was overrated. But what is business genius, or political genius, except ability to perceive the truth just before it becomes obvious to everybody?

Here is the point at which the biographer must throw up his hands and confess defeat. Why Ochs did specific things—hired one man and fired another, negotiated one deal and turned down another—can usually be explained plausibly by digging into the records or by drawing reasonable inferences where no written evidence exists. But how he managed to see opportunity that was invisible to everyone else is inexplicable. If we could explain that, we could explain the mystery of personality, which has baffled all investigators since history began.

But once the fact is accepted, all the rest falls into place. Intending to be a purveyor of information, not a special pleader for any cause —except as the prosperity and general welfare of the community may be regarded as a cause—the publisher was under the necessity of finding and supplying such news as the community needed. Note carefully, in this connection, the first of his five points—his paper was to be the "indispensable" organ of business. It was not to be merely entertaining. It was not to be merely edifying. It was to be indispensable, that is to say, it was to supply the information that men needed in the conduct of their serious affairs. Incidentally it might entertain them, and, on occasion, persuade them; but primarily it was to inform them, and that was the service for which it expected to be paid.

The second point refers to professional methods and the third, the perfunctory announcement of allegiance to Conservative Democracy, probably was no more than a concession to the conventions. People expected some kind of political alignment, so here it was; but obviously it was a mere gesture.

The fourth, however, is important, although it is possible that when it appeared Chattanooga had no idea what it meant. All that talk about expecting support proportionate to benefits conferred upon the community perhaps struck the average Chattanoogan as so much gabble put in merely to give a dignified tone to the article. But it wasn't. On the contrary, it was an expression of Adolph Ochs's most profound conviction, not merely as a journalist, but also as a man. It was a repudiation of patronage and parasitism. He had valuable services to sell and he proposed to collect from the community what his services were worth, no more and no less. He was accepting no handouts, nor was he a free horse to be ridden for nothing. He undertook to furnish the community with the sort of newspaper it needed and desired, but he proposed to be paid for his labor, and he wanted that distinctly understood.

This is the most direct evidence of the man's early maturity. The respect that older men accorded him is corroborative testimony, but here it is in black and white. This is no unformed youth, uncertain of his place or his purpose in the world. This is a man who knew his own worth, knew his own purpose, and knew how he meant to set about achieving it.

He had not yet reached his majority, but for years he had carried the chief responsibility of the family. For some time to come he would be subject to occasional outbreaks of juvenility; indeed, as has been mentioned, when he had passed the Psalmist's span he still retained a youthful delight in simple pleasures. But in all important matters, youth was already behind Adolph Ochs when the first issue of the Chattanooga *Times* appeared under his proprietorship.

If it had not, it would have been soon, for doing business under the conditions he encountered was enough to give gray hairs to the very spirit of eternal youth. Of course he couldn't meet his payroll that first week, but somewhere he found a lender willing to take a chance and borrowed enough to satisfy the printers. During the second week a little money came in, but so did a great many bills. Sad experience with the *Times* had made all Chattanooga tradesmen extremely prompt about rendering statements, and frequently the bill came in before the cash.

Some amusing and some pretty dubious expedients were resorted to in order to keep the sheriff out and to build up credit. Even at twenty Ochs was no bad psychologist. He made it an inflexible rule from the beginning, when a bill was presented, to ask for a day that it might be "audited"; to most creditors this seemed not unreasonable, and many doubtless found it impressively businesslike. Then, having gained twenty-four hours, he would set out to raise the money. Banking laws were far less rigid then than they are now and Ochs was one of a group of young businessmen who skinned through many a tight place by swapping checks on different banks, trusting to have the money on deposit before the checks could be cleared. Check-kiting was risky business, but it saved the credit of more than one business enterprise, the *Times* among them.

The creditor, returning for his money the next day, was given a second impression of the business methods of the establishment. With a printing plant at his disposal, Ochs refused to use the ordinary forms provided by the bank. He printed checks of his own, very handsome ones too,[11] and bound them in an opulent-looking book. The bill, duly "audited," was then paid. Presumably in the beginning those beautiful checks were rushed to the bank with all speed, but when they were promptly honored their appearance began to have its effect. The next time the creditor might not be in so great a hurry, and ere long he was in no hurry at all. Remarkably soon most businessmen were ready to deal with the *Times* on a basis of thirty to sixty days[12] and the initial crisis was past.

Hard on its heels, though, trod others. Exactly twenty-four days after its first appearance under the new ownership the *Times* was sued for libel and lost the suit. In reporting a police raid on a local amusement resort one of its reporters had quoted a police description

[11] Govan and Livingood; Edwards MS. These checks must have been exceptionally well designed, for they were remembered fifty years afterward by several people who had done business with Ochs in the early days.
[12] Govan and Livingood.

of the place as "a house of ill-fame." At the trial it was established it was not in fact a brothel, but merely a disreputable beer garden. The jury accordingly found against the *Times*, but its estimate of the situation is indicated by the fact that it awarded the plaintiff damages in the sum of thirty-five cents.[13] The *Times* paid up and in addition volunteered a disavowal of any intent to injure the plaintiff, "his house or his guests." Perhaps this incident was not altogether a misfortune. Every publisher, no matter how blameless, eventually must learn about libel suits; Ochs had his instruction early and at a relatively low price.

Less than a month after taking over the paper the new publisher got it into better quarters. The third floor of a building near the corner of Eighth and Market streets—a fairly central location—had been occupied by the old *Dispatch* and was now available. Ochs moved the *Times* there, perhaps with a certain satisfaction in now having control of the premises where he had once been impotent to prevent failure, even though the paper was gone forever.

But in late summer another crisis developed, more appalling by far than any of the others. Chattanooga was invaded by a familiar but dreaded enemy, yellow fever, then the scourge of all the southern states. It did not come without warning. In early June New Orleans had been stricken, and through June, July and August the plague had been slowly, but inexorably, creeping up the Mississippi Valley. Nothing definite was known then about the method of transmission, but there was a vague idea that it was somehow connected with climate, and admission of the presence of the disease was tantamount to admission of the presence of some poison in the air. Naturally, towns were reluctant to do anything of the sort and a policy of denial to the last was common.

In the early days the *Times* followed the custom. It vehemently repudiated the possibility that Yellow Jack could ever reach Chattanooga; but it was realistic enough to urge better enforcement of sanitary regulations, and it is interesting to note that one reform it emphasized was drainage of stagnant pools and of the puddles that studded the unpaved streets. It called for action to relieve yellow-

---

[13] Govan and Livingood.

fever sufferers in other cities and Ochs was made secretary and a member of the executive committee of an organization formed for the purpose; later he became chairman of a special Jewish committee with the same object. By the end of August Chattanooga had forwarded fifteen hundred dollars to the sufferers.

But in spite of the bold face the newspaper put upon it, the situation was sufficiently alarming to cause something very like a stampede from the city. At length, while Ochs was absent on a business trip to Louisville and Cincinnati, the Board of Health publicly admitted the existence of four cases and one death—that of a refugee from Memphis. Instantly Chattanooga was cut off from the rest of the world and its people lived virtually in a state of siege. Business was practically at a standstill and even the necessities of life were hard to procure.

Ochs, luckily out of it, didn't go back. There was nothing he could accomplish by returning, and he could drum up some business for the paper among the refugees. But there is some reason to believe that the deciding factor was Julius Ochs.[14] For once the ordinarily mild-mannered father asserted his parental authority in no uncertain terms; but the son, being intelligent, was probably content to submit.

Now MacGowan proved his worth. Throughout the epidemic the *Times* never missed an issue. Furthermore, once the cat was out of the bag it faced the facts resolutely and told its readers the whole story. Indeed, as the situation grew darker and darker the old soldier developed a grim humor and filled the column of local items with startling comments: "The hospital is awfully handy to the graveyard"; and on October 9, "Eleven deaths yesterday and more coming. Trot out your next funeral."

Furthermore, although business was paralyzed the *Times* explicitly opposed the premature return of the refugees. As late as October 23 while it paid high tribute to the courage and devotion of those who remained to administer relief and care for the stricken, it pointed out that those with no definite duties to perform would only be in the way. "The fewer people here, the quicker we can whip Bronze John."

With practically no advertising and with conditions growing con-

14 J. E. Govan to the author.

stantly more difficult, the paper came down to a single sheet; but it continued to appear and it continued to carry the essential news. In the bearded Scot the new publisher had a man who was utterly reliable. It was the first conspicuous demonstration of Ochs's remarkable ability to obtain and retain the services of trustworthy men. Mac-Gowan stayed with him to the end of his life, becoming, incidentally, a power in the state of Tennessee and a sort of institution himself.

The publisher, meanwhile, was scurrying about from Knoxville to Louisville to Cincinnati seeking desperately for funds to keep the editor going. By November 1, when the epidemic was officially declared ended, the paper was in the red to the extent of about $600— three-fourths of the total value its owner had put upon it six months before. Within that time Ochs faced the dismal necessity of making his paper pay for itself twice. Fortunately, the future was hidden from him. He was unaware that before securing final possession he was going to have to pay the original price seven times more. But to buy a paper priced at eight hundred dollars and promptly have it lose six hundred was sufficiently appalling. It was the closest shave Adolph Ochs had in his whole business career.

V

But with the end of the yellow-fever epidemic fate relented. Frost having disposed of the mosquitoes, no more cases appeared and the town came to life with a rush. The toll had been fearful. There had been three hundred and sixty-six deaths in a population of less than twelve thousand and the monetary loss to the city treasury was estimated by the mayor at half a million.[15] But Chattanooga had the spirit of the frontier, the spirit of post-Civil War America. No sooner was the immediate danger past than all its confidence in the future revived, as roseate as ever.

The *Times* led the revival. It assumed the position of civic trumpeter with unbounded enthusiasm. " 'He that bloweth not his own horn will

15 Govan and Livingood.

not have it blown.' We have a good horn and we intend to blow it."[16] In later years Ochs was to become known as the very embodiment of dignified, conservative journalism, but there is little trace of that in the ebullient journal fighting the battles of Chattanooga in the administration of Rutherford B. Hayes. "Monumental liar" was its retort to a contemporary that dared criticize Chattanooga, but its own comments on the town were uninhibited, to put it mildly: "There is a filthy mudhole in the lot back of the courthouse that would be a disgrace to the deadest town in the country."[17] Sanitation and education were the two central pillars of the *Times*'s civic program and in view of conditions then prevailing it was a good program. Chattanooga could stand plenty of both teaching and cleansing.

With the revival of business the paper prospered remarkably. The new publisher introduced no sensational changes of policy, but he organized news coverage of the town thoroughly and he introduced business methods in the conduct of its affairs. This was by no means as simple as it sounds. It took courage, as well as intelligence, to fix an advertising rate of eight cents a line or seventy-five cents a month for a standing ad, and collect it. It took courage ruthlessly to cut off subscribers who were in arrears. But Ochs did both and it paid in the end.

It also took a certain amount of ingenuity to collect for all advertising. The whole country was still suffering under the handicap of an inelastic currency and in the hustling, growing towns of the frontier —and Chattanooga was socially and economically, if not geographically, of the frontier—the shortage was chronic. An astonishing volume of business was done with a minimum of cash and businessmen had learned to be resourceful at getting along without money. Many merchants in Chattanooga who were in a basically sound position and who wished to use the advertising columns of the *Times* were flatly unable to pay cash without inconvenience so serious that they preferred to get along with a minimum of advertising. To demand cash on the nail simply meant that they would cut down their purchases of space or withdraw altogether.

[16] *Chattanooga Times*, July 10, 1878.
[17] *Ibid.*, July 11, 1878.

To cope with this difficulty the *Times* adopted a weird and complex system of barter. The principle of full and prompt payment for all advertising space was the important thing; as for the means of payment, it was willing to accommodate itself to the convenience of the customer. It would allow a merchant to settle his bill partly in merchandise, which the paper, in turn, used to meet its own obligations. Thus a printer on the *Times* at the end of the week might find himself paid off with a dollar or two in cash, supplemented with an order on a grocer, another on a dry-goods merchant, perhaps one on a drugstore, all payable in goods.

A modern publisher may shudder to think of proposing such a system to the Typographical Union; but it was the custom of the time and the place, and everyone seems to have been satisfied. At any rate, the *Times* flourished like the Scriptural green bay tree.

In December, 1878, at the insistence of his son, Julius Ochs brought his family to Chattanooga and became treasurer of the *Times*. He had come once before, in July, but only to affix his signature to the legal documents connected with the sale—a necessity arising from the fact that his son was still a minor. Perhaps the success of the paper's intricate system of financing is due more to him than to any other individual; for it was a system affording endless occasions for dispute and only a rigidly upright man could have kept all parties satisfied that they were being justly treated. In any event, Julius Ochs at last had found the work for which he was suited. As treasurer he had to deal with the local financiers, who found him careful, scrupulous and completely trustworthy; so within a few years he became one of the most respected men in the business community and a material addition to the prestige of the *Times*.

George and Milton, the younger sons, were put to work, too, George as a reporter and Milton in the business office, but they did not go on as year-round employees for some time, because Adolph demanded that they finish their schooling first. He was already feeling the handicap of his own scanty education, and he would not allow his brothers to incur that handicap merely to lift somewhat the burden on his own shoulders.

So the Chattanooga *Times* swung into the year 1879 with something like three thousand dollars less than no money at all, but rich in energy, in enthusiasm and in confidence; and from that time there never was a day when it wasn't a money-maker, while in some years it was almost fabulously profitable. At the end of the first year Ochs found that he had spent ten thousand dollars, including his own salary of nine hundred dollars, and had taken in just about twelve thousand dollars.[18] He was on the road to fortune and never once was he turned back.

VI

One may assert with the strongest emphasis that Adolph S. Ochs was a newspaperman twenty-four hours of the day, but it is not quite true to say that his newspapers were his whole life. The publisher was also a man and in these early days a man materially different from the one whom all the world recognized by name but who was really known to only a few fifty years later. Superficially the young man in Chattanooga bears hardly a trace of resemblance to the old man in New York; one must dig beneath the surface to find the foundation of the career that was erected later.

But if one does go beneath the surface, the man in Chattanooga is certainly not less interesting than the one in New York, and perhaps more attractive. He was still a bit raw and sometimes even raucous, but he had youth, which the judicious have ever found the most attractive thing in the world. He had a great deal yet to learn, both about the world and about himself. He was still capable of doing silly things, sometimes downright idiotic things, and without doubt there were times when he was thoroughly ashamed of himself, with ample reason. Yet nowhere in the written records, and nowhere in the memory of any survivor of those days, has the investigator encountered a mean thing charged against this man. There must have been some, for he was profoundly human and no human being is wholly blameless in that regard. But they must have been trivial indeed to have been

18 Edwards MS.

so completely forgotten, especially as there was ample cause for envy to have kept them alive.

This is not an assertion that he was saintly. On the contrary, it is a reasonable assumption that the roving eye that never missed a pretty girl led him into his share of youthful devilment; but whatever his adventures under the banner of Eros, they never blossomed into scandal. He was a discriminating and appreciative judge of liquor, too, which is an accomplishment not picked up in Sunday School; but his adventures under the banner of Bacchus never led him into debauchery. He kited checks and engaged in some other pretty dizzy financing when caught in a jam, but no man has come forward to allege that Adolph Ochs ever betrayed his trust or swindled him out of a cent. There are plenty of incidents in his career that are hardly to be held up as models for earnest young men to follow; but in one thing he was a model. He never welshed. He paid the bill for his own mistakes and never saddled them on others. In the severest trial of his professional career he could have laid the blame on another man; but he did not try it for an instant, although the experience put him in a hospital with a nervous breakdown.

A man of that sort is sure to have friends and this one had them. It is a temptation to dispose of the matter at a stroke by saying that he had one friend, to wit, the population of Chattanooga, but that would eliminate him professionally. No newspaperman worth his salt was ever without enemies. If he does his duty, he is bound to enrage every man who is seeking his own advantage at the expense of the general welfare. Ochs had plenty of enemies of this sort. George shot one and was himself very nearly shot by another. But these hatreds, although violent enough, were based on professional, not personal, activities; and they are not inconsistent with a very genuine respect and even a grudging admiration.

Considering the manners and customs of the times, the wonder is that the publisher escaped personal violence. He was of barely average stature and therefore offered temptation to every large-sized bully in the community. That the risk was real is sufficiently demonstrated by the fate of two of Ochs's most brilliant contemporaries in southern journalism, Edward Carmack, of Nashville, and N. G. Gonzales, of Columbia, South Carolina, both of whom were shot down on the street by men whom their papers had attacked.

There is on record, however, only one instance of a personal attack on Ochs, and that was made not by some town bully but by a man who was later to achieve a national eminence equal to his own. The assailant was William Gibbs McAdoo, who was to rise to the cabinet as Secretary of the Treasury under Woodrow Wilson. McAdoo at the time was connected with an engineering concern operating in Tennessee and certain contracts for public works granted to this concern had been criticized by the *Times*. Doubtless this irritated McAdoo, although Ochs did not view it as a personal attack.

But a little later Ochs made a recommendation to President Cleveland concerning the appointment of a Federal judge. He liked his man and made it strong, particularly as regarded his probity. But McAdoo took a different view. This judge had tried certain cases in which McAdoo was involved, and the litigant told the President that the man was certainly prejudiced, intimating that he was something worse.

When news of this came to Ochs, his temper exploded. It seemed to him that McAdoo was trying to make it appear that he had deliberately lied to the President, endeavoring to betray him into making an unsuitable appointment. He therefore instructed MacGowan to go for McAdoo, and that grim Caledonian went, with the terrific thoroughness of a Highland fighter.

Apparently this relieved Ochs's surcharged bosom and he regarded the account as closed. Not so McAdoo. Having already been rapped over the knuckles by the *Times* in the matter of the contracts, he seems to have construed this second assault as proof that the newspaper was pursuing a vendetta against him and he was, in the vernacular, fit to be tied.

Accordingly, when he entered a Pullman car at Knoxville one day and found Ochs seated there, all his resentment blazed up and he considered not at all the other man's attitude. Ochs, being entirely placid himself and seeing an acquaintance come in, started up and offered his hand. Possibly McAdoo mistook the movement, or perhaps he didn't even see it. In any event, what Ochs got was not a hand-clasp, but McAdoo's fist to the jaw, coming fast. McAdoo was thin, but he was long and that blow had weight behind it. In any circum-stance it might have floored Ochs, but as things were he had no chance at all, for the arm of the Pullman seat was right behind his knees. He did a swift back dive into the cushions and before he could extricate himself and get to his feet the Pullman conductor had rushed between the belligerents and the encounter was over.

In view of the positions held later by the two men it would be interesting if one might trace the effects of this affray upon the sub-sequent history of the United States; but the dull truth seems to be that it had no effect at all. In 1924, when McAdoo came close to cap-turing the Democratic nomination for the Presidency, and Ochs was publisher of the New York *Times*, this matter could not have affected the situation, for the *Times* had long been committed to the can-didacy of John W. Davis, and it could not have switched to another candidate without self-stultification, even if it had wished to do so. While the two men were never personal friends, when Ochs died in 1935 McAdoo sent to his brother, Colonel Milton B. Ochs, a telegram of condolence that bore every evidence of sincerity.

In general, however, life in Chattanooga went along amicably enough, although by no means tranquilly. On the contrary, it was an unbroken series of excitements. Adolph Ochs was squarely in the middle of everything that went on in the town. This is remarkable in view of his conspicuous abstention from civic and social activities in New York, where he gave such matters as little attention as his position would permit. But he had not learned as yet that a newspaper is as jealous a mistress as the law. At this time, bursting with energy and youthful enthusiasm, he was a member of all known committees, he was a promoter of all suggested projects, he was a leader of all sorts of movements with the single, but significant, exception of party politics. He did become a member of the school board, but that was his only public office.

He bought a huge house—another startling financial operation, for it was plainly beyond his means—in which he installed the family. They were all more or less involved in the production of the *Times*, Julius Ochs as treasurer, George and Milton on the staff, the three sisters and Mrs. Ochs always informed although Adolph would not permit the women of his family to work in the office. All of them had ideas about how to run the paper and the town and no hesitation in expressing them. It was a battling household but withal a conspicuously happy one.

As the years passed the house gradually took on another function. It was an imposing two-story-and-attic structure of gray painted brick on the corner of Fifth and Cedar streets, a good, although not swanky, residential neighborhood. It had a series of pleasant, ground-floor apartments large enough to accommodate considerable numbers of people—that is to say, a house well adapted to entertaining. So its master became in time a sort of unofficial municipal host. When Chattanooga was honored by the presence of a guest too distinguished to be consigned to a hotel, the Ochs home was made available. When important conferences were necessary, but too much formality might give rise to misunderstanding, Ochs could be relied on to arrange a dinner at his house, giving the meeting the color of a social event. Even when persons of importance were not guests under his roof, he was always on the entertainment committee looking after them. No eminent man came to Chattanooga without encountering the publisher of the *Times*, and many came. One who pleased Ochs greatly, and whom Ochs pleased, was Grover Cleveland, President of the United States. It was a meeting that had important results later.

The publisher also made a point of cultivating roving newspapermen. As a propagandist for Chattanooga he wished to give them pleasant impressions of the town for patriotic reasons; but he was also widening his circle of acquaintance in the newspaper world for professional reasons. Among those with whom he talked shop during a visit made pleasant by his cordiality was a certain Harry Alloway, New York newspaperman doing a series of articles on the South— a man who will reappear in this narrative.

The impression of these years that one gets from the existing records is primarily that of intense vitality combined with an insatiable curiosity about men and events. Yet there was little of the dramatic in them. The *Times* was a success, but it was made a success by a constant succession of little things. To become indispensable is a feat rarely achieved by one spectacular coup; rather it is brought about by unremitting alertness, by one small service today, another tomorrow, and a third the day after, until in sum the small matters become great. It was the way of the *Times*. The improvement in its news service startled nobody, but it was steady and consistent. MacGowan's editorial page indulged in a certain amount of fulmination, but no more than custom demanded; it became more and more conspicuous not for its thundering but for its logic and cool realism. More and more people felt that they had to have the *Times* in order to know what was going on, not in police court, nor even in politics, but in the everyday affairs of everyday men, the affairs that meant bread and butter and shelter, not to the exceptional, but to the ordinary, not to a few party leaders and workers, but to every man, woman and child in the town. The paper really was becoming an indispensable part of the city's life.

Note this—it worked. Note it well, for Adolph Ochs noted it. The money came rolling in and more than money came in. Prestige came. The respect of the respectable came. A definite, solid place in the world, and a desirable one, came. The policy outlined in the first issue under the new management produced the results that the publisher desired. This success crystallized and fixed his conviction that it was the only right policy for him to follow; and this happened in the early and middle eighties. It is a point to be remembered if one is to understand the Ochs of later years.

But he was not yet the master of his craft. His ebullience occasionally broke into print in a way that is startling to those who knew only the Ochs of metropolitan journalism. On March 12, 1879, for example, he edified his readers with a remarkable pronunciamento. It read:

We do not regard it as necessary to make any apologies for the remarks that follow. We are but human, and have our full share of self-admiration. This is a happy day with the publisher of this paper, and it is almost impossible to keep our happiness out of these columns. Though born in Cincinnati, Ohio, we have not until today become a citizen. Our happiness comes from the fact that today we are 21 years of age and have become a citizen—a man. Long have we looked to the time when we would have attained our majority, and many have been the bright pictures we have fancied ourselves the center of at this time. How many of these hopes have been realized we need not say.

We take this occasion to state that notwithstanding a boy has published the *Times* since last July, the *Times* has under his administration steadily increased in circulation and patronage, so that today we can boast that the *Times* has as large, if not a larger circulation than any paper in East Tennessee. We return our thanks to the citizens of Chattanooga and vicinity for the liberal encouragement given the present management of the *Times*, and we hope to merit a continuance of same.

It is easy to imagine MacGowan grinning behind his beard as he read this naïve declaration; but if he smiled it was privately. He was too well aware of the real ability that had gone into the management of the *Times* during the past year to make the mistake of deriding the publisher on account of his youthful exuberance. Nor did the town find it amusing. Letters of congratulation from readers poured in. After all, it was a young and hopeful city, that could understand hopeful youth.

Nevertheless, it is part of the evidence that Adolph Ochs did not yet fully comprehend the nature of power. He still associated it, as immaturity usually does, with its trappings—with legal majority, with public position, with respectable associations, with such pomp and circumstance as the locality afforded. Only in one aspect of this matter was he wise beyond his years. He had freed himself from the delusion that the real source of power was political office.

Why he escaped cannot be determined definitely, but probably the local environment had much to do with it. Chattanooga was definitely a two-party town and it was definitely becoming an industrial town. In such a locality the emptiness and sterility of what passed then for political debate was much more apparent than it was in places where crops and politics were the only subjects of public interest. Everyone in Chattanooga was aware that with the iron and coal in the hills and the rail and water highways available, there was a great new world to conquer and a more interesting world than that of party politics. Everyone in Chattanooga believed that the general welfare was promoted by working more rapidly and more surely than by voting. The city, in fact, did not participate effectively in state politics. To this day its citizens assert grimly that it is the stepchild of Tennessee, never receiving at the state capital the consideration that its size and economic importance warrant. Perhaps the reason is that its ablest men have rarely made politics a career, preferring business instead.

Certainly Ochs seems never to have been tempted to put himself forward for political office. It was not innate modesty, for he did put himself forward, frequently and energetically, for every other kind of public position. Reference has already been made to the innumerable committees on which he served. He also became more and more a factor in the business world.

Patten, whose own success is evidence that he was no mean judge of business ability, persistently sought an alliance with Ochs. Patten knew from hard experience how difficult it was to run a successful newspaper in Chattanooga. It is probable that he never expected to get his $1,500 out of the *Times*, but when Ochs took it over he did get it. More than that, he had been one of the arbitrators who determined the value of Cunningham's half interest when Ochs had had the paper two years. What he thought of Cunningham's moral claim we do not know; but his legal claim was unimpeachable and Patten found it worth $5500. That value was the creation of Ochs's work and skill. No wonder Patten would like to have such a man in his organization. He induced Ochs to make a small investment in stock of the Chattanooga Medicine Company and promptly made him a vice-president.

Ochs held the position for a short time only. Then he found that it was distracting his attention from things that interested him more. Perhaps, too, he was not altogether satisfied with the nature of the business. The federal pure food and drug laws were still in the distant future, nor had the medical profession and crusading writers as yet begun their heavy attack on the patent medicines; but there was even then some stirring of suspicion about the trade. This may have influenced Ochs's decision to withdraw, regardless of his high personal regard for Patten which never wavered while he lived; but the main reason, without doubt, was the demand upon his time and energy by other interests.

He was not yet ready, however, to concentrate exclusively upon his newspaper. Only through a long series of adventures was he to be finally persuaded of the wisdom of that course.

VII

Four years after taking over the *Times* Ochs was in an admirable position for a man of twenty-four—sole proprietor of a profitable newspaper in a growing city, a man of standing in his community and coming to be recognized as one of the leaders in southern journalism, he was the type that a wise father of marriageable daughters is not displeased to see about the place. True, he was not yet rich; but he had brains and character, which are much safer reliances than money.

Whether the Rev. Dr. Isaac M. Wise was a parent of that sort is somewhat open to question, but he did not object when young Ochs began to frequent his home in Cincinnati, obviously with an eye on his daughter, known informally as Effie, but entered in the birth register as Iphigene. Rabbi Wise was an eminent man, a learned man, a man of prodigious intellectual and moral force, but it is not to be denied that his attitude toward his parental responsibilities was somewhat casual. It is a part of family tradition that on the occasion of the arrival of this daughter he was in his study absorbed in composition of an essay on Euripidean tragedy. "It is another girl," they said. "What shall we name her?" "Ah, another girl," said the scholar vaguely, adding, as his eye fell on the papers before him, "name her Iphigenia," and with that he returned to Euripides. This offhand decision was modified only to the extent of making it the French form, Iphigene.

A MAN MASTERS HIS ENVIRONMENT

To assume, however, that Isaac M. Wise was no more than an absent-minded savant would be a grotesque error. It would be to overlook one of the strongest intellectual and moral influences brought to bear upon Adolph Ochs when he was a young man—an influence that unquestionably modified both his thinking and his conduct through the rest of his life. No one came close to Dr. Wise without feeling his influence, for he was one of the great religious leaders of his time, and while his influence was most profound upon his own faith, it was not confined to Judaism. He included among his friends liberals of all sects and some of none; and his house was frequented by everyone in Cincinnati who was genuinely interested in the battle of ideas.

A native of Steingrub, in what was to become Czechoslovakia, Isaac M. Wise was a product of the intellectual ferment that stirred Europe in the first half of the nineteenth century, culminating in the outbreaks of 1848. In his case, however, the impulse took a religious, more than a political, turn; he was interested in the reformation of Judaism, rather than of the state, and his long and profound studies were directed to that end. He came to this country in 1846 to find American Judaism hardly touched at all by the intellectual storms that were sweeping Europe.

Indeed, the faith was in a pretty low state at that time, in all respects. The Jewish element in this country was then small and widely scattered. Most of the adherents of the faith were poor and many were ignorant. Few organized congregations existed and still fewer were served by rabbis with anything like adequate training. The inevitable result was that in many places all spiritual content had departed and the practice of religion had degenerated into a dry formalism dangerously close to mere superstition.

Against this degeneration Wise, highly educated and cultivated, set out to do battle, at first almost singlehanded, with the traditional zeal of the crusader and with the usual result. He was misunderstood, misinterpreted, maligned. As a matter of course all those who were profiting by the existing state of things opposed him bitterly; but worse than that, many good and sincere people regarded him in the beginning as a mere malcontent and troublemaker. For years his career was stormy in the extreme; at least once he was actually mobbed.

In the end, though, his sincerity, backed by his splendid fighting ability, began to tell. Largely through his influence the Union of Hebrew Congregations came into existence and eventually the great dream of his life materialized—Hebrew Union College, an institution to train adequate religious leadership for Judaism. In 1883 he had been for eight years president of the college and was a power in the land, even though some of his coreligionists continued to regard him as an archheretic. He was still a fighter, for a fighter he remained to his last breath, but the desperate days were in the past, and he was beginning to acquire the mellowness that was to make him before his death in 1900 one of the most popular men in Cincinnati and indubitably the best conversationalist—witty, wise, urbane and tolerant, a delightful companion of all intelligent men, Jew or Gentile.

Naturally, such a man made a tremendous impression upon young Ochs. He made an impression upon everyone, but in Ochs's case it was doubled, for Effie was very much her father's daughter. She might have denied it vigorously in 1883, but it was true, and if it seemed doubtful at the time that was only because she was young. Petite, dark and vivacious, she was vastly more interested in the latest waltz than she was in the Greek classics; but at bottom she had a profound respect for her father's learning and for all intellectual achievement. This bundle of driving energy that burst into her life from Chattanooga certainly did not lose in her estimation because he had a head on his shoulders. But he also had a merry eye, a glib tongue, and a first-rate knowledge of how to get about on a dance floor, so it is not so clear what it was that took Effie's fancy. Grown older and more sedate, she contended that of course it was her recognition of Adolph Ochs's ability that attracted her; but one may be permitted a bit of skepticism about that. Marriages of the head and not the heart seldom endure the battering of the years, and this one did. All his life when Adolph Ochs really put his mind to the business of being charming he was a wonder; starting, then, with the advantage of youth and trying as he probably never had tried before, or ever afterward, it is easy to believe that he must have been irresistible.

At any rate, he won. On February 28, 1883, he and Effie Wise were married in Cincinnati. By that time he was a person of sufficient importance in Chattanooga to make the occasion an impressive social event; and the bridegroom was still sufficiently enamored of that sort of thing to throw himself into it with enthusiasm. It is the only time in his life that Adolph Ochs ever went in for swank, frankly and without reserve. To take the wedding party to Cincinnati he chartered a special Pullman, and the send-off at the railroad station almost assumed the proportions of a municipal celebration, with fifty employees of the *Times* raising thunderous cheers for the boss. On the return from the honeymoon, there was a formidable round of receptions, attended by everybody who was anybody in Chattanooga, and the man who was later to develop a marked distaste for all large, formal entertainments enjoyed them at this time and enjoyed them hugely.[19]

The sophisticated may smile at the bridegroom's exuberance, but no one can smile away the solid fact that Ochs believed that when he got Effie he had achieved the most brilliantly successful coup of his career; and for more than half a century he never changed his mind. Need more be said of her? Can more be said of her?

VIII

The five years following the marriage were perhaps the most decisive period in Adolph Ochs's life, yet their annals are almost bare of genuinely significant data. There is a plethora of incident, but most of it means nothing. There were journeyings up and down the land, a constantly extending acquaintance with the great, the illustrious and

[19] Chattanooga *Times*, February 27, March 1, 2, 8, 11, 16, 1883. Cincinnati *Commercial-Gazette*, February 29, 1883. Washington *Republican*, March 5, 1883. The Cincinnati paper in its story of the wedding described the bride as a "petite brunette of the most pronounced and brilliant type, with magnificent black eyes and level brows, and an extraordinary wealth of raven hair. She has been highly educated and inherits much of her distinguished father's intellectual acumen, as well as that gaiety of temper and brilliant wit which make him a most enjoyable companion."

the merely notorious—he and Effie were received by President Arthur in Washington during their honeymoon, for instance—and a growing influence in the newspaper world. Ochs took a leading part in the organization of the short-lived Southern Associated Press. He strengthened his ties with many newspapermen outside of Chattanooga, notably with Walsh in Cincinnati and Kohlsaat in Chicago. He labored diligently at improving the *Times*, typographically as well as in its news coverage. He was making it more and more indispensable; and in proportion as he did so, it became more and more profitable.

Occasionally he achieved dramatic newspaper sensations. For example, he learned that by some strange oversight the newspapers of Knoxville were ignoring the fiftieth anniversary of the founding of that city; so he prepared a special edition of his own paper, ran it over to Knoxville between midnight and dawn, and the amazed burghers learned from the Chattanooga *Times* that their town was fifty years old that morning, the information being accompanied with illustrated articles reviewing at length all that Knoxville had accomplished in its first half century.

In brief, he gave the town an alert, reliable and well-printed newspaper, one that was good and constantly getting better as its publisher perfected his knowledge of all the innumerable branches of his complex business. It is the picture of an able, energetic and successful businessman, assiduously cultivating his field and determined that no smallest patch of it should go untended.

Yet all the time he was running after false gods. In this very period of apparently high success, with money rolling in, with prestige and influence constantly increasing, with his own intellectual horizon constantly expanding and his knowledge of his business broadening and deepening, Adolph Ochs was driving straight toward ruin as a newspaperman.

The outward aspect of it can be described in a line—he was getting too many irons in the fire. But the inner aspect, what made him do it, is far more difficult to describe. Avarice? Certainly not; avarice is a vice from which he was conspicuously free. Vanity? No; he had his small vanities, but they never amounted to a passion, much less a ruling passion. Lust for power? Partly, perhaps; like every strong man, he enjoyed wielding power, but his lust for it was always strongly curbed by common sense. None of these, nor the combination of them all is enough to explain why he plunged into a labyrinth of business activities that all but ruined him.

A more probable explanation is that he still cherished a certain misapprehension of his place in the world. This is the time when Adolph Ochs came nearest to falling into the error that has trapped countless able journalists—he almost began to believe in himself as a Great Man. Not a great newspaperman, for he was well on the way to becoming that, but just a Great Man in general, an eminent personage, a community powerhouse, a man on whom everyone would rely for leadership in every conceivable community enterprise.

It is not an ignoble ambition. It is not necessarily based on selfish motives; indeed, it is nearly always linked with civic enthusiasm and intellectual energy. A man with a restless mind sees what obviously needs to be done and since nobody else seems to be attending to it, plunges in to do it himself. Let this happen a few times and presently the community turns to him almost automatically in every crisis. Sometimes the leader makes money out of his projects; more frequently he doesn't, but he inevitably becomes influential and useful.

In Chattanooga there were a thousand things to be done and very few with the resourcefulness and energy to do them. Ochs had both, and soon he was into everything. Whether it was an opera house to be built, a monument to be raised, a park to be established or a real-estate development to be laid out, he was always among those present and frequently in the lead. It is interesting to note that, with the exception of his brief connection with the medicine company, practically everything in which he took a hand had some sort of civic aspect. Even real-estate development, in which he became more and more involved, contributed to the enlargement of Chattanooga.

It is incontestably true that this sort of activity was useful to the town, and a little of it no doubt is the duty of every man of any considerable standing. But it was not Adolph Ochs's primary function, nor his primary duty; he was a newspaperman, and nothing else he could do for Chattanooga was half as important as giving it a first-class newspaper. He did not yet understand this quite clearly. He was still a little tainted with the heresy that he might serve the community better by offering it civic leadership than by offering it reliable news.

Possibly at this time he was also a little inclined to the idolatry of bigness. This cult was approaching its apogee, for its first stern challenge came in 1893, in the Sherman Anti-Trust Act. Between 1883 and 1888 Americans showed little disposition to question the excellence of size. Chattanooga was determined to be a bigger city, assuming that that meant a better city; for was not size itself a virtue? It would be strange if the publisher of the town's leading newspaper and one of its most prominent citizens had escaped entirely the illusion that seized everybody else.

Evidence that he did not escape is to be found in the grandiose nature of the projects that engaged more and more of his attention. In these years Chattanooga was seized with that strange sort of madness through which nearly every growing American city has passed at one time or another. It developed a real-estate boom. With coal and iron, timber and transportation available, what could stop it? The answer was Birmingham, but that became clear only by slow degrees. Birmingham's transportation was as good, its coal as abundant, and its iron ore better, because it contained less sulphur. Chattanooga's boom rested on an insecure foundation, but in fairness it must be admitted that it would have taken a soothsayer to detect the flaw in the structure as early as, say, 1885.

Adolph Ochs did not detect it. He became convinced that Chattanooga was destined to be a second Chicago. This was an error, but an excusable one. Less excusable was his second error, namely, that it was his duty to devote his time and resources largely to speeding the consummation. He bought land and planned housing developments, first on the outskirts of the city and then farther and farther afield. Presently he was clear across the river, miles beyond the last scattered houses, offering building lots with subscriptions to the *Times*, with great visions of a suburban development to be called Timesville.

In 1945 a survivor of the boom was asked how long, with the trans-

portation facilities then available, it would have taken a man to proceed from Timesville to the *Times* office. "About two days," was the
significant answer. The basis of the scheme was to be a railroad, starting from the river and climbing the mountain to bring Timesville
within practicable distance; but there was no railroad in existence as
yet. It was all on paper, but on paper it proliferated amazingly and led
to a still more gigantic project, one that all but finished Adolph Ochs
financially.

IX

At the moment, though, he must have been a rarely happy man. He
liked to work, and in these years he had a tremendous amount to do.
More than that, it was exciting work, apparently successful and, from
his viewpoint, a contribution to the general welfare.

This is a point that deserves some elaboration, for it is an index to
the man's character, but one that is easy to misread. Up to this point
every act in Adolph Ochs's career, viewed in the light of twentieth-
century conditions, is consistent with a philosophy of rank, unrelieved
materialism. His faith was in factories, mines and quarries. His notion
of a great contribution to society was a new railroad. Apparently he
would rather see Chattanooga acquire a new ice plant than the Par-
thenon. Had he no social vision whatever, no interest in humanity except as a labor force, no comprehension of the battle of ideas, no
delight in the thrust and parry of intellect not linked with financial
gain? What possessed people to regard this obvious money-grubber as
an enlightened, progressive and idealistic leader?

The explanation of this apparent mystery is not to be found in the
man, but in his environment. What to 1945 seems to be materialism of
a singularly dull, not to say sordid, aspect is, to borrow a theatrical
term, a trick of the lighting effect. For an adequate perception of
what the man really was it is necessary to turn out the lights of the
twentieth century and turn on those of the nineteenth, particularly
the lights by which the South was moving in the century's fourth
quarter.

It is a formidable job to re-create in the imagination the moral and intellectual climate of another century, but unless it is done at least passably well history becomes misleading. The industrial and commercial ruin wreaked upon the South by the Civil War is common knowledge, but the spiritual paralysis following that conflict is far more difficult to portray, yet it lasted longer and is more significant than the material wreckage.

Adolph Ochs began his career at the moment when that paralysis was at its worst. The purse of the South was empty but, worse than that, the mind of the South was ridden by the incubus of defeatism. The long and brilliant line of political philosophers that had shaped the nation had run out in John C. Calhoun. Since his day political thought in the South—if one by courtesy gives it the name of thought —had degenerated into a dreary threshing over of old straw. Religion in the South was becoming bogged in the morass of doctrinal disputation; it was like the shock of a new revelation when a wandering evangelist "preached powerfully" that providing work for starving people was a religious duty.[20] What artistic impulse survived in the South brooded over old wrongs and expressed itself almost exclusively in passionate defense of the old order and nostalgic paeans to a glory that was largely apochryphal and entirely vanished.

Into this atmosphere of listlessness and both moral and physical lethargy came Adolph Ochs proclaiming the doctrine of salvation by labor. Today he and his like—one thinks at once of his brilliant colleagues, Henry Grady, of Georgia, and Walter H. Page, of North Carolina—are accused of apostasy in that they preached that there is no god but the Almighty Dollar. But it is not true. They never preached faith in the dollar; they preached faith in the man, the ordinary, common southerner. If they were insistent on his getting up and seizing a dollar, it was because that was the obvious first step; the main thing was to make him get up.

They were frankly scornful of fine-spun constitutional theories, or

---

[20] See Broadus Mitchell, *Rise of Cotton Mills in the South*, for a curious account of religious influence upon industrialism.

disputes over predestination and free will, or essays attempting to prove the superiority of Timrod over Whittier and of Longstreet over Sherman. Specifically, Ochs had no patience with the journalism that filled its columns with endless arguments over microscopic points, excluding news of the building of a new cotton mill to devote two columns to a political speech by a candidate for Congress, and refusing space to chronicle the activities of an energetic businessman in order to make room for the vapid opinion of somebody whose father had been a Confederate brigadier. Thus he is accused of having no interest in the things of the mind and the spirit; the truth is, he had no interest in nonsense posing as intellectual and spiritual activity.

It is true enough that his was an incomplete philosophy. It is true enough that the impulse he aroused in the South was frequently turned to base purposes. The industrialism that he supported, while at first it made for economic freedom, was capable of being used to establish economic slavery, and sometimes was so used. No doubt Ochs would have been a greater man had he possessed a deeper knowledge of the triumphs of the human spirit and been a more fiery crusader for social justice. Had he been thoroughly grounded in the classics and trained in the cultural traditions of the great universities, he probably would have done better; at least he might have done better. But he wasn't. He was a common man himself, poorly educated, poor in purse, poor in influence, down on the same level with the people he undertook to lead.

To his honor be it said he led them upward. He could do it because he had faith in them—not in money, but in men. And because he had faith in the common man when very few possessed it, people regarded him as conspicuously enlightened, conspicuously progressive, quite definitely an idealist. "Man shall not live by bread alone," to be sure; but bread is none the less necessary if he is to enter into the larger life of the spirit. The group of leaders to which Ochs belonged stimulated a languishing South to bestir itself to obtain the means of sustaining its physical life; to denounce them now because they concentrated on the obviously necessary first step is to misread history, for

[81]

when the wandering evangelist referred to above proclaimed that "Next to the religion of Jesus Christ this town needs most a cotton mill," he wasn't preaching materialism, however it may sound now. He was preaching practical idealism, he was announcing a vision, he was holding up a torch to people who went darkling. Men who do that cannot rightfully be listed among the money-changers in the temple.

CHAPTER IV

In Which a Man Demonstrates the Practicability of Lifting Himself by His Bootstraps.

I

THE years between 1883 and 1888 brought to bear upon Adolph Ochs certain influences other than those connected with his business and public activities, influences that have left almost nothing in the written record, but which must have been as important in shaping his mind and character as anything else. During this time he met grief and fear and stood by open graves. Such experiences have more powerful and lasting effects upon a man than anything that can happen to him in the business world, but there is little that can be said about them. They are the common lot of man; and like many of the most important things in the world, they elude the captivity of the world.

When Effie's first child was born, there was trouble, and the baby did not survive. When the second one came, there was more trouble. The child survived only a few weeks, and for a long time Effie herself lay between life and death, exhausted beyond the point where life itself held much interest for her.

In all probability modern gynecology would have made light of the difficulties, but this was fifty years ago and hers was then an old, familiar story, too familiar to be regarded as noteworthy. Such things happened, and that was all there was to say. Indeed, it was regarded as a bit unmanly to be shattered by misfortune so commonplace. So there is little concerning it to be found in the record. Ochs shut his mouth grimly and went about his business.

Still, it takes no soothsayer to divine behind the curtain of silence heats and pressures sufficient to shape any man's spirit. Adolph Ochs was completely devoted to his wife and he had his full share of the intense family consciousness characteristic of all clannish peoples. Here was a threat to both. More than that, it came, with savage irony, at a moment when his business and professional success seemed to be assured—a grim reminder that, for all the wonders he seemed to be working, he was no more than a man and like all men the plaything of relentless destiny.

It is easy to dismiss all this with a shrug, for it was merely a part of the process of growing up. An individual to whom terror is unkown, to whom grief is a stranger, one who has never felt himself in the clutch of forces beyond human control or stood beside his dead, may be brilliant and attractive and successful, but he doesn't know much. He may be a wonder, but he is hardly a man. Furthermore, sorrow and fear are great catalysts, precipitating whatever may be in suspension in the unformed character. In an essentially small man their touch brings out bitterness and misanthropy; in a big one it broadens his sympathy and quickens his perception of the distress of others. To measure the quality of Adolph Ochs in this regard, consider what they said of him, not in praise, but in disparagement. In New York cynics agreed that he was notoriously a sucker for every hard-luck story that came along, especially if it were one involving domestic troubles. If his critics said that, it is needless for his friends to argue that he was a man of quick and lively sympathies.

This is a quality that cannot be dismissed with a shrug, and tracing its development is an important part of the story of any man's life. There is every reason to believe, in this case, that the development began, or certainly was greatly advanced, in the years when, in spite of his public success, his private life was shadowed by anxiety and re-curring disappointment.

Yet perhaps the same quality that made the man forget the carrier boy's suffering and remember the Christmas gift may account for the scantiness of the records of this sorrowful time; for after all, it ended well. The third child was born, not in Chattanooga, but in Cincinnati, a larger city with much more modern facilities and at least one cele-brated doctor. The maternity hospital was then practically unknown, so accommodations were secured at the Hotel Alms, one of Cincinnati's best, and Effie went there sufficiently far in advance to be sure of first-rate attention. It was successful, and mother and child came back safely to a father whose delight was unbounded—unquestionably all the greater by contrast with the somber years.

The child was a daughter, whom they named Iphigene, after her mother. Her father's joy in her was complete, but it did not prevent his taking impish note of one circumstance connected with her arrival in the world; he never let her forget that she was born in the Alms House.

II

In the late eighties a real-estate boom hit Chattanooga.

The statement seems simple, plain, matter-of-fact, dull. But to any man more than forty who spent his youth in an American town or small city, it is loaded with implications intricate, sinister and frequently strange to the point of incredibility.

The real-estate boom is doubtless an inevitable accompaniment of the sort of development this country has undergone. Great speed precipitates curious economic reactions, some of them apparently illogical; but the economic effects of a real-estate boom are simplicity itself by comparison with the intellectual, social and moral effects upon the participants in the affair. A sort of frenzy seizes upon them, and if the boom is extensive enough the frenzy mounts until it attains a level not far from that of outright madness.

It is a peculiarly American phenomenon, because nowhere else do the necessary conditions exist—nowhere else, except in regions taken over by the military in time of war or some comparable emergency, has the howling wilderness been transformed within the span of a single lifetime into a crowded city, with the colossal increase in land values that accompanies transformation of a rural into an urban area. The suddenness of it is the characteristically American feature. People have been enriched elsewhere by the same process, but not quickly. The Duke of Westminster is, or was until recently, the richest peer in the realm by reason of his ownership of a large area in the heart of

London. But London has been building for a thousand years, and even its relatively sudden increase since the Industrial Revolution has been spread over two hundred years. The growth of the fortune of the house of Westminster, therefore, has not been exciting enough to threaten the normal tranquillity of the Duke's existence. His Grace has observed it with satisfaction, no doubt, as his father observed it before him, and his grandfather and his great-grandfather in their time. But there was no reason for any of them to come near going mad about it.

But if Westminster had seen the market price of his possessions doubled, or tripled, not within a generation or two, but within a week or two, it is not hard to believe that even traditional British phlegm would have been unable to withstand the jolt and the peer might have run as wild as the wildest Chattanoogan between 1885 and 1890.

It is an extreme statement, for they were wild indeed. Even as level a head as that of Adolph Ochs was quite appreciably tilted by the impact of the boom; and many were upset so completely that they ruined themselves irretrievably. What happened is an old, familiar story. During the early part of the town's extremely rapid growth real-estate prices did not rise to the extent that the increase of population justified. After some years the lag was very considerable and the smarter traders realized it suddenly. Then there was a tremendous jump almost overnight and everyone realized that Chattanooga property was much more valuable than people had thought; so there was a rush to buy that swept prices far beyond any reasonable relation to possible returns.

It was bad judgment, extremely bad; yet before we, who have the advantage of hindsight, laugh too loudly at the stupidity of the Tennesseeans, let us consider their environment. If they expected miracles, why not, when miracles were happening around them every day? This was the period of the immense growth of American cities in the Mississippi Valley, with Chicago leading. The conversion of the lonely outpost of Fort Dearborn into a giant metropolis was an event that had not been paralleled since Peter the Great, with millions of slaves at his command, converted a frozen swamp into St. Petersburg. No such feat had ever been performed by freemen, working on their own initiative.

And Chicago was unique only in its size. Cincinnati, Cleveland, Pittsburgh, St. Louis and a dozen others were going up at nearly the same dizzy speed, with Detroit still to come. Why not Chattanooga?

No reason, said the Chattanoogans, provided they were sufficiently vigorous and alert. They had iron ore, timber, coal and transportation, both rail and water. Labor was pouring in, and there were large reserves of manpower on which to draw. Nothing more was needed except brains and organizing ability, and the Chattanoogans believed they could supply both. How could they lose? They decided, Adolph Ochs among them, that they couldn't and proceeded to make ready for a population of a million or so.

All the time, of course, there was a villain lurking just around the corner of the future, a ruthless villain with a big stick. But they didn't see him. They saw lesser villains in plenty—rival towns, railroads whose freight rates were too high, Congressmen who wouldn't vote funds to deepen the Tennessee River and, most villainous of all, pessimists in their own midst who wouldn't work for Chattanooga or at least whoop for Chattanooga. Against all these they did battle, cheerfully and powerfully.

But the real villain they did not perceive because, not being a man, or a rival town, or even a railroad corporation, he was actually imperceptible. He was a thing called Technology and he was even then putting skids under Chattanooga's imperial dreams by introducing the age of steel, in which Chattanooga's sulphur-laden iron ore would be handicapped. The fact that he passed unnoted does not set the town's businessmen apart from their class. Who has been able to foresee unerringly the line that scientific development would take?

The point of real significance, as it affects the career of Adolph Ochs, is that in it there was a sort of exaltation hard to describe in words, but familiar enough to anyone who has passed through a boom. Such an affair begins with the perception of an immediately realizable profit, but it soon passes out of that stage to become interested in profits realizable only in the more and more distant future. Inevitably imagination is called into play at an accelerating rate; and as vast, glittering projects take form in men's mind the profit motive plays a diminishing part until, in extreme cases, they become convinced that they are hardly working for money at all but engaged in an idealistic crusade for the betterment of the community.

Unfortunately, when that point is reached, rational thinking goes down with a crash and men who ordinarily are shrewd and able bargainers plunge into schemes so wild that later they are unable to give any coherent account of how it all came about. It is a form of intoxication both more insidious and more effective than the intoxication produced by alcohol. If it usually results in a more dreadful hangover, at the time it also gives a far greater lift. Men drunk on their own enthusiasm in a real-estate boom are drunk indeed; but if their conduct is likely to be irrational in the extreme, it must be admitted that they have a wonderful time while it lasts. In the late eighties Chattanooga went on a terrible spree; but for a period of two or three years it was unquestionably as happy a town as could be found in all the country. To this day the few survivors of that period—old men now—shake their heads and describe it as a completely crazy time for which they are unable to account; but there is a gleam in their eyes as they remember it.

III

Squarely in the midst of this almost fabulous business orgy was Adolph Ochs busily learning, although he did not yet suspect it, the third great lesson in the textbook of a newspaper publisher—the lesson that the shoemaker should stick to his last.

In justice it must be admitted that he could not have escaped some involvement. The publisher of the leading newspaper in an American town must support what seem to be the town's interests, or he will not be a publisher very long. For the Chattanooga *Times* to be anything but enthusiastic for the boom would have been unthinkable.

But he could have given it journalistic support without plunging into the affair up to the neck—that is to say, he could have done so in theory. In practice, being the sort of man he was, to stay out was a psychological impossibility. Two of his most valuable qualities combined on this occasion to betray him into folly. In the first place, he was a man of imagination, and in the second place, he was a man of tremendous enthusiasms. Without both qualities he could never have rehabilitated the Times; but with them he could no more stay out of the current excitement than a fire-horse can stay quietly in his stall with the bells clanging all around him. Add to this that he was still in his early thirties and had never been really badly burned, and the impossibility of his pursuing the prudent course is evident.

He didn't. Dabbling in real estate at first, he soon became an operator in a really big way on his own account and in a vastly bigger way in partnership with others. He became president of a river steamboat company. He invested in a scheme to make paper out of tobacco stems. He became a leader and frequently the prime mover in every sort of civic enterprise, from erecting a fountain on the public square to building an opera house and beginning the construction of a public park system. He actually bought land in Texas.

He had a fine time. In later years he didn't like to admit it, maintaining that this was a period of heavy labor and of stress and strain without any compensation. As far as the labor and stress are concerned, it is true; and as far as financial compensation is concerned, it is true. But he was the sort of man who is never happier than when he is doing too much. Routine drudgery he disliked, but when work was diversified and exciting there was no such thing as too much of it to suit him. Proof of this is plain. It is in the fact that few of the huge number of jobs he carried in these years were really forced upon him. Most of them he did not merely accept; he went out and gathered them in. He was on the way to ruining himself but he was having a wonderful time doing it.

Nor is it by any means certain that it was all futility and lost motion. Chattanooga was penalized for this boom in many ways and for many years; but some of the ideas generated at this time have survived to make it appreciably a better city than it was before. At least the Chattanoogans learned to think in ways that went beyond the provincial. Ochs, in particular, gave the town an ideal of public service that has never been forgotten. What a standard of that sort may mean to a town cannot be computed in material measures but no rational man denies that its value is great.

The climax came in the organization of what was known locally as "The Over-the-River Company," more formally as the Chattanooga Land, Iron & Coal Co., a project so grandiose that the accounts of it today are all but incredible. It was basically a real-estate development, but a development in the imperial style. It strode across the Tennessee River—whence the local name—and plunged into the hill country on the other side. It involved iron mines, coal mines and large tracts of timber. It involved the creation of a mountain resort and the erection of palatial hotels to accommodate the expected tourists and citizens escaping the heat of the river valley. It involved the building of a railroad from the river up the escarpment to serve both the summer resort and the mines and sawmills. It involved an investment of something like twelve million dollars.

Nearly all Chattanooga plunged into this harebrained adventure with blind enthusiasm, but across the river were country dwellers some of whom were untouched by the excitement. Among these was one Hampton, the owner of a large tract that seemed to be essential to the purposes of the company. Approached by agents of the syndicate backing the project he displayed an extremely languid interest in selling to a group about which he knew nothing. Yes, the price was satisfactory, but he didn't know anything about any syndicate. The fact that Adolph Ochs was a member didn't impress him; yes, he knew Ochs, and if Ochs wanted to buy, he would talk business, but he was flatly not doing business with a syndicate.

The situation was critical. Protracted negotiations would certainly start rumors, and rumors would send skyrocketing the prices of other property the syndicate needed. Prompt action seemed imperative, so in the end Adolph S. Ochs bought the property individually, giving his personal note for a great deal more money than he could easily raise. He was acting for the syndicate, of course, but he made the purchase individually, and transferring title to the syndicate did not relieve him of his obligation to the original owner. Morally, it was the syndicate's debt, but legally Ochs was responsible for seeing that the man got his money.

When the syndicate failed to meet the notes as they fell due Hampton sued Ochs. The defense pleaded that the purchase was made in behalf of the syndicate; that Hampton knew it was for the syndicate; that other members of the group were actually in the next room when the papers were being signed. The plaintiff's answer was that there was not a word about all this in the papers, and it rested its case on the documents. Ochs's lawyer was still making a gallant and voluble effort to argue around this fact when his client suddenly threw in his hand.

"Mr. Swaney, you have won this suit," he said to the plaintiff's attorney. Judgment was entered and a few days later Ochs delivered to the court his check for $103,000. Hampton was justified of his wisdom, whatever the moral quality of his case, when he chose to deal with Ochs alone.

This was the straw that broke the camel's back—except that instead of a straw it was a boulder of enormous size. This is the deal that put his head under water definitely; but it did so many other things that its nature and effects are worth examining in some detail.

It was by no means his only error in these years, but it was the fatal one. The steamboat company, for example, was a losing proposition from the start. The real-estate developments in and around the city dragged on for years before the property began to assume anything like its expected value. The story of his multifarious ventures is long, elaborate and involved, but almost the only significant fact about the man that it reveals is proof that his business judgment was ordinarily good, for nearly every one of them paid out in the end. As long as he was operating strictly on his own account, trusting altogether to his own judgment, he kept, if not within the bounds of prudence, at least within the bounds of reason. Even without the Over-the-River Company he would have been in a tight place, especially when the panic of 1893 struck, but his situation would hardly have been desperate and the story of his life might have been altogether different.

He enjoyed life in Chattanooga and was genuinely fond of the town. Had he been able to squeeze through this financial pinch he might have been content to spend the rest of his life there, dying as a prosperous citizen possessed of large blocks of valuable urban property and, incidentally, of a newspaper. Doubtless it would have been a good newspaper, but it is hard to believe that it would ever have become a conspicuous contribution to American journalism. Doubtless its owner would have been a worthy citizen, but it is hard to believe that he would have been known far beyond the bounds of Tennessee.

What changed all that was his signature on those notes, so it is of prime importance to any true appreciation of the man to understand how it got there.

Simply to write it off as one of those follies that even good businessmen occasionally commit is to lose a large part of its significance. It was foolish, of course, but that proves no more than that Adolph Ochs was not superhuman, and was capable of falling into errors like any other man. What is really interesting is the peculiar nature of this folly, for this peculiarity gives a clue to the mystery of why Ochs did not follow the usual course of a businessman who is caught over-extended. The fact that he did not follow the usual course in this instance throws a flood of light on his subsequent career in New York.

All available evidence indicates that in this deal he considered that he was acting simply as agent for the syndicate and an unpaid agent, at that. Certainly he expected to profit by the deal, but only as a member of the group. There is no indication that he endeavored to make a separate, individual profit out of the purchase of this property; which is to say, he assumed a huge risk without taking measures to assure himself a commensurate profit in case all went well. Clearly, then, he had some motive over and above the profit motive. He expected the Over-the-River Company to be a profit-making enterprise, but he expected it to be something more—he expected it to be an institution with a profound influence upon the social and cultural, as well as the economic, development of Chattanooga. Therefore he was willing to go somewhat beyond the point that would have been his limit in an exclusively profit-making enterprise.

This, not the folly of the deal, is its significant aspect. There is no point in trying to excuse the folly. It was inexcusable. He should have known better—indeed, he did know better in his sober moments, but at this time he was, to put it baldly, drunk, not on alcohol but on the far headier spirit of boom times. So was practically everybody else in the town, but the fact that it was a general orgy does not excuse the individual participant. But what betrayed him into folly was not the common reason, greed, overreaching itself, but the man's desire for something more than a financial profit.

This is the key to Adolph Ochs's character—he liked money, but he always wanted something more.

Let it be admitted at once that this does not make him a knight in shining armor. If he wanted something more than money it was, perhaps primarily and in any event certainly, for his own satisfaction. But while his desire for other things than money does not in itself make him an altruist, it does make him interesting. In all the world there is nothing more commonplace, nothing duller than avarice. A man whose whole being is dominated by the acquisitive instinct may be spectacularly successful, but he cannot be interesting. Precisely because this man, in his mistakes and failures as in his most brilliant achievements, was animated by something beyond the mercenary, he becomes worthy of study.

It was this, too, that made him most thoroughly an American of his period. This aspect of the Imperial Age of business is not one that appeals strongly to writers of the period, simply because it does not lend itself readily to dramatization. Presented truthfully, it spoils the picture of the big businessman as a sordid, soulless money-grubber; on the other hand, presented truthfully, it does not fit into the picture of him as the patriot hero devoted to selfless promotion of the common good.

Nevertheless, the best men of the period had it. Not all—on the contrary, the most lurid portrayals of the muckrakers did not exaggerate the character and deeds of some contemporaries of Adolph Ochs who looted the continent with the remorselessness of gangsters going through a bank. Naturally, their spectacular careers made a deep impression on the minds of men and it is of them that most people think when the post-Civil War period is mentioned.

Yet the truth is that, except for their effect upon public morals, these men were of secondary importance. The men who laid the foundations of the national economy were, practically without exception, bigger than their fortunes. This is not to say that they were necessarily praiseworthy, even in their non-mercenary aspirations. Sometimes these aspirations took the form of a lust for power, or of a vindictive fanaticism, or of megalomania no more admirable than avarice itself; but oftener than not the things that engaged their interest beyond the acquisition of money were things that command respectful attention.

John D. Rockefeller, for example, unquestionably felt that he was creating more than merely a profit-making enterprise in building up the Standard Oil Company. In sober truth, he was. He established order in a fearfully chaotic business. In a sense, he substituted the reign of law for the rule of force and blind chance. He may have done it with a ruthlessness that sometimes made the remedy worse than the disease, but the fact remains that his conception was broader and bolder than the profit-and-loss account, and was based on a sense of social responsibility.

Andrew Carnegie was a philanthropist long before he built a library. It is easy to call him a hypocrite because he first took good care to make sure that his steel business returned a profit; but it is not so easy to dispose of the mass of evidence that the man felt and accepted a very definite responsibility for improving the condition of his less fortunate fellows.

The railroad builders—to be sharply distinguished from the railroad financiers, who were frequently no more than banditti—were after money, without a doubt, but they also sincerely desired to play a part in subduing the wilderness and converting it into a civilized region supporting a prosperous and numerous population. They did it, too. The textile barons, first of New England and then of the South, were not insincere, at least in the early days, in their claim that furnishing employment was as important a part of their function as making a profit.

It is doubtful that in any other nation undergoing a period of vast industrial expansion have the industrialists accepted as readily and as nearly unanimously the theory that a large share of responsibility for the general welfare lay upon them. The reason, undoubtedly, is the absence of an aristocracy of blood in the United States. In all Europe the tradesman, rising to wealth and power, could salve his conscience by shifting social responsibility to the nobility, theoretically the ruling class, therefore responsible for good government. But here there was no nobility. Businessmen were patently the ruling class themselves. So, indeed, they were in Europe, but here there was no convenient theory of a superior class to mask the truth.

Thus in the United States, at the very moment when industrialism was coming into flower, the natural human tendency to buccaneering was complicated and somewhat ameliorated by the American businessman's consciousness that he was not the tradesman, pure and simple, whose function was discharged when he had made money by any means that did not land him in jail, but a social being, indeed, a social leader with responsibilities to society as well as to his ledgers. This makes him the most interesting businessman in the world. The fact that he frequently failed to measure up to his responsibilities is beside the point; his struggle to measure up, sometimes languid but sometimes vigorous and remarkably successful, gives his story its fascination.

Thus Adolph Ochs's acute perception that a man is in business to do something more than make money not only makes him interesting as an individual but proves his essential Americanism. It was the distinctive idea of his time and country, the very insignia of the American businessman. The suggestion may provoke the wrath of the radicals, but perhaps this spirit also accounts for the fact that what was built between 1865 and 1900 has lasted as well as it has, despite the assaults of ideologues of every shade from blood red to leprosy white.

IV

The final blast that blew the Chattanooga boom out of existence came with the great crash of 1893, but as a matter of fact the boom was already dead. It had died lingeringly, not with the swift finality of a blown-out tire, but rather in the manner of a slow leak, every day a little softer, a little flatter, a little more discouraging.

In some ways this is more painful than a financial catastrophe that comes like the crack of doom. It permits men to continue hoping when there is no hope, struggling long after the struggle is in vain. It keeps them on the rack, turning and toasting them with a fiendish leisureliness. It inoculates them with despair in homeopathic doses, not massive enough to kill, but poisoning their spirits cumulatively. Against such an experience the dashing courage of the beau sabreur is of no avail; only the courage of the stoic, the Spartan, can carry a man through.

This was by no means Ochs's strong point. He was the man for the flashing coup, the long shot, the risky circling raid around the flank. He had the cold nerve required for such operations, but the dogged stubbornness needed for a long pounding was something wholly different. The wonder is that he came through as well as he did, considering the agonizing length of the process of his deflation. All around him men who were his friends, men whom he respected, and men less heavily involved than he was were taking refuge in the shelter of the Bankruptcy Act. Some of his advisers urged him to follow suit and he knew that their advice was wholly sincere, not tainted with any selfish motive. But he would not. There was something in him that could not quite stomach the idea of failing to meet an obligation he had voluntarily assumed, no matter how legal the means of escape. For one thing, he could never have been his father's true son if he had taken any questionable means to ease his situation. Nor was it Julius Ochs alone—it was all that the Rabbi stood for in his official capacity, all the long and honorable line who had sworn to their own hurt, back

[96]

to the Old Testament prophets. Ochs did not denounce those others. Many of them he blamed not at all; but for himself, well, voluntary bankruptcy was simply not possible.

His optimism died hard. As the boom sagged and sagged he clung bitterly to the theory that it was a mere temporary recession and he exhausted his ingenuity in expedients. He borrowed from every bank in Chattanooga. He borrowed in Knoxville. Presently he was borrowing small sums from country banks in villages throughout east Tennessee—when a note fell due in one town going over into the next county and borrowing enough to meet it, then reversing the process.

He kept going for an astonishingly long time because he was receiving a handsome income from the Chattanooga *Times*. Through the whole period, including even 1893, there was never a year in which the paper did not show a profit and in most years it was a gratifying profit. But what he made on the *Times* was swallowed up by the other ventures, and presently they were swallowing more. Eventually Adolph Ochs came to the place where he was borrowing money to pay interest and that was too much even for his almost incurable optimism. He was insolvent.[1]

He had, it is true, one resource remaining. Through all his struggles he had somehow contrived to keep the paper clear. This was, of course, good judgment, but it is easy to believe that there was an emotional drive involved also; and emotion may have had as much to do with it as wisdom. All the other things, the land, the houses, the steamboats, the mines, the railroads, were mere property, but the *Times* was something more than property. The newspaper was the expression of its owner's personality, his creation, in a very real sense his life. The Chattanooga *Times* was Adolph Ochs's excuse to the world for cumbering the ground, his payment to society for the rights and privileges he

[1] For obvious reasons everything possible was done to keep the true situation concealed at the time and the records are fragmentary, except as regards the *Times*. The outline presented here was pieced together in part from the researches of Govan and Livingood, but largely from interviews with survivors. The writer is especially indebted to Colonel Milton B. Ochs and to E. Y. Chapin, of Chattanooga, for information on this period.

enjoyed, his claim to the respect of his fellows. Therefore to lay violent hands upon the *Times* would be, for him, almost like maiming his own body.

The day came, though, when even this possibility had to be faced. The proprietor of the newspaper consulted his legal counsel and banking connections quietly and arranged a bond issue of $300,000 on his newspaper property. For the moment, at least, these bonds were not to be marketed, but were to be used for collateral to support existing loans;[2] Ochs had not yet quite given up all hope of pulling out by increasing his income, but he had to do something to gain time.

V

From Chattanooga in general all this was hidden. A few bankers and lawyers among his close business associates may have had a pretty good idea of the real situation and perhaps some of the more astute businessmen guessed that Ochs was in a tight place, but the public had a quite different impression. The public had before its eyes visual evidence of the power and prosperity of the *Times* in the shape of its magnificent new home whose golden dome, soaring above the rest of the city, was a landmark for miles around.

The new building was not the least of the publisher's worries, but whether it was an asset or a liability is hard to say. He had projected it before the air had all leaked out of the boom and had made sure that he extracted the full publicity value from his plans. Before it was completed, however, things had begun to tighten up, and the question was whether to proceed under difficulties or by abandoning the project advertise the difficulties.

He proceeded. It was a characteristic decision in that it was bold and yet based on common sense. In the first place, the *Times* needed the building. In addition to the daily, the shop was now turning out a weekly edition, and a commercial weekly called the *Tradesman*, as well as printing several other periodicals whose ownership was vested in others. Crowded quarters were reducing efficiency of operation and

[2] E. Y. Chapin to the author.

[98]

adding to expense. The new building would cost $100,000 and call for additional equipment; but the business was now of a size that justified such a plant.

Furthermore, the very fact that a man's affairs are becoming more and more involved makes it highly desirable for him to maintain his prestige until he has weathered the crisis. To turn back after having announced a large project is inevitably damaging and by shaking confidence may precipitate the very crisis it is most necessary to avoid.

So the new *Times* building rose, story by story, above the roofs of Chattanooga, magnificent in its granite, its arched windows, its corner tower with a curving entrance, six full stories with a cupola on top surmounted by the golden dome. It was, for the time, a highly efficient newspaper plant, but it was also a civic monument, an architectural triumph that added to the pride of Chattanooga.

It was natural, therefore, on the night of the formal opening, December 8, 1892, for the town to turn out to have a look. Ten thousand persons crowded into the building that night, to admire and wonder at the elevators, the huge, plate-glass windows in the counting room, the big press in the basement and, above all, the newfangled typesetting machines that Ottmar Mergenthaler had recently introduced but that so far had been adopted by very few newspapers south of the Potomac.

But the town was not content merely to stare. Chattanooga felt that it ought to make some more formal acknowledgment of what was plainly a municipal adornment as well as a business establishment. So at nine o'clock in the evening a space was cleared in the crowded front office, Adolph Ochs was brought into it, supported by his wife on one side and his mother on the other, while the venerable Judge D. M. Key, once Postmaster General of the United States and now leader of the bar in Chattanooga, advanced and fired an oration at him, ending by presenting him a morocco-bound volume and a grandfather clock eight feet high.

The book was a testimonial signed by two hundred and seventy citizens who had clubbed together to purchase the clock.

"No one citizen has done more to place Chattanooga in the front rank of progressive cities than yourself," read the testimonial; "and as a slight token of the high regard in which you are held as a friend, a good citizen, an enterprising business man, and a public benefactor, we present to you . . . this testimonial and Grand Father's Clock; and as the clock ticks off the days, weeks, months and years, may each succeeding one bring to you and yours more of the world's goods and more happiness than the preceding one, is the earnest wish of your friends."

In his presentation address Judge Key touched a note of prophecy. The young man who had come to Chattanooga as a boy only a few short years before had accomplished much, he said; but "there are grander heights for you to ascend, broader fields in which to carry your triumphs, and brighter victories still to obtain."

It was all highly gratifying to a worried young man, especially as the whole business had been carefully concealed from him. The clock had been brought in while he was out at supper, muffled in cloth like a monument to be unveiled. But, although taken by surprise, he caught his cue promptly, ending his speech of thanks with a statement of his journalistic philosophy that was as precise as it was appropriate to the occasion.

"I shall endeavor not to go too fast or too slow," he said, "but keep a regular, steady gait in the path of truth and fairness. Every evening before the paper goes to press I shall try to see that everything it contains will be timely and in season and I hope that the reader next morning will find it so. I believe this will be the case if I continue to have the encouragement, support and confidence of the people as I have in the past. I thank you deeply for this kind expression of your friendship and hope that I may continue in your estimation to be deserving of it. I cannot say anything more."

Yes, it was gratifying to have come so far in no more than thirteen years—from the position of an obscure printer to that of proprietor of the city's principal newspaper, now housed in its finest business building, equipped with all the latest machinery for the swift transmission and publication of news It was gratifying to be publicly praised by the town through the voice of its most distinguished citizen, and by others—the Hamilton County Court has sent an engrossed testimonial, and the Southern Associated Press a silver loving cup, flatteringly inscribed. "Friend," "good citizen," "enterprising businessman," "public benefactor"—no doubt the words chimed sweetly enough in Adolph Ochs's ears, and no doubt Effie and his mother were supremely happy. For that matter, Adolph himself was happy, too, for this beyond question was one of the incidents that inspired his lifelong affection for Chattanooga.

But he was not carried away. The slave was at his back, the slave that followed Caesar in the moment of his triumph to whisper in his ear a reminder that he was bald. The slave in Adolph Ochs's case was the memory of all those notes in all those banks; as a newspaperman he was indeed riding the high tide of success, but as a promoter, real-estate dealer, impresario and financial magnate he had been, in the southern phrase, "snatched bald-headed," or was plainly about to be. There is no reason to doubt that he found the moment of his triumph sweet; but it must have had enough of a wry aftertaste to prevent its going to his head.

It was only a few months after this glowing December night that he arranged the bond issue which meant putting the *Times* in hazard to save him from the results of his follies.

VI

Yet it was precisely now, at what was, financially at least, the nadir of his career, that Adolph Ochs demonstrated his possession of the indomitable spirit that is an element and perhaps the basic element of a great man.

He had learned in the last five years that there were a dozen things at which he was no good; but he dismissed that knowledge. He had learned also that there was one thing that he could do, and upon this item of information he concentrated all his energies. He could run a newspaper. Through all the ups and downs of his other enterprises, through good years and bad, the *Times* had steadily paid a profit, had steadily increased in circulation and influence, had steadily improved its service and raised its standards. Obviously the course for Ochs to pursue was to devote himself to running a newspaper, attempting nothing else.

This must have occurred to any man of ordinary good sense, so the fact that this one perceived it is no indication of genius. But his situation did not permit his simple retirement into the publisher's office. He was too badly involved for that. Although the *Times* was returning a net profit somewhere between twenty and thirty thousand dollars a year[3] a great deal of it went to amortize the cost of the new building. Deduct, then, the publisher's living expenses and those of his family, and there was hardly enough left to meet interest payments on his outside liabilities, to say nothing of paying off the principal.

Yet the *Times* was being run at a high level of efficiency, which is to say, it was already doing just about all it could be expected to do. Its current profits were really a tremendous income for a newspaper in a town no larger than Chattanooga and it was idle to hope that they could be increased materially except as the town itself grew; and the collapse of the boom had extinguished hope of any great and rapid growth.

Two courses were open to Adolph Ochs, one prudent and conservative, with no high returns but a fair promise of safety, the other a hair-raising gamble.

The prudent and conservative course was to recognize that he was whipped, ditch his outside enterprises, make the best settlement possible with his creditors, going through bankruptcy if necessary, but trying to wangle through still in control of the newspaper. It would have been difficult, but it was not impossible. Eventually he might have emerged somewhat singed but with a small, sound property that would keep him in comfort for the rest of his days. A small man, or a timid man, would have found that the only course even thinkable.

The other course was to back his own ability to the limit, to plunge on the one thing he knew he could do well. He had to have more

---

[3] Exact figures are not available. This estimate is that of various people more or less familiar with the situation, corroborated by indirect evidence in the statement for his bankers prepared by Ochs at the time of the bond issue.

money. He could make money out of a newspaper. Therefore get another newspaper and make more money. But this meant to add more liabilities to those under which he was already staggering—a suggestion to appall any man except one supremely confident of his own capacity, a genuinely indomitable man.

Adolph Ochs bought the New York *Times*.

VII

The pungent irony in the whole transaction is that he didn't mean to do it.

In the beginning no deal so colossal entered his mind. Yet in the beginning he made the crucial decision, the determination not to accept the small man's way out, but to bet on himself to the limit, throw everything he had into the pot and cry double or quits. This really was the test of the man; what followed was to some extent fortuitous but the decision to back his own ability while he had a single chip left was the decision of a man of size and courage.

There were in the region contiguous to Chattanooga a number of newspaper properties being badly managed. Ochs knew of several that he was convinced could be made to produce far better returns than they were producing at the time and he hoped to secure one of these on terms that he could manage. He made effort after effort[4] to do so, but something always intervened—the price was too high, or the title was defective, or single control could not be secured, or someone cut in ahead of him. Word spread through the craft that Ochs was in the market for another newspaper and suggestions began to be volunteered. The most promising seemed to be the Nashville *American*, which was suffering from what Ochs regarded as bad management, complicated by factional fights among the stockholders. Ochs approached Colonel A. M. Shook, Nashville lawyer and industrialist, who owned part of the stock, and began to dicker.

---

[4] His papers contain a voluminous correspondence covering two years on this subject. There was hardly a newspaper within a radius of two hundred miles about which he did not make at least tentative inquiries.

The negotiations were protracted, but he had expected that. The asking price was far too high, ownership of the stock was scattered, the financial setup was complicated by various notes and liens. The correspondence with Shook lasted through the whole year of 1895 and into 1896, but the parties seemed to be getting closer together. Ochs believed he was on the way to securing the newspaper.

But while the deal dragged an idea of a different sort began to appear with curious pertinacity among his advisers. His friend John R. Walsh, of Chicago, suggested that instead of fooling along with Nashville, or any other small place, he try to get into the New York field. His friend H. H. Kohlsaat, also of Chicago and a publisher for whose judgment Ochs had a high respect, also suggested that he try New York. His friend Leopold Wallach, New York lawyer, not only advised him to come there, but told him of an opening; the New York Mercury, said Wallach, was practically on the rocks and could probably be purchased at a bargain.

This was an idea bound to arrest the attention of a bold and confident man. The Mercury was not a particularly desirable property, but it was a going concern and it was located in New York. It was a Democratic paper, but recently it had been flirting with the free-silver idea, then rending the party, and it was generally believed that its owners were hoping to unload it on the silver crowd, who needed a journalistic spokesman in New York. Ochs's investigation convinced him that the paper had possibilities and he became seriously interested.

But there were obstacles in the way. Again the asking price was too high—a total of $160,000, when Ochs's estimate was that $100,000 was the most he could afford to put into it, since he must expect to operate at a loss for a considerable time before he could build it up into a profitable enterprise. Negotiations hung on this snag for weeks, and then another question arose. The Mercury was operating under a United Press franchise granted under conditions which made it uncertain that it could be transferred; Ochs asked for definite information on this point and couldn't get it. The whole project began to take on a sickly aspect.

The idea of owning a New York newspaper, however, had taken

hold. The terrific competition he would face there daunted him not at all, for he had developed the interesting notion that the worst of it would soon be eliminated. "There is going to be a great change in the newspapers in New York in the next five years," he wrote a friend in May, 1895, "for I believe in less than five years Mr. Dana will die of old age, Pulitzer of nervous prostration and Bennett of riotous living."[5]

In any event, as he wrote Walsh, he knew the New York publishers and there was not a man among them he was afraid to face in business competition. "I am exceedingly anxious to conduct a newspaper in New York if I can do so under favorable circumstances. I must confess I have no suspicion of doubt as to my success in publishing it."

To Kohlsaat, however, he was less jaunty. Years later one of his favorite anecdotes was of a conversation with the sardonic Chicagoan about this time.

"Sometimes I doubt that I am a big enough man to run a newspaper in New York," Ochs confessed.

"Maybe you aren't," said Kohlsaat, dryly, "but just don't tell them so and they'll never find it out."

Summer and autumn and winter passed. The year 1896 came in, and still the negotiations dragged. There was a moment when Ochs turned away from the Mercury altogether and tried to secure the Commercial Advertiser instead. It was a more desirable property but the price set upon it was altogether beyond his means. He returned to balancing the Mercury and the Nashville American. For a time he toyed with the idea of buying them both, putting Milton in charge at Chattanooga and George at Nashville, while he went on to New York.

But in the middle of March, 1896, everything collapsed. The Mercury people definitely rejected his final offer; almost simultaneously the factions at Nashville suddenly burst into open warfare, tangled the paper in litigation and made it impossible for anybody to buy it.

Ochs was profoundly depressed. His position in Chattanooga was

[5] Ochs to Casper H. Rowe, Ochs MSS., May 17, 1895. Details of the negotiations for a New York newspaper come almost entirely from the same source.

growing slowly but steadily worse and every avenue of escape seemed blocked. All the energy and resourcefulness he had displayed for the last two years had gotten him exactly nowhere. He seemed to be staring at a blank wall across the end of the road.

It was at this black moment that he opened a telegram from Harry Alloway, a New York newspaper reporter. It read:

WOULD NEW YORK TIMES PROPOSITION BE ATTRACTIVE NOW? ANSWER CONFIDENTIAL.

Five months later, almost to the day, the paper was his.

It was his greatest moment. Later he did many things that brought him more acclaim, many things that seemed more important in the eyes of the world, many things that appeared to be and perhaps were nobler. But he never did anything that more severely taxed all his personal qualities simultaneously—his courage, his resolution, his judgment, his vision, his ingenuity, his energy, his tact, his eloquence, his patience and his knowledge. It is the superstition of New York that Ochs grew into a great man in the atmosphere of the great city. The truth is that he was never greater than at the moment when he turned his Tennessee defeat into a broad highway to his New York triumph.

CHAPTER V

Interlude Devoted to the Chaos That Was New York About the Year 1896.

I

NEW YORK newspaperdom was mildly astonished when Adolph S. Ochs, of Chattanooga, Tennessee, showed up in control of the remnants of the New York *Times*. The better informed newspapermen knew him as an able and successful small-town publisher, and the handful who had been dickering with him over the *Mercury* had reason to know that he was a shrewd trader. Leopold Wallach, the lawyer, knew more. He had seen genius in the man. But beyond that, and beyond the acquaintances he had made in negotiating the deal, New York knew nothing about Ochs and perceived no reason for learning.

He had bought the wreck of a once great newspaper. Well, what of it? The general assumption was that he had a backer, some millionaire, or some political or commercial group who for reasons of their own did not care to appear in the open and so had put forward this obscure southerner. Nobody believed for a moment that Ochs had done the thing on his own responsibility, for nobody believed it could be done. Certainly tremendous things were being done in New York journalism every day, but they were being done by men with millions and with powerful banking and political connections. No impecunious stranger could possibly invade that field, hence it was obvious that Ochs was, if not exactly a figurehead, at least a false front for some unidentified power.

Not only was this believed at the time, but for many years the smartly sophisticated who pride themselves on having inside information were to expend vast ingenuity on "proving" that Ochs's invisible backer must be whatever figure suited their fancy. A favorite in 1896 was Grover Cleveland, then President of the United States, but a few years later most of the guessers swung to J. Pierpont Morgan, the banker, although some held out for August Belmont. All they were agreed on was that it couldn't possibly be Ochs.

It is a fact that Ochs did have dealings with both the President and the banker. But Mr. Cleveland's entire contribution to the enterprise was a friendly letter, expressing confidence in Ochs's ability as a publisher and hope that his new enterprise would be successful. Mr. Morgan's contribution was an agreement to accept 5 per-cent bonds that might be—and, as the event proved, were—perfectly sound in exchange for certain notes he held which were obviously worth little or nothing. In other words, Mr. Cleveland did only what any good politician would do for a faithful supporter and Mr. Morgan did only what any good banker would do to protect his investments. Neither man had any part in instigating the deal and neither held or ever sought to acquire the slightest degree of control over the newspaper.

Yet the skepticism of New York, although without foundation in fact, is easily understandable. The maelstrom into which the Tennessean stepped blithely was terrific. The great newspaper war between Joseph Pulitzer and William Randolph Hearst was roaring toward its resounding climax at the time of the Spanish-American War, two years later, and all the other newspapers in the city were being buffeted mercilessly by the combat of the giants. The Times, indeed, had been battered down, which explains why it was on the market; and all the rest were suffering great annoyance, if not heavy damage, from the disturbance.

It was a period of conspicuous personalities in the newspaper world, the spectacular sunset of the old-style personal journalism. In a few years editors were to become as anonymous as bank tellers and most publishers would develop an aversion to personal publicity verging on the morbid. It is true enough that journalism would remain personal, as it always had been and doubtless always will be; for a newspaper, like an army, cannot long remain great without a powerful personality somewhere in the high command. But the time was passing when people would look to see what Greeley or Raymond said, rather than what the *Tribune* or the *Times* said, and when editorial controversies quite commonly were decided with horsewhips or pistols on the street.

But as late as 1896 the great moguls of the newspaper world were celebrities in New York whose idiosyncrasies were as much a matter of public interest as those of cabaret singers half a century later. As a matter of fact, the leading newspapers were in the hands of a group of salient personalities and as one looks back it is hard to believe that such salty characters could have been inconspicuous at any time. Whitelaw Reid, controlling the *Tribune*, was the least spectacular, but there was something momentous in the very intensity of his respectability and his aristocratic aloofness from the brawls and uproars all around him. The *Tribune* was the solidest of all New York newspapers, the recognized mouthpiece of the Republican party. Its influence in a chronically Democratic city was limited, but its clientele was assured. Nothing could divorce lifelong Republicans from the *Tribune*, so it could afford to be imperturbable while the heathen raged.

The *Sun* was still directed by the incomparable Charles A. Dana, now drawing near the end of his long life, but still exercising upon fellow members of the craft the fascination that had made him above all others the newspaperman's editor. Long ago Eugene Field, out in Chicago, had written a jingle with a refrain that expressed it all—it was about a wandering craftsman who was obviously a bum yet who was regarded with something like awe in every shop he entered because "he used to work with Dana on the New York Sun." Cynical, scintillant, much more occupied with the right phrase and the play of ideas than with news coverage, the *Sun* was the delight and despair of newspapermen from end to end of the country and, of course, the newspaper of the sophisticates in New York.

The more ponderous intellectuals were equally well served by E. L. Godkin in the *Post*, as strange a genius as the American newspaper world has ever seen. Born in Ireland, trained first in London and then as a roving correspondent all over the world, a man of superb intellectual equipment splendidly developed, he was admittedly the most learned editor in the country. But he had more than learning; as one of the founders and the first editor of the *Nation* he had won a reputation for uncompromising fidelity to high and austere ideals—and for the bitterest tongue in the country. This equipment he had brought to the *Post* in 1881. Fifteen years later that newspaper was celebrated throughout the country as being always morally correct and always infuriating, a situation summed up in the celebrated *mot* of the New York woman who asked how New Yorkers could hope for salvation "with the *Sun* making vice attractive in the morning and the *Post* making virtue odious in the afternoon."

Looming over the field was a monument of departed glory in the *Herald*, already badly damaged by the eccentricities of the second James Gordon Bennett, but still impressive and still supplying the best foreign service in New York. Sixty-five years earlier a raw-boned Scot named Bennett used to foregather with a group of cronies, all but himself printers, in a saloon near Printing House Square. They included a man named Benjamin Day, who was obsessed with an idea for revolutionizing journalism. The ordinary price of a newspaper in 1831 was a "fip," or 6¼ cents, which was also the price of a dozen eggs. Workmen didn't buy newspapers, largely on account of the price, but also because they were filled with long political orations by Mr. Webster and articles clipped from the latest newspapers arriving from England, but with never a word about last night's riot in the Bowery and who had landed in police court as a result. Day's idea was to print the local news in a sheet that would sell for one cent. After years of idle talk, and spurred to action by a cholera epidemic, he did it; and his New York *Sun* was such a resounding success that his cronies followed suit. Bennett set up the New York *Herald* with equipment consisting—or so he afterward maintained—of a board laid across two barrels. Others in that group were the founders of the Philadelphia *Public Ledger* and the Baltimore *Sun*, which, together with the New York papers, constituted the original "penny press" that did, in fact, revolutionize American journalism.

The elder Bennett was full of startling and unpleasant characteristics, but he was a publishing genius. He filled his paper with vulgarity, vituperation and scandal, but he got the news. He was reckless in his attacks and when extra-legal vengeance was visited upon him he never failed to publish the details. Tradition has it that he ordered his composing room to keep ready a standing head, reading, "Bennett Thrashed Again." But the money he made in the early days he plowed back into the business. He built up the most alert and aggressive staff in the country and kept it tuned to a high pitch. For one thing, he established relays of horseback riders across Nova Scotia to pick up dispatches from ships touching there and race them to Annapolis whence they could be brought down to Portland, Maine, then the end of the telegraph line; and when the Mexican War began in 1846 he joined with some others in establishing a combined telegraph and pony express service all the way to New Orleans. He frequently gave news of the war to the War Department itself. His culminating feat was sending the explorer, Henry M. Stanley, into the heart of Africa to find Dr. David Livingstone, the missionary. Before his death he had made the *Herald* one of the greatest newspapers in the world.

But the second Bennett inherited his father's eccentricity without a compensating measure of his genius. Ochs's remark about "riotous living" reflected current opinion. Bennett as a young man became involved in an affair that never has been fully explained. A young woman's name was mentioned; there was talk of a broken engagement, and the scandal broke into the open when Bennett was horsewhipped in public by the young woman's brother. He retired to Paris and never returned to New York except for brief, occasional visits, usually productive of prodigious upheavals in the staff. Yet he did maintain and strengthen the foreign service and a certain prestige clung to his paper even after Bennett was haled into court and heavily fined for publishing advertisements of brothel keepers.

II

But the *Tribune*, the *Sun*, the *Post* and the *Herald*—with the shattered *Times* left far behind and plainly sinking—were the old-line battlewagons of New York journalism, and they were receiving far less attention than a new sort of craft that had recently appeared. The *World* and the *Journal* were having an effect on the press roughly analogous to the effect the aircraft carrier has had on navies in our time.

They were regarded as a new sort of newspaper and, as respects their methods and technique, so they were; but the idea behind them was not new. It was merely a readaptation to different conditions of the idea adumbrated by old Ben Day two generations earlier, the idea that had given the *Herald* and the *Sun* their original impetus. It was the idea of mobilizing and employing effectively the strength of numbers by appealing to the common man. Its practitioners called it democratizing the press. Its opponents called it vulgarizing the press. In fact, it was an application to newspaper work of the idea that was taking shape, dimly at first, but now more and more clearly, in commerce and industry and that worked out into what we now call mass production.

Some ten years earlier a fury had fallen on New York out of the West. From St. Louis had come a thin man, half blind and apparently frail but really composed of whipcord and spring steel, who had blasted Park Row out of its somnolence of many years. Joseph Pulitzer, making a success of the St. Louis *Post*, had combined it with the *Dispatch* of the same city, making a still greater success of the combination. When he had accumulated a quarter of a million he bought the moribund New York *World* and, like Ben Day before him, went out looking for readers that the other papers were neglecting.

His first problem was to make the city aware of his presence and, like Bennett, he determined that the quickest and easiest way to accomplish that was to shock, to startle and to entertain. This he undertook to do and no man was better equipped for the job. Nothing that interested humanity was alien to Joseph Pulitzer, or lacked a place in his columns. Nothing that moved the emotions of large numbers did he deem trivial. He put the ablest writers he could hire on human-interest stories that the more staid papers relegated to the back pages. He used pictures and cartoons lavishly. He went in for colored inks.

He made the *World* as sensational as it was humanly possible to make it and the circulation bounded.

Among his innovations was a comic strip—later to become a bone of contention between him and Hearst—drawn by F. Opper. The hero was a street urchin, garbed in a single shapeless garment which was printed as a block of orange-colored ink. He was known as "The Yellow Kid" and when Hearst captured Opper and Pulitzer tried to carry on with another artist, the Kid became a kind of insigne and the sort of newspapers in which he appeared came to be designated as the "yellow press."

Joseph Pulitzer was cynical, but not the complete cynic. He had, indeed, many of the elements of a very great man. While his play to the groundlings in his early New York days was a deliberate, conscious effort to capitalize on intellectual immaturity, and while his methods of smashing competition frequently resembled those of Captain Kidd rather than those of Lord Nelson, there was underneath it all a genuine faith in democracy. Once he had been beaten at his own game he abandoned it, but he did not abandon his conception of a newspaper as a champion of the underdog Dropping extreme sensationalism when it had served its purpose the *World* developed into a great protagonist of liberalism and so remained to the end of Pulitzer's life.

The real cynic was a man who moved in under Pulitzer's shadow, a tall young man with a long face, so immaculately dressed as to take a place at once among the dandies of the town and so rich that he impressed even New York. Heir to a huge fortune in California, William Randolph Hearst was attracted by journalism. He had his eye on the San Francisco *Examiner* and he came to New York frankly to learn the trade under Pulitzer, whom he regarded as its greatest contemporary master. He studied the setup and methods of the *World* diligently for some months, then returned to the West and applied them on the *Examiner* with resounding success. Within little more than a year he had satisfied himself that he had learned the ropes, whereupon he returned to New York.

At the time, the *World* was occupying only part of its great new building on Park Row and had office space to rent; and Hearst had the impudence to rent an entire floor under the golden dome for his head-quarters in the war which he proposed to wage against his landlord. After looking over the field he purchased the *Journal*, another tottering newspaper property, and launched his campaign.

The battle that followed was Homeric. Nothing like it had ever been seen in the American newspaper world. With millions at his command, Hearst set out to take Pulitzer's clientele away from him. But by this time Pulitzer had millions of his own and he did not propose to have his tenant ride roughshod over him. Every new sensation that Hearst produced Pulitzer promptly capped with one of his own. Every startling advertising campaign to promote the *American* was met by a new move on the part of the *World*.

Pulitzer's superb staff, carefully selected and rigorously trained, was soon riddled. Hearst would pay any price for a first-class man, and salaries shot to amazing heights. This affected the other papers as well as the *World*. Dana sneered, Godkin snarled, Bennett howled by cable from Paris, but the young man with the bottomless purse went serenely along, taking what he thought he might require from the cream of the profession, and the saloons and "lobster palaces" of New York became familiar with the faces of newspapermen enjoying an unprecedented affluence. Tradition has it that Hearst sunk eight million dollars in the *Journal* before he drove it ahead of the *World* in circulation and began to collect. The cost to Pulitzer has never been authoritatively estimated, but that it was prodigious is beyond doubt.

III

Into this shambles stepped Adolph Ochs with $75,000 to try conclusions with men who were throwing millions around as if they were tossing beanbags.

Small wonder that New York scornfully rejected the truth and assumed as a matter of course the presence of some invisible backer whom Ochs was representing! It was so easy to prove, in so many ways, that the thing couldn't be done that none of the wise in their own conceit could possibly accept the facts.

Indeed, to this day there are many phases of the affair that remain obscure. For instance, where did he get even $75,000? The most plausible explanation is that bond issue of the Chattanooga *Times*.[1] There is no evidence in the records that they had even been issued; Ochs seems to have been holding them as a last desperate expedient if bankruptcy became imminent. If it was really upon these bonds that he raised the money, the evidence of his confidence in himself is impressive. He was so certain of success that he was willing to do what he had never done before, pawn his Tennessee newspaper, in order to get a chance to compete with Hearst and Pulitzer!

As a matter of fact, though, that was only the superficial aspect of the situation. In a more exact sense, a sense that New York did not perceive, he did not intend to compete with them. He had the wit to descry a corner of the New York field that was not trampled by the boots of the contending forces and it was this that he proposed to occupy.

Adolph Ochs was not a cynic. This is the crucial fact that must be kept in mind if his achievement in New York is to be made intelligible. He was not a sentimentalist, either. He was well aware that the method pursued by Hearst and Pulitzer—pursued earlier by Bennett— is a very effective means of building up circulation and thereby commanding advertising; but he never cherished the cynical delusion that it is the only possible method. It was his firm conviction that from the masses a response can be evoked by an appeal based on nothing more sensational than fairness, accuracy and intelligibility.

In all New York nobody was making exactly that appeal. Dana's appeal was to intellectuality, Godkin's to morality, Bennett's to curiosity not untinged with snobbery—if one leaves out the appeal to pruriency of his advertising—that of the yellow press to emotion. The cynics might point out that the *Times* itself had been making just the

[1] E. Y. Chapin, who probably knows more about the circumstances than anyone else, inclines to this theory; and certainly at the moment of the sale one New York bank made a temporary loan of $25,000 on those bonds.

sort of appeal Ochs had in mind and the *Times* was sinking; but Ochs would have denied it. In the past the *Times* had indeed been just the sort of newspaper he had in mind, but it was so no longer. A period of bad management had ended by impairing its editorial policy, and it was now padding its columns with stuff that was not news but shameless flattery of advertisers or politicians who might be in position to aid its fortunes. But it was bad management, not any lack of validity in its original policy that had brought it low. Ochs knew he could supply good management; and he believed that nothing more was needed to restore the *Times* to the great position it had held of old.

For it had once been great. On that point, everyone at all acquainted with the history of American journalism was—and is yet—agreed. The *Times* had been created by two young men who were idealists, indeed, but who yet had their feet on the ground. That is strictly figurative, for it is literally true that at the moment when they first conceived the idea of their newspaper their feet were not on the ground at all; instead, they were on the ice in the middle of the Hudson River.

In the winter of 1858–59 the river froze over and two young men, one named Henry J. Raymond, the other George Jones, were making an adventurous expedition. They determined to cross on the ice and it was during this trip that they decided finally to undertake a project they had been thinking over for some time. They founded the New York *Times* as a Whig newspaper, but it did not remain long in that party. The forces of liberalism and idealism were pouring into the new Republican party, which claimed to be the legitimate heir of Jefferson. As is the way of new parties, it was collecting not only the genuine liberals but also the restless and impatient, every type of fanatic except fanatical supporters of slavery, most of the disgruntled Whigs and Democrats and a small but potent group of political janissaries who perceived in service under the new flag tempting opportunities for glory and loot.

These last, however, were invisible in the early days. To able and sincere young men, such as Raymond and Jones, the new party seemed to represent every element that made for decent and intelligent government. It stood in glowing contrast to the dubious motives and rheumatic thinking characteristic of the old parties. They had not started their newspaper to be a party organ; they intended it to support honest and intelligent government without regard to party label. While they were in general agreement with Whig principles, they took the stand that character and ability in government take precedence over any party program. Within a year they went over to the Republican party, thus committing the *Times* right at the beginning to the principle that brains and honesty come first and party allegiance afterward.

It is a fine standard for any newspaper, but it is a bruising one to uphold. Within six years the *Times* was doing battle against the leaders of its new party. Raymond, as much a politician as an editor, got himself elected to Congress and eventually became chairman of the Republican National Committee; but he was not enough of a politician to go along quietly when the party entered upon a path that seemed to him suicidal. Completely convinced of the wisdom of Abraham Lincoln, he was sickened when Thaddeus Stevens and his followers jettisoned Lincoln's policy of reconciliation after the war and substituted for it one of bitterness and revenge. Above all, he fought furiously against the madness of impeaching President Andrew Johnson.

This pretty well finished him as a party politician and it brought down the wrath of the party leaders upon the paper; but the paper suffered less than Raymond. There were enough fair-minded people in New York City to support a newspaper in a course that seemed to them right. The *Times* emerged from the battle with its Republicanism somewhat in question, but with its honesty and courage established beyond doubt. Raymond, however, died in 1869 when he was less than fifty years old.

Later under George Jones, the surviving partner, the *Times* conducted a tremendously effective battle against the Tweed Ring that was looting the city. From the journalistic standpoint this was one of the *Times's* finest achievements, but it tells less about the character of the paper than some other fights, for in this case there was no question of divided loyalties. Tweed and his crew were Democrats and the *Times* could lay on with the approval of all its own party.

A far more severe test came with the scandals in the Grant administration. When they broke the *Times* went flatly into open opposition. It suffered, too, for the period was one in which public standards of political morality had sunk to one of the lowest levels they ever touched. It was not merely that men in high office had been caught in brazen crookedness; it was also that the public reaction was dull and apathetic. It was one of those dismal epochs in which the moral vitality of the nation seems to burn as low as the physical vitality of an exhausted man. In business, in politics, everywhere, the test of public approval of almost any act seemed to be the agent's ability to get away with it. There were times when the Republican party's leadership apparently resented most, not the crimes of the Whisky Ring and the others, but their stupidity in getting caught. So the *Times's* thundering denunciations of dishonesty simply because it was dishonest, not only brought reprisals from the politicians, but came dangerously near boring its own constituency.

Yet, after all, there were those who had not bowed the knee to Baal. In the Grant administration the fight was a fight against plain, unmitigated corruption and the courage of the *Times* did bring it some support—perhaps as much as the indignation of the partisans cost it. In the material sense it gained nothing by the fight, nor did it lose much; but its prestige was enhanced.

What finally brought it down was its revolt against James G. Blaine in 1884. Here the case was somewhat different. Blaine was not an out-and-out crook, he was merely a politician with a somewhat smelly record. Nobody accused him of stealing, but only of having used his position in Congress—he had been Speaker of the House—to advance legislation favorable to companies in which he had a financial interest.

To the *Times* it seemed horrible to nominate for President of the United States a man whose financial integrity had even that much of a stain on it; but partisanship was running so high that a great many Republicans deemed it worth almost any price to keep the Democrats out. It was plain that Grover Cleveland, the Democratic candidate, would put up a tremendous fight, and every possible vote would be needed. True, the Republican candidate might smell a little but, after all, there was nothing in his record on which he could be sent to jail. Therefore, when the *Times* bolted to Cleveland a great many people felt that it was assassinating the Republican party for an unimportant scruple.

Cleveland won, but the *Times* lost. Republican readers deserted it in shoals and Democrats did not come swarming to the support of a paper with a long record of Republicanism. Furthermore George Jones was already well up in the seventies and perhaps the ingenuity and resourcefulness necessary for an adaptation to a new situation were not in him.[2] In any event, profits began to decline even before Jones's death in 1891, and his passing removed the paper's mainstay. He bequeathed the property to his heirs, but he couldn't pass along his managerial genius and within a year they found that they had inherited a white elephant indeed. Profits had vanished altogether and the deficit began to mount. Soon the heirs' one thought was to get rid of the thing with all possible speed.

This came to the knowledge of the staff, and there ensued one of those gallant, but hopeless, efforts with which the history of journalism is studded. The *Times* was served by many men to whom the paper was far more than merely a means of livelihood. Its honorable record was a part of their honor, its fine traditions were a part of their mental and emotional history. Its sale to the first comer might mean its extinction and would certainly mean a radical alteration in its character.

It was a prospect which the men on the *Times* found literally unendurable. The traditionally cynical, hard-boiled newspaperman is really one of the world's great sentimentalists, and the extinction or degradation of a once great newspaper is literally as painful to him as the death of a beloved friend. So the men on the *Times*, headed by

---

[2] Elmer Davis, in his *History of the New York Times*, denies that the political change had more than a temporary effect on the fortunes of the paper. Most of the ground lost in 1884 had been regained in three or four years, he says, and the collapse was due largely to the expense incurred in erecting a new building. But he admits that profits, which had run as high as $100,000 a year, by 1890 had sunk to $15,000. The new building didn't do that.

Charles R. Miller, the editor, threw everything they had into a desperate effort to save the paper. They formed a company and by prodigious efforts managed to borrow or beg a million dollars,[3] for which price the heirs had agreed to sell.

What they got was little more than a name, for the equipment was largely worn out and the real estate, including the building occupied by the paper and "erected with its profits and its credit,"[4] went to the Jones estate. Then, within a few months of the purchase came the panic of 1893, with a disastrous falling off in advertising, especially financial advertising, in which the *Times* was pre-eminent. Since everything they could raise had gone into the purchase price, the new owners were without operating capital. Somehow they managed to sell debentures of the new company to the amount of $250,000 and this money kept the paper going for a time; but in fact only a publishing genius could have pulled it through and they had no genius— a good editorial staff, yes, but no publisher of the first rank. The amazing thing is that it kept staggering along for three years.

But it was absolutely at the end of its rope when Harry Alloway sent his telegram to Adolph Ochs in the spring of 1896.

IV

Charles R. Miller was more than a superb newspaper editor. He was also a stouthearted gentleman, but he did not appear to advantage in March, 1896, for at that moment he was a whipped man. All that he had of energy, of ability, of courage and determination, had been thrown into the effort to save the *Times*, and he had lost. Holders of the paper's promises to pay had exhausted their patience, and at that moment they were dickering with the proprietor of what Miller regarded as a rather noisome picture sheet with the avowed purpose of allowing him to purchase the *Times* and combine it with his rag.

[3] To be precise, $950,000, for at the last moment one man who had promised $50,000 was unable to make good; but the heirs, impressed by the loyalty and energy of the staff, cut the price by that amount. Davis, *op. cit.*

[4] Davis, *op. cit.*

The journal that Miller had served and loved through the last thirteen years was not even to be allowed the grace of a quick, clean death.

All the fight was out of Miller. Apparently he had sunk into a sort of numb apathy and was simply awaiting the end. He was past caring. Even when they told him that a new man had entered the field and was considering the purchase of the *Times,* he was not much interested. He didn't want to see the follow. Why waste time and harrow up his soul again by repeating the dismal tale to some fantastic hick from the back of beyond who thought he could accomplish what the best newspaper brains in New York had decided was an impossible task? Repeatedly Miller refused to grant an interview to this—what was his name?—oh, yes, Ochs.

But Harry Alloway was persistent, so to get rid of him Miller at last agreed that if the man would come to his house he would give him fifteen minutes one night after dinner. But he meant fifteen minutes and no more, because he had promised that night to accompany his family to the theater, and he didn't propose to miss the first act to accommodate the intrusive Tennesseean.

The proposal was accepted and the visitor arrived on the minute. Miller told the family to get into their coats and hats while he disposed of the caller, who was ushered into his study. The door closed behind him, the family prepared to go out and then began to fidget. At the end of a quarter of an hour the door opened and Miller looked out. He instructed them to proceed and he would join them at the theater, since the interview was taking a little longer than he had expected. They went, expecting him by the time the curtain rose; but the first act ended—no Miller. The play went on to its end, and still no Miller. The family came home to find the study door still closed with the head of the house inside. It was close to one o'clock when he emerged, showed his visitor to the street door and turned back into his home, somewhat dazed and incredulous but with at least the suggestion of a new gleam in his eye. The man, he said, had ideas; as far as the editorial policy of the paper was concerned, they were substantially identical with Miller's own ideas, but in addition to that the newcomer was full of notions about pulling the paper out of the hole financially. Many of these had never occurred to the editor, but they were extremely plausible and Miller was almost daring to hope that they were sound.

This was the critical moment that decided the success of Adolph Ochs's effort to acquire the *Times*. There was still a vast amount to be done. All Ochs's energy, ingenuity and resourcefulness were to be strained to the limit before the deal was completed, but without the co-operation of Charles R. Miller there would have been no chance of a successful outcome.

And it is precisely at this point that the biographer is defeated. "What song the sirens sang" Sir Thomas Browne thought not beyond conjecture, and the substance of what the caller said that night may be gathered from subsequent statements that he and Miller put on record. But how did he say it? That is the all-important point, and that eludes the chronicler as the central mystery of personality must always elude those who seek to capture and imprison it in words. But the inference is inescapable that it must have been one of the greatest sales talks an American businessman ever made. For the circumstances made the task doubly difficult. In the first place, Ochs had to inspire in Miller confidence in a complete stranger of unknown ability and character. This was formidable enough, when the subject was a veteran New York newspaperman of high intelligence and long experience, but at that it was the lesser difficulty. More formidable by far was the equally necessary task of re-establishing a beaten man's confidence in himself.

The armament of letters that Ochs had brought with him was utterly useless for that purpose. Realizing the handicap of his lack of acquaintance in the city, he had applied to nearly everybody he knew for letters of introduction, starting with President Cleveland.[5] They were doubtless more or less valuable in establishing the credit of Adolph

[5] The President wrote, "In your management of the Chattanooga *Times* you have demonstrated such a faithful adherence to Democratic principles, and have so bravely supported the ideas and policies which tend to the safety of our country as well as of our party that I would be glad to see you in a larger sphere of usefulness."

Ochs, but they could do nothing toward re-establishing the credit of
Charles R. Miller in his own mind. They could not put a fresh will to
fight in a man with all the fight knocked out of him and conjure up
a vision of success before the eyes of a man only too bitterly conscious
of his own failure.

That miracle must have been worked, not by the arguments, but by
the dynamic personality of the man from Tennessee. It was the electric
contact that had inspired the jobless printers after the *Dispatch* had
failed and that had magnetized the hard-bitten MacGowan into following the lead of an adolescent. That it struck a spark in the dispirited
Miller was perhaps a somewhat larger achievement, but it was the same
sort of achievement. Ochs was playing on a broader scale the role that
he had learned in Chattanooga.

Yet in this connection "learned" is a doubtful word, unless one un-
derstands it in the sense in which one might say that Napoleon learned
the art of war and Raphael learned the value of color. No doubt as
he grew older Ochs did learn more and more about the art of handling men; but in the beginning there must have been an enormous
capacity that was never acquired by study.

Yet granting that there was born in the man a faculty of leadership
that forever escapes analysis there are certain aspects of his accomplishment that are indubitably related to his time and his country. Fully
to appreciate the situation one must bear in mind that when Ochs entered Miller's study that night he was a whipped man himself. His
adventure into real estate and multifarious other non-journalistic enterprises had been a failure as disastrous as Miller's emergence from edit-
ing into publishing. Indomitable courage is a gift of the gods and no
doubt Ochs would have had it whatever might have been his native
land; but it is extremely doubtful that his courage would have given
him the bounce that he had anywhere except in America, and perhaps
not even in America at another period.

But this was a moment when the United States had not merely an
expanding economy but one expanding at a rate never approached
before, a rate that seemed more like explosion than expansion. The

last frontier had been closed just three years before and the whole vast continent was now open to development that was proceeding with incredible speed. The country was cramming into decades economic changes that everywhere else had required centuries, and changes of fortune were accomplished with an abruptness and a dizzy speed never witnessed before. One curious effect of this was to establish in the American mind a lordly contempt for financial ruin. So often had a man made a fortune, lost every cent, and then turned to and made another and greater one that the occurrence, far from being regarded as a miracle, was almost commonplace.

In 1896 Adolph Ochs, who had once rated himself as worth $300,000 over and above all liabilities, was actually insolvent. He was a man of courage, therefore had he been a European he would have met the situation with fortitude; but it is doubtful that anyone but an American, and especially an American of the post-Civil War period, could have met it with the resilience that he displayed. When opportunity is boundless it is not mere rodomontade to say, as they said in those days, "A man may be down, but he's never out." This was the proclaimed slogan of the Salvation Army, but it was also the tacit assumption of the Chambers of Commerce, the trade associations and, to an astonishing extent, even the banks.

It is inadequate, therefore, to say that Miller was inspired by contact with a man of courage. It is essential to remember that it was a peculiarly American form of courage widely prevalent in 1896. It was that combination of hope based rather solidly on experience and of keen vision ranging over an all but illimitable prospect that was at the very moment creating the trusts and the transcontinental railroads, the American standard of living and the American mechanization of life, mass production, mass education, mass regimentation, and that was fumblingly and gropingly moving toward some tremendous goal— whether the democratization of culture or the degradation of the human spirit remains to be seen. There were giants in the land in those days and they were creating with a lavish hand and startling impartiality magnificence and monstrosities that dazed the world. Kipling, observing this sort of American, wrote acidly that

[124]

                                                        elate
He greets the embarrassed gods, nor fears
To shake the iron hand of Fate
Or match with Destiny for beers.

Miller, perhaps, was one of the embarrassed gods, but only momentarily. Within a matter of days he had become convinced that here was
the man to save the *Times*, and with the conviction his fighting spirit
revived and he became Ochs's invaluable ally in the intricate negotiations that followed.

V

Those negotiations were long and difficult, not because there was
any angry and determined opposition, but simply because Ochs was
trying to persuade a group of hardheaded businessmen to embark upon
what was, on the surface, an insane adventure. Here was a business
enterprise losing more than $2000 a week; and he coolly proposed that
they put more money into it and turn it over to him.

More than that and, if possible, more startling than that, he coupled
his proposal with an announcement that he did not intend to change
the *Times* at all, as far as its editorial policy was concerned. On the contrary, he proposed to continue the same staff in charge because he regarded it as a very good one—and this in face of the terrific losses.

It is indicative of his persuasive powers that by the time he had seen
all those most concerned they, instead of calling for a straitjacket, were
making a counterproposal and a handsome one. Charles R. Flint, who,
at the solicitation of Miller, had invested $50,000, was convinced that
the only hope of salvaging anything was to sell the *Times* to the proprietor of the picture sheet; and as Flint' controlled three of the five
directors, he had the power to make the sale. But he had been stopped
temporarily when Miller and Edward Carey, who was also a holdover
from the Jones regime, took the desperate step of throwing the paper
into bankruptcy. This was gambling on Ochs with a vengeance, but it
did gain time. With Alfred Ely, a New York lawyer, as receiver, the
paper was carried on for four months.

In the meantime other stockholders headed by Spencer Trask, the banker, had been strongly impressed by Ochs's ability. While at first they did not take seriously his proposal that the paper be handed over to him, lock, stock and barrel, they did decide that he was just the sort of manager they had been seeking. So they offered him the job on a salary basis, starting at a large figure and, as they became more and more enamored of the idea, going up step by step until it reached $50,000 a year.

This, they believed, would prove irresistible to a man from Tennessee. Indeed, it would have been irresistible to most newspapermen in New York, for in 1896 a salary of $50,000 was much more impressive than it is half a century later. Ochs knew it, and in letters to his wife he confessed that he was flattered; but he was not tempted for a moment. When negotiations had been in progress a little more than a month he made his position plain in writing:

It is well that we should have a clear understanding of the terms and conditions under which I am willing to assume the management of the New York Times, and invest $50,000 with the new capital.

To that end I submit in general terms the conditions to which I am willing to subscribe.

I begin with the hypothesis that it is generally conceded that the New York Times, as now circumstanced, is bankrupt; that its assets cannot be sold for an amount sufficient to pay its debts, which are estimated to aggregate $350,000; and that, for some years past, even under the latter year management of the Jones Estate, the receipts fell short of expenditures; and that for the past three years this deficit has exceeded $2,500 a week.

I hope to be able to so manage the property, while conducting it as a decent, dignified and independent newspaper, that this deficit will be extinguished, and that it will earn and pay 5% interest on $500,000, and create a sinking fund of $15,000 a year; thus turning an annual deficit of more than $100,000 into a surplus of $40,000, requiring more than $140,000 per annum increase in the receipts, as compared with the last two or three years.

I contend that a man capable of accomplishing such results as outlined in the foregoing paragraph, is entitled to fully one half of the earnings in excess of so large a sum as a fixed annual charge.

Let me say at this point that at a fixed salary I would not undertake the task, even if the salary were made three times that I hereafter mention. I have no need to seek employment. I say this, for I do not wish the salary hereafter mentioned to be considered as full compensation for my services, but rather a provision for my necessary living expenses.

I am impelled by only one desire in these negotiations, and that is to secure permanent control of the New York *Times* which I believe I can make a successful and very profitable business enterprise, and at the same time make it a model American newspaper, a model high-standard daily journal, a model for fairness, cleanliness, independence and enterprise, a welcome daily visitor in the homes of intelligent and respectable people.

Unless I can be assured that under reasonable conditions (alike fair to me and to those who now or hereafter may have money invested in the New York *Times*) I would secure the permanent control of the property, I would not care to further pursue these negotiations. I would not entertain a proposition that means anything less, which involves a surrender of any of these principles, on which I know, from past experience, I must succeed.

And furthermore, unless I am in absolute control of the property and of all who are employed therein, I would not undertake the management at any price, for I am certain that I would not succeed as manager with any abridgement of almost autocratic power.

Now assuming the foregoing conditions to be understood and accepted, I agree to invest $50,000 and give my best efforts to make the business a success, make it earn a dividend on its capital stock while maintaining its high standard.[6]

This was bold to the point of arrogance—"the supremacy of gall for a country newspaperman burdened with debts" Ochs himself called it in a letter to his wife. Momentarily it floored Trask, and the negotiations hung fire for a few weeks, leaving Ochs in an agony of apprehension. Yet within five years men were calling it the best move he could possibly have made and wondering where this inexperienced countryman acquired the extraordinary wisdom that led him to his decision.

They overlooked the fact that while he was a countryman he was far from inexperienced. There was a ghost standing between him and acceptance of Trask's offer—the ghost of the dead-and-gone Chat-

[6] To Spencer Trask, May 9, 1896. Ochs MSS.

tanooga *Dispatch.* New York had never heard of the *Dispatch,* and if it had would have regarded the extinction of an insignificant village newspaper as unworthy of note in the history of journalism. As regards the paper itself, New York would have been right; but its death is a different matter. The death of the *Dispatch* taught young Adolph Ochs a lesson that he never forgot, namely, that if a newspaper organization is to succeed, somebody must be boss. The most brilliant staff in the world will not operate well for long unless authority is concentrated in competent hands. A manager, no matter how able, who has to explain every move to a group of stockholders with no technical knowledge of newspaper work is in a hopeless position. The odds against his success are overwhelming and never again did Ochs propose to occupy that unhappy position.

It is a curious fact that this principle is hotly denied by many newspapermen, especially those engaged in writing the paper. There is a good deal of artistic temperament in the craft, and it is difficult in the extreme for an artist to understand that artistry does not comprehend the whole of intellectuality. Brilliant men chafing under what they regard as the plodding mental processes of a publisher who never emitted a spark in his life are prone to delude themselves with the idea that a committee of brilliant men could do a much better job than one dull fellow who moves carefully and cautiously, therefore slowly. As regards the writing of the paper, there is something to be said for the theory; brilliant minds are burnished by contact with each other. But getting the paper printed and distributed is a manufacturing and merchandising operation for which the brilliant writer as a rule is poorly equipped; and a committee cannot supply the deficiency. Indeed, a committee in control of anything involving mechanical production nearly always does, not a better, but a worse job than would be turned out by its least competent member if he were in control.

It is true enough that a competent newspaper publisher cannot be exclusively a manufacturer and merchant. He must have the rare ability to understand men whose minds are of a different fiber from that of the successful businessman; to understand what they are doing and to stimulate them when they are right; and always to keep in mind the whole picture of which the brilliant writer nearly always sees only a part. But this presupposes an intellectual range and power of impressive proportions; and a man with a powerful mind must have authority commensurate with his strength if he is to function efficiently. The really great publisher, in fact, is a much rarer bird than the powerful writer; and to get in his way is a more antisocial act than to frustrate the artist.

Nobody was going to get in Adolph Ochs's way—not any more. It is highly improbable that he ever spent much time analyzing his own temperament. But he knew that the *Dispatch* need not have died if competent hands had held adequate authority; also he knew that it did die and that because of its death he and MacGowan and a group of printers were all thrown on the street with no jobs. Once was enough. That mistake he was not going to make again, in New York or elsewhere; and neither Spencer Trask nor anybody else could tempt him into that trap, not even with $50,000 as bait.

But candor and clarity paid. Trask himself was a man of high ability and therefore able to appreciate the force of Ochs's reasoning. If he was momentarily taken aback by the flat rejection of his own scheme, it was not for long. One month and three days after submitting his proposal Ochs was able to write to his wife that he had "captured Trask." His appreciation of the importance of this victory is reflected in the satisfaction with which he reported it. "It is no little accomplishment to get a man not only to abandon his own pet scheme, but to accept one which is much less profitable to him," he wrote.

As to the latter part of the statement one may be permitted to cherish a doubt. Spencer Trask was a banker, but not one of the unimaginative sort whose utmost vision is bounded by the dream of 4 per-cent and safety. He was capable of understanding what Ochs was talking about. They sat in Trask's home one night from ten o'clock until half-past one; and Ochs went away not only with Trask's agreement to accept his scheme, but with the banker's promise to put up $25,000 of new money to help put the scheme through.

On the face of it, this seemed to be from the banker's standpoint a dead loss. Under the Ochs scheme Trask's stock would be reduced in value by fourth-fifths—that is to say, in face value. But the stock, as things stood, was really worth nothing. Eventually, under the new management, the stock became worth much more than five times what Trask had paid for it; hence the fifth that he retained in the end recouped his losses and more. The deal was unprofitable only in appearance. It was a case of accepting a temporary reduction in value in order to profit by a later rise, and before Ochs had quit talking that night the shrewd banker knew it.

This was the Tennesseean's second personal triumph as the conversion of Miller had been his first. Trask brought in Flint, and after that it was easy to round up the rest of the stockholders. Only the security holders remained to be dealt with; but they included such formidable people as J. P. Morgan, August Belmont and the Equitable Life Assurance Society.

VI

The Ochs plan of reorganization was frankly a gamble on the ability of the proposed management. A new corporation, the New York Times Company, was formed with 10,000 shares authorized of a par value of $100 each. The old company likewise had had 10,000 shares and its stockholders were offered one share in the new company for each five of the old one, which is to say, 2000 of the new shares were exchanged for all of the old ones.

The bondholders and other creditors, who held obligations of the old company to the amount of $300,000, were offered $300,000 in 5-percent bonds of the new company, thereby funding the outstanding debt.

There remained the question of raising working capital. To take care of this Ochs proposed to offer at par $200,000 additional bonds of the new company. To induce purchasers to take them, he offered a bonus of 15 shares of the new stock with each $1000 bond. Seventy-five of these he took himself, which gave him 1125 shares of the stock.

Finally, there was the matter of his compensation. He had named a salary of $10,000 a year, but he had explained that this was to cover his living expenses. If he succeeded in pulling the paper out of the hole, all its stockholders would profit enormously and his services would be worth far more than $10,000—if he didn't, they would all be exactly where they then were, to wit, in bankruptcy. He therefore made his real compensation contingent on his success. There were to be deposited in escrow 3876 shares of stock. When, and only when, the paper had showed a profit for three consecutive years, this stock was to be his without further payment. Added to the 1125 he had secured by purchasing the bonds, it would give him 5001 shares—a clear majority of the stock and therefore absolute control.[7]

The trick, of course, was the sale at par of $200,000 of the bonds of a bankrupt newspaper; or, rather, of $125,000, since Ochs himself was taking the rest. How he did it, nobody can tell. He was never an eloquent man. He wasn't even a smooth man—polite enough, but not endowed with the suavity of a Chesterfield or a headwaiter by any means. He had no particularly commanding presence. Of barely average height, he was at this time still slender and almost frail in physical appearance. If the term "sales psychology" had then been invented, which is doubtful, the chances are a hundred to one that he had never heard it.

All he had was a tremendous belief in himself and in the potential value of the *Times* coupled with an extraordinary facility at putting his ideas into plain words. Even these ideas, as far as we have any record of them, were not in the least startling, nor what the average man would describe as brilliant. The response of the typical businessman to an argument by Adolph Ochs was rarely to exclaim, "Amazing!" but usually to say, "Why, of course." Yet when the effect of a man's argument upon you is to make you feel like kicking yourself for not having thought of that long ago, he is almost irresistible. The ability to produce this effect Adolph Ochs had in a high degree; everyone he approached in New York felt that at least he was a man of sense. At this time perhaps only Leopold Wallach realized that the force in the man was more than common sense in any ordinary definition of the term—that it was common sense intensified, multiplied, raised to a power that made it indistinguishable from inspiration. To most men

[7] The scheme is explained in detail in the Ochs MSS. and its substance has been published repeatedly. The summary above follows Davis, *op. cit.*, pp. 185–186.

"inspired common sense" is a contradiction in terms, since they are accustomed to regard inspiration and common sense as opposites; yet this is a case that defies classification in ordinary categories.

We know that he did not propose any new, untried methods to revive the newspaper that was obviously dying of dry rot. We know that he had none of the fanatical zeal that inspires protagonists of utopias. We know that he had no tricks of speech or manner, no histrionic fascination whatever. We know, in short, that he was the very opposite of dazzling. Yet at the same time we know that he not only convinced Spencer Trask that his own scheme was a bad one, but made him a convert to the Ochs scheme. We know that in an interview lasting less than twenty minutes he persuaded J. P. Morgan to accept bonds of the new company for the securities of the old. We know that in an hour's interview with Marcellus Hartley, chairman of the board of the Equitable, he not only had Hartley's agreement to accept the bonds, but came away with Hartley's personal check for a substantial investment in stock of the new company.

Furthermore, we know that the language he talked was not any jargon comprehensible only to businessmen and financiers. There is a story that in these days Ochs struck one nut that he couldn't crack. A man from whom he had expected $25,000 couldn't, or wouldn't, put up the money. But it happened that the man's daughter, who did not pretend to know anything about business, was present at the interview in which Ochs did his best. When he rose to go, defeated, the girl suddenly spoke up. Some relative had recently left her a bequest of $5000 and she was looking for an investment; on the spot she bought bonds of the Times Company[8]—sufficient proof that Ochs's sales talk

[8] Incidentally, that investment is worth tracing. By purchasing five of the bonds, the girl got seventy-five shares of the common stock. From the beginning she received $250 a year interest on her bonds; in the course of time the bonds were retired and she got back her principal; in the meantime she was receiving dividends on her common stock, and as the years passed they included not merely cash payments, but shares in subsidiary enterprises, such as the various *Times* buildings, the paper mills, and the like, which in turn paid dividends. In the end from all these sources she was receiving an annual income approximating the amount of her original investment—which she had already recovered!

had in it nothing mysterious and obscure, nothing but plain language comprehensible to anyone of reasonable intelligence.

There is, however, an element in his success less mysterious than the magic of his personality. This was his terrific energy. Among his papers is a letter to his wife in which he noted down his schedule for that day, not by any means an unusual one during the four months of his negotiations. It reads:

At Flint's office at 10 o'clock.
Wallach's office, 10:20.
Belmont's, 11.
Hanover Bank, 12.
Wallach's, 12:30.
Wilson & Wallace, 12:45.
Western Union, 1:20.
Lunch, 1:45.
Western Union, 2.
Hartley's, 2:30.
Hanover Bank, 3.
Wallach's, 3:20.
Hartley's, 4.
Glen Falls Paper, 4:15.
New York Sun (Laffan), 4:45.
Van Doren's, 5.
N. Y. Post Job Printing, 5:15.
Julian F. Davis, 5:20.
Charles R. Flint, 5:35.

He explained that since all these places were in downtown New York within relatively short distances of each other it was not worth while taking a cab. He was doing his errands on foot, tramping the streets from ten to five thirty-five, with fifteen minutes off for lunch. The country editor had a drive and an endurance that not many men could equal.

Yet he thrived on it. The suspense harried him at times, and delays and postponements occasionally exacerbated his temper, but in the main his letters at this period portray a man in high good humor. It was Chattanooga and its boom times all over again—he was never happier than when he was doing what most men would have regarded as entirely too much. But this time he wasn't endeavoring to run the town, he was sticking strictly to his own business. He had taken on a job that was taxing the resources even of Adolph Ochs to the extreme limit; if it was a job that certainly nobody else could do and that frequently seemed beyond even his powers—well, that was precisely the sort of job he liked. Except at moments of extreme fatigue, he was not cast down, he was exhilarated. By that time, "How long, O Lord?" was the cry of the despairing family, but he did not echo it. To an aunt who expressed impatience with the long delay, "I said, 'Aunt, if it took me ten years to make a million dollars would you think that a long time?' She understood me."[9]

Even his incessant peregrinations from office to office did not exhaust his physical energy. He bought a "bicycle suit" and in the evenings rode a rented wheel in Central Park. In the mornings, before the Wall Street magnates had thought of coming to their offices, he made long excursions about the city, always entertained, always curious, always picking up items of information to be stored in his memory and suddenly produced, perhaps years later, to the astonishment and sometimes to the confusion of his associates.

Only one thing in this period he found really hard to bear and that was the separation from his family. He had a haunting impression that the baby was growing up without him. "Kiss my little darling for me," he wrote to Mrs. Ochs, "and tell her her papa would like very much to see her and carry her around on his shoulders and on his back; that he fears that if he prolongs his absence much longer she will be too large for him to carry around. Just think of it—I have been the best part of three months away from home."[10]

Living alone in the old Madison Avenue Hotel, he looked upon the city with the eye of a newcomer and found it good, but a long way from perfect. By this time it was pretty well understood in the *Times* office that Ochs would be the new owner and he was therefore permitted to view the inner workings of the place about as he liked. When

[9] Ochs to his mother, June 7, 1896. Ochs MSS.
[10] Ochs to his wife, June 20, 1896. Ochs MSS.

he first came to New York it was ostensibly to examine the *Mercury* proposition and he did, in fact, spend a few days satisfying himself that it was a poor one; but all his attention had now been concentrated on the *Times* for three months and such things always get about. There was uncertainty and apprehension in the staff and no one cared to displease the man who might be in charge any day.

The result of this close inspection was that Ochs saw any number of reasons for the deplorable condition of the paper. Some of these reasons really existed, but some were certainly based on the misconception of New York formed by nearly every newcomer. The deceptive casualness of the city's businessmen nearly always fools and frequently scandalizes the late arrival from a small city, where the boss commonly handles far more routine than he does in New York. What the man from the small town fails to take into account is that a great deal of his ordinary schedule at home is mere clatter, not work. When a high-salaried administrator himself attends to details that might be looked after as well, or even better, by a low-salaried clerk, the boss is merely making noise, not doing his real work. But he is extremely likely to begin in time to associate bustle with labor and fall into the error of assuming that a man who isn't bustling isn't working.

Miller, for example, shocked the Tennesseean by his way of drifting in and out of the office in an apparently aimless fashion. As a matter of fact, at this time Miller was in a very low state indeed. An editor who has had his paper shot from under him is not likely to be a model of energy and industry, and there was probably some basis for Ochs's criticism. "Mr. Miller has not been in the office today, and when he does come he remains only an hour or two, and always goes home or to his club by six or seven, and seldom appears at the office at night."[11]

Everybody above the grade of the veriest leg man seemed to have a secretary, which didn't comport at all with the ideas of Tennessee. "There is going to be a cyclone in this office when I blow in." But this was a private impression, shared with nobody but Effie. In public Ochs showed an impassive countenance and to the staff he was affable.

[11] Ochs to his wife, June 13, 1896. Ochs MSS.

He was too sensible to destroy morale by premature thunderings; more than that—and in this he differed from a good many visitors from afar —he was keenly aware that he didn't know everything and that certain customs of New York that seemed to him foolish might have a reasonable basis. He moved carefully until he was certain of his ground.

Sometimes it was difficult. Miller, in particular, was in a trying position. He had come to believe in Ochs, but he had no very firm assurance that Ochs believed in him. He had been assured that his position as editor-in-chief was secure; but exactly what did that mean? It could be merely the position of a glorified office boy, carrying out the publisher's orders, and Miller was not the man for that sort of thing. Moreover, what about salary? Was his standard of living to be reduced to that of a beginner? While the negotiations were still pending he sat down and wrote Ochs with complete frankness that he would not consent to work as a mere employee and that he would require at least $300 a week to live in New York.

"He don't get it," wrote Ochs privately. "I won't give him a contract and I won't pay over $200 a week to him; and then he has to prove himself worth it."[12]

But that was in private. To Miller himself Ochs wrote a masterly letter. There was no question of Miller's being a mere hired hand. "Your distinguished ability, high and honorable purposes and popularity as an editorial writer, and your wide knowledge of public affairs, men and measures all combine to make you the man I most desire as editor-in-chief." Any two men whose ideas of the proper conduct of a newspaper agreed so exactly and whose conceptions of public service were identical should be able to get along together amicably. As for compensation, that depended on what the paper might be able to pay; but Miller could rest assured that once income exceeded expenditures the publisher would "endeavor not only to be just but liberal."[13] This was plain truth, for $200 a week was the salary Ochs had fixed for himself.

[12] Ochs to his wife, June 15, 1896. Ochs MSS.
[13] Ochs to Miller, June 15, 1896. Ochs MSS.

On the other hand, sometimes encouragement came from sources whence it was least expected. There was Jacob Schiff, for example. When Miller and his fellow employees bought the *Times* Schiff had put up $25,000 cash for 250 shares. At first he heard Ochs's proposal noncommittally, but a few days later sent for him and handed over the 250 shares. He had been a mugwump, said Schiff, but was now a straight Republican and no longer interested in supporting a Democratic newspaper; however, he was convinced that Ochs proposed to maintain a decent journal, creditable to the city, and he would not stand in the way of such an enterprise, therefore he offered his shares as a gift. Ochs, of course, insisted on the usual exchange, one share of new stock for five of the old, and Schiff's holdings eventually were worth more than he had paid for them; but the generous gesture inspirited the hard-working negotiator enormously, and it was never forgotten. Like Father Ryan's Christmas present to the carrier boy, it was one of the things that Adolph Ochs loved to recall in his old age.

Spring merged into summer and summer slowly wore away. One by one the obstacles fell. Even the courts' delay and the circumspection of lawyers yielded to time. Wallach had intrusted the details of Ochs's affairs to a young associate, one Alfred Cook, with whom the publisher struck up a lasting friendship. They bicycled all over New York together. "I am going with Alfred Cook, the young lawyer in charge of Wallach's office, to Atlantic Highlands to call on Mr. and Mrs. Oscar Straus and from there we are going to ride on bicycles to Elberon, where we will dine with the Wallachs."[14] Long years afterward, when Wallach was dead and Alfred Cook was head of a stately law firm that acted as counsel for the *Times* such memories put into the relation a zest that no sort of retainer could have supplied. All through his career Adolph Ochs was well served, in part because he paid well for good service, but in part, and in very large part, because he liked most of the people with whom he was associated; and because he really liked them, they couldn't help liking him.

The long delay that perplexed his aunt was probably extremely fortunate; for in those months he laid the foundations of friendships that

[14] Ochs to his wife, July 25, 1896. Ochs MSS.

were to be invaluable in the years ahead—Cook (Wallach was a friend already), Miller, Hartley, Schiff, Trask, Belmont, Morgan and many others who were potent in New York came to know him. He had arrived in New York almost unknown; but by August 17, 1896, he was well and favorably known to a group of men whose power in the financial, business and political worlds was out of all proportion to their numbers. On that day the sale ordered by the court took place. Trask made a pro forma bid of $75,000. Ochs put in his bid. There were no others and the property was formally knocked down to him.

VII

On August 18, 1896, he took possession and that same day he wrote two extremely revealing letters. They were addressed to the two women who had shared his struggles and to whom he did not hesitate to bare his thoughts; and they offer a strange contrast to what the staff of the Times saw. The staff observed a quiet, unassuming man who came in during the afternoon and occupied the office of the publisher in a matter-of-fact way; the letters reveal behind that quiet exterior an interior turmoil in which all sorts of impulses, divergent and even contradictory, battled for dominance. Pride clashed with humility, complacence with nervous apprehension, shrewdness with a Napoleonic belief in a star; and right through the confusion of this greatest day so far in the man's life drove a shaft of human sympathy. A little elevator boy in the Chattanooga Times had died; and on the very day of his triumph Ochs was not so elated that he forgot to write the boy's mother a note of sympathy.

The first letter sheet of the New York Times is used to send my love to those who are dearer to me than the great prize I have won, if it were many times more valuable than my most extravagant dream [began the letter to Effie].

I was formally installed at 3:30 P.M. today and an army of men stand ready to carry out my wishes.

I have succeeded way beyond my fondest hopes, and by the help of God I will maintain myself in this high position with credit to myself. I am certainly a lucky fellow; I hope my luck may continue to the end.

Occupying as I do tonight the position that death made the greatest newspaper publisher in America[15] vacate, fills my heart with a yearning for you to be here to share my pride and satisfaction.

The transfer was made quietly and without ostentation; I will try my best to be modest and unassuming and wear my honors easy.

Even at this glorious moment of my short life, I must drop a tear at the thought of the awful death of that dear little elevator boy in our office at Chattanooga, little George Wood, which occurred Saturday. I wrote to his bereaved mother last night.

I will tomorrow move from the Madison Avenue Hotel to the Astor House where I will be until you come to reside.[16]

To his mother, who knew, even better than Effie, how long was the road he had traveled and how bitter had been the struggle in the days when actual want was never far from the household, went the second letter of this day:

It is a matter of the greatest pride to me that I have enabled my mother to say that she is the mother of the publisher of the New York Times. I am here safely in the position which puts me in the front rank of the newspaper men of the world; a position which I one time, not long ago, thought as impossible for me as the throne of Great Britain. If I have succeeded far beyond what is ordinarily man's lot, I owe much to the influence of a mother who is the noblest and purest of mortal beings. God bless her and preserve her for many years to see her son prove himself worthy of the good fortune which has befallen him.[17]

These letters are revealing, yet it may be argued with some plausibility that nothing in them is more revealing than what is not in them. It must be borne in mind that these were the most intimate of private letters, written to the two people to whom the man would have least

[15] The reference is to George Jones, Raymond's partner, and it throws an interesting light on Ochs's estimate of his contemporaries, none of whom resembled Jones.

[16] Ochs to his wife, August 18, 1896. Ochs MSS.

[17] Ochs to his mother, August 18, 1896. Ochs MSS.

hesitation in telling all that was in his mind, assured that his confidence would not be violated. It is a fair assumption, therefore, that these letters set forth not only what the writer was thinking at this climactic moment in his life, but all that he was thinking. What was not in these letters was not in his mind; and there are some amazing omissions.

Of these omissions the most astonishing are the Messrs. Hearst and Pulitzer. At the moment of his entry into the New York newspaper field Adolph Ochs apparently never gave a thought to the two most formidable publishers already in that field. Indeed, in all his voluminous correspondence of that period there is no reference to these men except the most casual comment—such remarks as that the *World*'s display of news bulletins was good, but could be improved, and that the *Journal*'s use of lighted signs was interesting. These men were simultaneously detested, dreaded and reluctantly admired by every other newspaper publisher in the city, but the newcomer's interest in them was too languid to produce emotion of any sort. He sincerely believed that they were working in a different field from the one he intended to occupy and therefore were not true competitors. Literally, they didn't matter.

Again, the sole touch of anxiety in the two letters turns upon the possibility of a run of bad luck. Like every businessman of experience, Ochs had a healthy respect for the damage that can follow when Fortune turns spiteful. But on this day of days no other possibility of failure seems to have entered his mind. He was taking over a wreck. Even his backers regarded it as a hazardous, not to say desperate, venture in which the odds against success were heavy. Not so Ochs. In his most private communication, to the mother from whom he had no reason to conceal anything, he declared that his new position had already put him "in the front rank of the newspaper men of the world." He was not merely on the way, he had arrived. The fact that a terrific fight was to follow was a detail; he had a newspaper, and with a newspaper only an incredible run of bad luck could stop him, not any ordinary difficulties.

Conceit? Well, you can call it that, but men in general have chosen other words to describe it. One thinks rather of the mad admiral when he stepped aboard the *Bonhomme Richard*. She was a rotten old hulk, she was waterlogged, she was cranky, she was unfit to keep the sea; but she was a ship, and her master was serenely sure that any ship would do when John Paul Jones was in command.

CHAPTER VI

In Which the Man Increases in Wisdom and in Stature, Not Always to the General Approval.

I

THE battle began promptly enough. On the very day the new publisher took over an old employee in a confidential position led him aside and told him *sotto voce* the truth about the circulation. The 19,000 that the *Times* claimed was largely for publicity purposes. True, 19,000 copies were being printed, but more than half were returned by the news dealers unsold; actual, paid circulation was running about 9000 copies a day. When the new chief remarked that he thought circulation might be increased, the employee made a comment indicative of the low morale prevailing in the office. "Increased!" he exclaimed. "Increased! Mr. Ochs, if you could keep it from going down any further you'd be a wonderful man!"[1]

But that was by no means the worst of it. Presently hidden liabilities began to show up, bills that for one reason or another had not been disposed of in the legal proceedings and had to be paid by the new management. By the time they were all in, they reached the appalling total of $100,000. His utmost efforts had provided Ochs with only $200,000 of working capital, and half of it was swept away before he got a start.

Not for nothing, though, had this man started the Chattanooga *Times* on $12.50 and kept it afloat to the amazement of all beholders. The figures were bigger in New York, but the situation was essentially the same and he met it with the same resourcefulness, ingenuity and agility. Ways and means had to be different. There was no question now of kiting checks with friendly, if impecunious, pals. But it was still a matter of keeping one jump ahead of the creditors and that, to

[1] Davis, *op. cit.*, p. 203.

[142]

Ochs, was an old, familiar game. A man who had dodged and twisted his way through Reconstruction days in Tennessee and through the panic of '93 after that had very little to learn about the art of dodging and twisting. His skill proved as effective in New York as it ever had been in the South.

He regarded as the first necessity the reduction of that deficit of $2500 a week. He went at it efficiently, but not by the obvious and easy method of ruthlessly slashing the payroll. This was what the staff had expected and when nobody was let out, other than obvious super-numeraries, relief and astonishment were mingled in the minds of *Times* men.

What they forgot, or did not know, was that they were working for a newspaperman who had come up the hard way, by slowly mastering, one after another, every detail of newspaper production. True, New York was strange to him, but no city room is altogether strange to an old reporter, no composing room to an old printer, no business office to a man who has successfully organized and managed one of his own. In his time Adolph Ochs had delivered papers, worked in the press-room, set type, made up forms, covered assignments, written editorials, solicited advertisements and subscriptions and supervised the work of others in all these lines. In the whole *Times* organization there wasn't a man to whom he couldn't talk in his own jargon, not a man whose work, or something very much like it, he had not done at one time or another.

Therefore he knew where to look for the leaks and no man knew better the difference between a leak and a necessary expense. For one thing, he promptly ordered the press run reduced to the number of copies that could actually be sold. For another, he ripped out of the paper the "reading notices" with which it had been padded in recent years—matter that is not news, but is designed to curry favor with some business, or political, or other interest. He ordered the enor-mously inflated commodity market reports swept out of the paper, but when howls of anguish resounded from the financial editor, he modified the order; he decreed that one commodity market report should be dropped, then another, and so on until there was a substantial protest from readers. His argument was that the commodity markets were adequately covered by various excellent trade papers, and it was on these that dealers depended. Events seemed to justify his reasoning. As the various reports were dropped, there was only one protest—a man wrote in to say that he missed the prices on naval stores, and that report was immediately restored.[2]

Such changes reduced the deficit briskly, yet cost nobody his job; more than that, every craftsman could see that they were making a better newspaper. So in the minds of the staff relief and astonishment, the first emotions, gave way to approval, then to admiration and within a very short time to enthusiasm. The Old Man[3] knew his business. That made an immeasurable difference to the man in the ranks, for under a competent chief good work would not be wasted, and nothing kills the spirit of a newspaperman faster than to have a really fine piece of work undervalued and unappreciated. Evidently this would not happen on the *Times*, and as a result a new spirit pervaded the place.

This was noted at once and has been repeatedly recorded as regards the editorial staff, but it extended all down the line. Miller was a new man, full of energy and aggressiveness. So was Lowenthal, the managing editor, who had also fallen into a mechanical routine; now he was not content with doing his regular work, but insisted on accompanying Ochs, when the first edition had been put to bed, on long walks through the night in which they discussed ideas for improving the paper. All this has been remembered and recorded by the writing men who experienced it.

What has not been emphasized, although it is just as important, is that this breath of fresh air swept through every department. Ochs could write an acceptable news story or an editorial; but he was not primarily a reporter or an editor, he was a publisher, and one of the

[2] Davis, *op. cit.* Eventually a demand grew up for commodity reports and they were restored, but in a much improved form, more compact and more easily understood.

[3] In newspaperdom as in the navy this term has no reference to senescence, but merely indicates the top authority; Miller and a number of other members of the staff carried more than Ochs's thirty-seven years, but as publisher he outranked them, therefore he was the Old Man.

best. This means that he knew the whole show, including the mechanical and commercial operations as well as the news gathering and news writing. If the editor in chief was delighted to find that the publisher knew a good editorial page when he saw one, the foreman of the composing room was no less impressed when he discovered that the big chief knew exactly when a make-up man was botching his job and how he was botching it, while the cashier found no small satisfaction in working for a man who knew the difference between a smartly efficient accounting system and a hodgepodge. From basement to roof the word spread through the office, "The Old Man knows," and while the news may have had an ominous sound to malingerers, the real workmen in every department pricked up their ears and took a fresh grip on the job.

A cyclone would hit the place when he blew in, Ochs had informed Effie privately. At the time he probably meant that any number of people would blow out as he blew in, for at the moment of writing he was irritated by the prevailing slackness and inefficiency of the place. But the event fulfilled his prophecy in a different way. Before he actually entered the office as publisher he had realized that much of what he disliked was due to conditions over which the men had no control; therefore he determined to change the conditions first and see what those men could do in a different atmosphere before he started a general clean-out.

That clean-out never materialized, for he found that, given a fair chance, his staff was an excellent one. A cyclone hit the office, all right, but its effect was not to sweep men before it, but to energize them and convert them from a spiritless assemblage into a team capable of generating the power, the speed and the smoothness of a steam piston.

II

When he assumed control the new owner issued the conventional "proclamation to the natives" that new owners seem to regard as indispensable to a proper transfer; and the proclamation was received by the public with the conventional bland indifference. New York had seen too many such declarations of intent to be much interested in a new one that repeated pretty much the same things; for it occurred to hardly anyone to suspect that in this case the things might be true.

But if readers of the announcement were merely bored in 1896, half a century later the pronouncement has a vivid interest; for we know now that the writer was going to make good the substance of what he said. It was in these words, printed on the editorial page:

To undertake the management of The New York Times, with its great history for right doing, and to attempt to keep bright the lustre which Henry J. Raymond and George Jones have given it, is an extraordinary task. But if a sincere desire to conduct a high-standard newspaper, clean, dignified and trustworthy, requires for success, honesty, watchfulness, earnestness, industry and practical knowledge applied with common sense, I entertain the hope that I can succeed and maintain the high estimate that thoughtful, pure-minded people have ever had of The New York Times.

It will be my earnest aim that The New York Times give the news, all the news, in concise and attractive form, in language that is permissible in good society, and give it as early if not earlier, than it can be learned through any other reliable medium; to give the news impartially, without fear or favor, regardless of party, sect or interests involved; to make of the columns of The New York Times a forum for the consideration of all questions of public importance, and to that end to invite intelligent discussion from all shades of opinion.

There will be no radical changes in the personnel of the present efficient staff. Mr. Charles R. Miller, who has so ably for many years presided over the editorial page, will continue to be editor; nor will there be a departure from the general tone and character and policies pursued with relation to public questions that have distinguished The New York Times as a nonpartisan newspaper—unless it be, if possible, to intensify its devotion to the cause of sound money and tariff reform, opposition to wastefulness and peculation in administering public affairs, and in its advocacy of the lowest tax consistent with good government, and no more government than is absolutely necessary to protect society, maintain individual and vested rights and assure the free exercise of a sound conscience.

ADOLPH S. OCHS.

New York City, Aug. 18, 1896.

Assuredly this is no masterpiece of English prose, nor is it an announcement of anything strange and new. If the New York of 1896 yawned and passed it by, the public indifference is understandable. Yet, as frequently happened in Ochs's writings, there is in the midst of its pedestrian measures a flash that lights up the whole landscape. "To give the news impartially, without fear or favor, regardless of party, sect or interests involved"—there is the whole duty of a newspaper man expressed in sixteen words; and there is the sincere intent of Adolph Ochs. It was his intent, not always his accomplishment, for who attains his ideal in this frustrated world? But it is a lordly intent, one of the highest goals of human endeavor; for to be impartial, truly and thoroughly impartial, a man must divest himself of all the passions, whether as low as lust and greed, or as high as the crusader's zeal, that subtly color his vision and draw veils between his eyes and naked Truth. It is, flatly, a goal no mere mortal has ever attained; but this man strove for it, and if in the end he won the respectful consideration of his country and his time, it was because men conceded that he had gone a long way toward that goal.

The strong emphasis upon what may be called the soap-and-water motif sounds a little odd to modern ears. A "clean" paper, for "pure-minded people" written in "permissible" language—today all this would suggest an obsession with dirt. Possibly the suggestion is justified, but the obsession, if it existed, was not individual in 1896. It was of the time and country, not distinctively of the man. Victoria still reigned and Anglo-Saxon society was far indeed from its present freedom of speech. One of the methods of advertising themselves that the yellows were working hard was that of shocking the fastidious by skating just as close to the edge of obscenity as the law would allow. True, what was daring then would be pretty dull now; but at the time the godly were racked with anxiety lest naughty words in newspapers undermine all morality, subvert religion and play hob with civilization in general.

There is little evidence that Ochs took this menace very seriously; but the class of people he wanted to attract took it seriously indeed, so it was good business to soothe their feelings. Moreover, that sort of thing wasn't journalism, anyhow. It was merely a circulation-building trick, and Ochs was always profoundly contemptuous of tricks, even clean ones.[4]

The political ideas set forth in the conclusion of the announcement are more certainly part and parcel of the man's intellectual endowment; but even they are strongly colored by the time. It was 1896, the year of Bryan's greatest popularity, and the theory of bimetallism was the dominant issue. Industrialization was largely an accomplished fact, but relatively few people were as yet aware of the extent to which it had invalidated Jefferson's faith in simplicity of government as a safeguard of liberty. Ochs was not one of the few. He was a conservative and he did a good deal to justify his later position in the minds of radicals as the very archpriest of conservatism; but in 1896 the position he took was conservative, not reactionary, as it sounds today.

III

For months a young fellow employed in the business office of the *Sun* had been bedeviling Ochs for a job. He wanted to be business manager, but that was out of the question. Ochs was going to be business manager himself; and Theodore L. Peverelly, the chief clerk in charge of the office, was too good a man to be thrown out for some stranger. Ochs brushed the applicant aside.

But he wouldn't stay brushed. Day after day, week after week, he renewed his suggestion. He was so small of stature that he was almost dwarfish, but his persistence was gigantic—matched only by the bland good humor with which he met refusal after refusal. Somewhat irritated yet somewhat pleased by the man's persistence Ochs wrote his wife that apparently he would have to give the fellow some sort of job

---

[4] On the other hand, he was equally contemptuous of the trick of suppressing news out of fear of the Nice Nellys. In later years a desk man brought him some sheets of copy hot enough to singe even a desk man's calloused fingers. It was a transcript of part of the evidence of an important case then being tried; furthermore, it was the vital evidence on which the whole issue hung. "Print it," said Ochs promptly; and when the subordinate wondered if they could get away with it, the publisher grinned. "Of course, we can," he said. "In the ....[naming a particularly sensational contemporary] that story would be dirt; but in the *Times* it's sociology."

to have any peace. The man's intelligence and alertness were obvious, and it was not unflattering to have such a youngster fix upon you as the coming man in the newspaper world and determine to attach himself to you. So when the purchase at last was consummated, the new owner yielded. In spite of his determination not to increase the payroll, he found for this applicant a small job at small pay.

Forty years later he said, "It was one of the best trades I ever made," and all the newspaper world agreed. For the persistent little man was Louis Wiley, who was to grow into something far more than a business manager, although he was one of the ablest of his generation. Because he was affable, witty and charming, able to make a sparkling after-dinner speech, to meet a great lady with a graceful compliment, a great statesman with urbane and subtle flattery and all newspapermen with intelligent interest and ready helpfulness, he became a sort of roving ambassador of the Times. He went everywhere, met everybody, and charmed them all. So widespread was his popularity, indeed, that a petty-minded publisher would have thrown him out; for the time came when half the world, noting how this fascinating figure showed up at conventions, at state dinners and other conspicuous occasions, cherished the delusion that Wiley was the power in the Times and disregarded Ochs.

Indeed, there is some fragmentary and inconclusive evidence that Ochs did feel an occasional twinge when Wiley was loudly praised for something the publisher had done; but he never showed it in public or to Wiley. He knew that the man was doubly valuable, first because he was a top-flight business manager, and second because his dazzling social talent was also an asset to the Times. It didn't hurt at all to have a representative of the paper helping the Prince of Wales pin on his decorations in a sudden social emergency, and strolling about the Riviera with the King of Yugoslavia, and dropping into the office of Mussolini for a chat when that office was barred to all other newspapermen. If Wiley outshone his chief in the social world, what of it, as long as the shining was good for the paper? The chief was too big a man to allow petty jealousy to interfere with his important aims.

This of course was merely one aspect of that curious, elusive quality that we call, vaguely, capacity for leadership. Adolph Ochs assembled, controlled and dominated a group of powerful men. Among his principal assistants there was none who was not in one respect or another a bigger man than the chief. Miller, for example, had a far richer and broader cultural background than Ochs possessed. Van Anda, the great newsman, was vastly more learned than his chief. Louis Wiley was his superior both at statistics and at small talk. Yet there was no doubt in anyone's mind that Ochs was the boss; and he remained the boss without feeling the need to suppress any individual's particular strength.

On the contrary, he urged his men to exert and build up their powers. Miller was encouraged to pour into the editorial page all the intellectual wealth that the libraries and universities could furnish. Van Anda was cheered on when he found that science was news and dug out fascinating stories in laboratories where Ochs would have been utterly confused. When Louis Wiley came home his breast aglitter with foreign decorations conferred by princes and potentates of Europe and Asia, he was applauded and sent back to get more. The result was that Ochs got out of his men the very best of which they were capable, both in quantity and in quality. Especially in the early years, when it was a question of survival to make every edge cut, the work the *Times* staff did provoked the envy and amazement of every other publisher in New York. Yet to say that Ochs drove his men is to miss the point; under his direction they drove themselves, furiously, incessantly, and with resounding success.

Of course the wags did not overlook the ubiquitous presence of the new owner. The "Bab Ballads" were relatively new at the time, and soon a parody was going the rounds of the office:

> I am the boss,
> The Editor bold,
> And the Chief of the
> New York *Times*.
> The Big Ad Man,
> The Office Boy
> And he who handles
> The Dimes.

"The little man who went around turning out the lights" was already established in his role, while the great publisher was as yet only beginning to appear. His appearance was beginning, however, for although he was everywhere he was never out of place. There was a reason for everything he did and—which is far more important in sustaining morale—the men under him could perceive the reason.

But he was more than efficient, he was also scrupulously fair. In the case of Miller, for example, the dark threats he had uttered to Effie were never carried out. Miller, with the assistance of friends, had contrived to buy 50 bonds of the new company, which gave him 750 shares of the new stock; his wife, who had had 500 shares in the old company, received 100 of the new. Then, during the course of the reorganization, Ochs decreed that Miller must be issued 500 additional shares, ostensibly in settlement of any claims he might have against the old company, but really as an expression of appreciation of his work in the past. At the time of Miller's death this stock was appraised for inheritance taxes at $1,270,000.

So the *Times* pulled itself together and was transformed, not by any spectacular, lightning-like stroke of genius, but by a multitude of small changes, each insignificant in itself, but each a genuine improvement in the service the paper was rendering. For example, at the time nobody was publishing the court dockets in full; Ochs inserted them and thereby made the *Times* more valuable to every lawyer in town. It was a small matter which passed unnoted by laymen; but the profession did not overlook it. He ordered the financial reports to be handled on a strict news basis. This meant cutting out a great mass of stuff that was repetitive, of uncertain accuracy, or that amounted to free advertising. This had two effects; it saved space, but in addition to that by stripping away useless verbiage the financial pages were made easier to read and understand. When a businessman discovered that he could find out what he wanted to know from the *Times* more quickly and easily than from any other newspaper, he thereafter looked at the *Times* first.

This process made an excellent newspaper, but it gives the historian of the paper a dull story. Hearst and Pulitzer were doing things far more entertaining then and far more colorful in retrospect. They were also running a long way ahead of the *Times* in both circulation and prestige. But Ochs was content. He was building more slowly, but far more solidly than his gaudier contemporaries. Other papers had their ups and downs, their triumphant years and their disastrous years, but the *Times* moved always in the same direction. It is literally true that from the day Adolph Ochs took control the *Times* never slid backward. Some years were more successful than others, but no year was a failure. Sometimes progress slowed down to a crawl, but it never quite stopped; on the other hand it rarely proceeded by leaps and bounds.

IV

As for the man himself, life took on a different meaning when Effie and the baby were installed at the Astor House. With the family assembled he was a whole man again, ready to face the heavy task before him with all his faculties at their full strength.

Even so, it was a temporary expedient. Hotel life was always to him an abnormal mode of existence, and one quite intolerable where children were concerned. Never for a moment did he propose to have his daughter brought up in a hotel and he set about finding more desirable living quarters even before the family arrived.

But he was not content to procure a house and occupy it. In the beginning he held one, briefly, but to him that was not a normal mode of existence, either. All his life he had lived in a crowd. There were six children in his boyhood home, and as soon as he was able to manage it—sooner than he could afford it by any ordinary means of calculating resources—he bought a big house in Chattanooga, brought the whole family there, after his marriage installed his bride there, and as time passed gathered in various unattached relatives.

All accounts agree that it was, as a rule, an amiable and rather jolly crowd. The explosions that occurred were neither numerous nor serious enough to do more than add spice to life. But like all big families it lived a noisy life. Its members might have anything within reason that they desired with one exception—quiet. But to the boy brought up in that environment it was incomprehensible that anyone should desire quiet.

Indeed, he seems to have cherished the belief that there was something slightly abnormal about a liking for stillness and privacy. He was determined that his one child should not be brought up alone, for only a house full of children seemed to him a normal establishment. Therefore he insisted on finding quarters where there were other children, so after a short tenure of their own house Effie and her daughter were moved to share one with a family blessed with numerous children.

Economic necessity was not the ruling consideration in this. It was Ochs's carefully considered policy; and it is worth more than passing mention because the adoption of that policy throws a flood of light on the man's attitude in other things.

There is a contradiction here. There is every reason to believe that Effie didn't like being thrust into partial occupancy of a house. There is every reason, in fact, to believe that Effie never had enjoyed a crowd. At the same time, there is conclusive evidence that Ochs was genuinely devoted to his wife, and equally conclusive evidence that he was a generous man. Why, then, did a generous man, not driven by necessity, subject the woman he loved to an environment that she didn't like?

The only possible answer is that he didn't realize her attitude. Even if she told him—and it is quite possible that she never did—he heard it with his ears only. It did not penetrate through his own experience to his understanding. As far as he knew, a large family, which meant a house full of people and noise, was the only normal, wholesome mode of existence. It had been his own way of life and he had thrived on it. So had his brothers and sisters. So had various aunts, uncles, cousins and assorted relatives. Obviously, it was a good way of life, and he took the easy step of assuming that it was *the* good way of life, and a taste for any other must be suspect.

Granting that the incident is trivial in itself, it nevertheless assumes importance by its implications. It marks quite definitely the limit of the man's genius. To say that Adolph Ochs was unimaginative is nonsense. The creation of each of his papers was an imaginative triumph of the first order. To call him unsympathetic would be to deny a mass of evidence scattered through his life from beginning to end. One conspicuous proof of both imagination and sympathy was an endless fairy tale he told his daughter as they walked together toward her school—a new installment every morning, about a Swiss governess (Iphigene had a Swiss governess) whose lover pursued her over continents and seas and won her in the end by the remarkable method of mailing himself to her via parcel post. How, then, did it happen that an imaginative and sympathetic man remained to the end a rock-ribbed conservative?

The answer is that he didn't—that is, if one construes conservatism to mean immobility. Adolph Ochs's social and political philosophy developed steadily in the direction of liberalism. He who couldn't stomach Bryan in 1896 was able to accept the second Roosevelt in 1932, and while the New Deal gave him some terrific shocks, it is doubtful that it ever terrified him as completely as free silver had done. At seventy-five his mind was more, not less, resilient than it had been at thirty-seven; which is certainly not characteristic of a moss-backed reactionary.

Nevertheless, while the *Times* followed the advance of American liberalism, it is indubitable that, like the Apostle Peter, it followed "afar off." It was so far behind the vanguard, indeed, that among radicals it became an article of faith that the *Times* was the very fortress of reaction. This was certainly their opinion, and it is not enough merely to deny the accuracy of the radicals' impression. It is necessary to account for it, and the incident of the family and the house offers an illuminating illustration.

Adolph Ochs's philosophy was empirical to a high degree. Partly, no doubt, this was temperamental and partly it was due to his lack of formal education in his youth; but the fact remains that experience furnished the only light which he followed with real confidence. What he had endured, what he had witnessed, what fell within the range of his own observation and experience, he comprehended with extraordinary thoroughness; but he lacked the speculative power that enables a great philosopher to enter and comprehend a situation utterly alien to his own way of life. The thing that enabled Jefferson, the aristocrat, to express with rare perfection the ideas, the hopes and fears of the common man, and that enabled Lincoln, the proletarian, to understand the highly educated and highly sophisticated better than they understood themselves, was not in Ochs.

But this does not mean that he was hidebound in his thinking. On the contrary, given the merest flash from the past, he was capable of converting it into a floodlight to pour upon the future. For example, to have seen in the collapse of the Chattanooga *Dispatch* a truth that would nerve him for the long battle with Spencer Trask over control of the New York *Times* was an intellectual feat possible only to an intelligence sinewy, active and swift in a high degree. But he had to have the flash, and he rarely, if ever, received it from inspiration.

As yet there was nothing in his personal experience to enable him to divine either that tranquillity might be Effie's great desire or that it might be an extremely wholesome and desirable influence in bringing up a child. The give-and-take of a large household he knew by experience to be invaluable social discipline; and it did not occur to him to study the possibility that a different sort of life might have a discipline of its own not less valuable.

Nor was his wife the sort of woman to help him much to attain a different point of view. Effie by this time was resigned to her fate. She was espoused to a whirlwind and a woman in that situation has only three possible courses of action open—to keep up, to withstand, or to sway. Effie swayed. Probably it was all she could do. Although she had made a satisfactory recovery after the birth of her third child she was never again the vivid, impetuous girl of Cincinnati. Her vitality was definitely lowered, and to attempt to keep pace with her exuberant and tireless husband probably would have killed her outright. On the other hand, to withstand him and try to stop him was unthinkable. It was the last thing she wished to do, for she loved him and was tremendously proud of him; and if she had wished it she knew that anyone who tried to stop Adolph Ochs was courting disaster. There remained only the third course—to let him go, influencing him, but by suggestion, not by opposition and not undertaking the hopeless task of keeping up with him.

So if he wanted to cram the family into a house already full of children, instead of setting up an establishment of their own, Effie would acquiesce. Naturally, her acquiescence did nothing to disturb her husband's faith in the reliability of his own experience as a guide. He was serenely unaware that conditions could have been better from the standpoint of his wife and daughter.

It is necessary to guard against making too much of this. Set down in black and white it sounds like an item from the casebook of a psychiatrist, one of those psychological conflicts from which the most terrific and devastating results may flow. Indeed, if the people involved had been highly neurotic and emotionally unstable, it might have been just that; but in fact it was nothing of the sort. At most it was a minor irritation in Effie's life, and one on which her daughter looked back years afterward with a mild exasperation tempered with amusement.

It is mentioned here not for its own importance but because it illustrates in a small matter a quality of the man that determined his course in many great matters. Some intelligent and quite sincere people regarded him as obsessed by an almost Chinese reverence for traditional institutions and ways simply because they were old—he who, with the merest glimmer of experience to guide him, was the boldest of innovators. But his innovations were always in the nature of improvements upon what existed, never establishment of complete novelties.

V

He had had the paper about two months when he introduced a phrase destined to become famous in newspaper history because it was to be vigorously attacked and spiritedly defended for more than half a century. First at the masthead on the editorial page and later on the front page Ochs had printed the words, "All the news that's fit to print."

It is hard to think of any group of seven words that have aroused more newspaper controversy. Critics called it arrogant, Pecksniffian, nonsensical; they said it implied approval of censorship; they said it assumed editorial omniscience; they raved and raged.

The uproar delighted Ochs for it proved that he had hit upon an effective phrase; but he professed to be amenable to reason. He offered to take down the offending line instantly if someone would provide a better one. He offered a reward of $100 for an improvement and called in Richard Watson Gilder, editor of the *Century*, a stately monthly review, to judge the suggestions offered. They came in a flood and some of them were good; but after wading through the lot the judge and then, with marked reluctance, the staff, admitted that not one was as terse and vivid as the original, so it rides triumphantly at the top of the New York *Times*'s front page to this day.

Even yet the phrase is occasionally denounced, but with the passage of decades the newspaper world has come pretty close to agreeing that the thing was a stroke of genius. True, in 1896 it had a certain timeliness that it has since lost for at that time there was a widespread tendency to make newspapers just as foul as the law allowed. Outright scavenger sheets have always existed and doubtless always will; but at this time smut seemed to be exercising a curious fascination upon managing editors of papers that were by no means scavenger sheets. Ochs realized that the time had come for a loud and emphatic repudiation of that tendency; and that was the primary purpose of his slogan.

Nor does "All the news that's fit to print" approve even by implication the principle of censorship. No rational man regards as censorship the laws against printing obscenity and libel, and to the average man the phrase meant simply that the *Times* was not even going to skate dangerously close to those laws as some other newspapers were doing.

Finally, when the newspaper philosophers began to analyze the thing, they were faced with the fact that the word was "news." Charles A. Dana's sardonic remark that if God permitted it to happen he was not too proud to report it did not really apply. The event itself is not news, but the account of the event. The account of an event may be written in any number of ways, including dirty ways. A sufficiently ingenious and unscrupulous reporter could make a bawdy story out of a Sunday school convention—indeed, a few years ago some dubious genius did take Mother Goose and by the simple process of blacking out a word here and there, adding nothing whatever, converted it into something very close to pornography.

The man at the copy desk is by the very nature of things a censor. He has at his disposal only a certain number of columns and he always has enough news available to fill more than that number, frequently enough to fill them twice over. The measure of his skill as a newspaperman is his ability to get a reasonably adequate account of all important events into the available space. To select out of the mass the news that's fit to print necessarily means to censor what is unfit; but since something has to be thrown out, what better selection can be made?

Here the boys who opposed the slogan at one time thought they had Ochs pinned down. "What is unfit to print?" they demanded.

"What is not true," he replied promptly.

As a riposte that was effective. It stopped them dead. But it did not cover all the ground. There were any number of things against which no charge of falsehood can be sustained but that Ochs considered unfit to print in the *Times*. Triviality was one. Sloppy writing was another. Confusion, ambiguity, all the varieties of fuzzy thinking, pomposity and pedantry he strove with all his might to eliminate from his newspaper; but so does every competent craftsman. If that is censorship, every good newspaper is guilty and proud of it.

What eventually justified the slogan, however, was no sort of argument, but the course of action that the paper followed. By deeds, not words, Ochs proved that in his own mind the emphasis lay not on the fifth word, "fit," but on the first word, "all." Fierce competition in the New York field had had the effect of dulling somewhat men's realization of the importance of printing all the news. The truth that Day and the elder Bennett had discovered two generations earlier, namely, that somebody, somewhere, is interested in affairs that to others, perhaps including the editor, seem ineffably dull, had been obscured because paper after paper had succeeded by slanting the news in such a way as to appeal to a particular constituency. The *Sun*, for example, appealed to the sophisticated, the *Herald* to the cosmopolitan, the *World* and the *Journal* to the emotional. Find your constituency and then play to it by every means that ingenuity can suggest seemed to be the formula for successful New York journalism.

The assumption that one's constituency may be the population in general was one of those that everyone accepted in principle and no one believed in fact. Tastes differ, said the wiseacres, and it is impossible to appeal simultaneously to all tastes. But clear and accurate information, said Ochs, is not a matter of taste; it is desired by people of all types. He would supply it, and as for taste his appeal would be a negative one—it would be directed toward those with a distaste for the sensational, the sordid, and the over-smart. It was his theory that if he printed all the news he would draw a considerable part of his clientele from readers of other papers, who would read the *Times* for the news and the other paper for stimulation, excitement and amusement.

The central element in this program was the fact that it was necessarily slow work. It may be argued with some plausibility, in fact, that the vital difference between Ochs and his contemporaries, Hearst and Pulitzer, was simply that they were in a hurry and he was not. Certainly there was nothing in his program that they didn't know, nothing that any good newspaperman didn't know; on the other hand, when it came to the technical processes of metropolitan journalism Pulitzer, at least, knew more than Ochs. The latter never hesitated to admit that he had learned a great deal from the sensational press. Indeed, he rather scandalized some of his strait-laced friends by contending that there is a place for such newspapers and that they serve a useful purpose.

At the same time, he went calmly and methodically along the course he had chosen, and it began to succeed. The deficit slid down and circulation began to creep up. The deficit could have been eliminated during the first year had it not been for the necessity of improving the paper; but the new publisher was not content with cutting out dead wood. He had to stimulate new growth and that took money.

His first conspicuous move in this direction took place three weeks after he assumed control. It was the appearance of the Sunday magazine, first offered to the public on September 6, 1896. A magazine section, so-called, was a feature of most New York Sunday papers, but the typical section consisted in large part of comics and for the rest of material more flamboyant, if possible, than anything in the weekday issues. The *Times* magazine was different. It was printed on a good quality of coated paper and the illustrations, including many photographs, were clear. The material was interesting, but not highly colored; it was news, but not spot news. In short, it was a genuine magazine, intended to inform rather than to startle.

On October 10, 1896, one month after the first appearance of the magazine, came the second of the two features in which the *Times* for many years was to lead the country. This was the book review section, edited by Francis W. Halsey, and at first inclosed with the Saturday paper. Ochs's attitude toward this feature is interesting. Literary criticism, he granted, may be an art, but books themselves are news and therefore within the province of a newspaper; if his reviewers could also write competent criticism, so much the better, but the thing of first and greatest importance was not to furnish definitive critical appraisal of books, but to keep readers of the *Times* informed of what was going on in the literary world.

Failure to understand this distinction has led to much irrelevant disparagement of the book review section, especially among the learned who frequently seem unable to conceive that it may please many people to know what a book is about without knowing how it compares with previous treatments of the same idea, or its precise rating as related to accepted literary standards. Other considerations aside, a daily newspaper can seldom wait for true critical appraisal, which involves comparison, reflection and unhurried judgment; but the news element in the publication of a book—its author and publisher, its theme, and at least a rough approximation of its literary quality—can be covered as rapidly as any other news event.

But Adolph Ochs, whose formal education was of the scantiest—perhaps for that very reason—understood the desires of the public better than the learned. His book review section was popular from the start and in the course of time it came to exercise a wider influence than he had planned. Eventually university professors of English were requiring their classes in contemporary literature to read the *Times* book review section as part of their work.[5]

Publishers, however, were not easily won over. Their first response, indeed, was distinctly unfavorable. Far from perceiving the advantage of collecting all literary news in one place, where it would be quickly and easily available, some of them conceived the idea that books were being segregated in a sort of journalistic ghetto and they objected strongly. It was months before the more recalcitrant would purchase advertising space in the book review section, and what eventually brought them around was no argument of the business office, but the demonstrated popularity of the section.

It did become popular—so popular, in fact, that it began to draw fire from another direction. The day came when the *Times* was being accused of perverting the public taste by the journalistic quality of its reviewing, which was so popular that it threatened to extinguish true criticism. This was an example of the curious position the newspaper as a whole came to occupy in the newspaper world—if what it did was unpopular, it was denounced, but if it was too popular the paper was denounced again. Someone was always denouncing the *Times*, frequently both sides at once; but this did not greatly disturb the publisher. He regarded it, rightly, as one of the inescapable penalties of leadership.

VI

The first storm of opposition came immediately after the change of ownership when Ochs threw the support of the *Times* to Palmer and Buckner, the gold Democrats, which was in effect aiding William McKinley, the Republican candidate, in the Presidential campaign of 1896.

Supporters of William Jennings Bryan, the regular Democratic can-

[5] Davis says that Dr. C. Alphonso Smith, then professor of English at Louisiana State University, was the first.

didate, instantly assumed that the *Times* had sold out to Wall Street, and those who had suspected that the paper was secretly backed by Morgan or Belmont were confirmed in that opinion. The demand for tariff reform in the paper's salutatory was dismissed as merely an effort to throw dust in the eyes of the public; Ochs was given a massive dose of the characteristic illiberality of the liberals.

Perhaps he was unduly ostentatious about it. Not content with coming out editorially in favor of the gold candidates, he organized a *Times* section in the great gold parade, staged during the campaign, and marched in the line himself. Afterward he wrote to his wife of his satisfaction in the smart showing the section made. It was the last outbreak of the touch of the flamboyant that had thrust him into the forefront of every sort of public pageant in Chattanooga. From 1896 on he displayed more and more reluctance to appear personally in any sort of stage show. He did not object to addressing a gathering of publishers, or speaking at the dedication of a new temple, or on some other strictly nonpolitical occasion; but he preferred more and more to remain in the background and exert his influence through his newspaper.

In 1896, however, he was ardent, not so much in his support of Palmer and Buckner—who were, indeed, such nonentities that ardor in their support was well-nigh impossible—but in his opposition to Bryan. Naturally, to Bryan men, this was a distinction without a difference; but after the lapse of half a century the difference is conspicuous, and to understand Adolph Ochs and the large group of men of whom he was typical it is essential to understand the difference.

Bryan headed one of those periodic popular revolts by which American democracy has been thrust along its jerky and uncertain course further and further away from the Roman republic of the Founding Fathers' dream. The uprising of 1896 was based on the discontent of farmers in the South and West who were being squeezed by an economic system consciously designed to build up industrialism. The farmers were aided to some extent by labor, for the industrial wage scale was still feeling the effects of the panic of 1893.

These people had real grievances, but to comprehend their course it is essential to keep in mind the fact that economic thought has undergone a great deal of sharpening and clarification in the last fifty years. Ideas that are commonplace to every college sophomore today were then understood dimly, if at all; and monetary theory, in particular, was even more confused and obscure than it is now.

But there was then, as there is now, one interest in the West that was extremely clear-eyed in all that affected its own welfare. This was the silver-mining interest, that has used every method from confusion of thought to political blackmail to levy billions in tribute upon the country. Into the turmoil of the popular revolt barged the silver interests, with a beautiful theory; it was that the distresses of the farmers were mainly attributable to high interest rates and that interest rates could be maintained at a high level only because the existing currency was based upon gold exclusively. If their product, silver, could also be made a monetary base, money would instantly become cheap and everything would be lovely. They saw no point in stressing the fact that this program would also be enormously profitable to themselves; and those who did stress it were promptly accused of being in the pay of the gold monster.

There was nothing obscure about the distress of the farmers. That was as distinct as starvation, as plain as poverty. But Bryan and the group he headed were confused as to the causes of that distress. They knew that the protective tariff, the monopolies, especially in transportation, and the concentration of wealth had something to do with it, but these things were obscure and difficult while the theory of the silver interests was beautifully simple and gradually dominated the minds of Bryan and his followers. The remedy they proposed, therefore, was bimetallism, specifically the unlimited coinage of silver at the ratio of sixteen to one.[6]

To Adolph Ochs this was sheer nonsense. He was not a trained economist, but he had kited too many checks in Chattanooga to have

---

[6] That is to say, the government would guarantee that one ounce of gold would always be worth sixteen ounces of silver, no more and no less, regardless of fluctuations in the market price of silver. It is an ideal that has never been entirely abandoned by the silver interests, and to this day the government guarantees silver a price well above its actual market value.

any superstitious reverence for a metallic currency of any kind. Those checks had nothing behind them but the recipient's confidence that somehow they would be made good; yet as long as that confidence lasted the checks were perfectly good money. Hence nobody could tell Ochs that the distresses of the country could be cured by as simple a means as meddling with the currency. Bryan's remedy was idiotic, so the plain inference was that Bryan was an idiot and his whole movement a crazy tilting against windmills.

The observation was accurate, but the inference was not. Yet it was an inference that could be made, at that time and in the existing circumstances, by a completely sincere man of liberal temperament. The assumption of the Bryanites that no one could oppose their man except those who were either antidemocratic at heart or moved by self-interest was one of those fanatical delusions that are propagated by every hard-fought campaign and that frequently result in the political destruction of some honest man. The victim in this case was Grover Cleveland. Today his name is a synonym for integrity backed by steely courage, so it is hard to realize that fifty years ago millions of his countrymen really believed that he was venal, timorous and pliant. But so it was, and although when the heat of the campaign subsided most people rid themselves of that folly not all did so. Cleveland had been dead for years before the whole country appreciated his worth.

To a certain extent Adolph Ochs was victimized by the same fury. He lined up with the goldbugs, which definitely listed him as a conservative; but in the storm of 1896 the radicals also listed him as a tool of Wall Street and an opponent of popular government, which he was not. Nevertheless for years he and his paper were favorite targets of abuse by every radical stump speaker and to the day of his death Ochs was regarded by some people who should have known better as the public spokesman for wealth and a believer in government by an oligarchy.

The charge that really lies against him is merely that of having failed to appraise correctly either the nature or the strength of the force that Bryan represented; which is, in essence, a charge that Ochs was neither a prophet nor a magician. Nobody else appraised it correctly, Bryan himself included; but although Bryan was confused as to the nature of the movement, he did feel its moral strength, while Ochs did not.

Why? He was well enough acquainted with poverty. He had fought his own way up against every sort of economic handicap, so it is a natural assumption that he was peculiarly well equipped to understand the distress of the handicapped farmers of the West and South.

Perhaps his early environment had much to do with it. Chattanooga had some of the characteristics of both West and South, but it was typical of neither. It was a frontier community, and on the whole a thriving one despite fluctuations in its fortunes. Men fought desperately to maintain a footing there, and many lost, but in the main ability, industry and character were duly rewarded. Adolph Ochs was a genuinely modest man. He never regarded himself as greatly gifted and he was quite honest when, as an old man, he declared that any boy of average ability could do what he had done if he applied himself.

Thus he developed an oversimplified philosophy of life. He had faced difficulties, but never hopeless difficulties. He had tasted the bitterness of failure, but in every case he could trace his failure back to some definite error of his own. He had never failed because forces altogether beyond his control broke his strength. Nor had he seen around him in Chattanooga any conspicuous number of men caught in a hopeless situation and beaten because they never had a chance to win. The same characteristic that prevented him from comprehending how his wife might prefer to live in a quiet house, inability to put himself imaginatively in a position of which he had no experience, kept him for many years from appreciating the true significance of such popular uprisings as that of 1896.

This is stupidity, if you choose to give it a harsh name; but it is a stupidity that is escaped only by those rare human beings who come to be known as saints and sages. If Ochs had perceived clearly all that the agrarian movement signified in 1896, his would have been the mightiest intellect of his time and he would have been, not merely a great journalist, but incomparably the greatest ever known.

As it was, with complete honesty and a sincere desire to promote the general welfare he fought against an economic fallacy and in so doing aligned himself in opposition to an effort of the people to free themselves from economic bondage. He knew that sixteen to one was no panacea and believed it was a poison; and, like all his contemporaries, he lacked the skill to separate the questionable policy from the profoundly right impulse that was the driving force behind it. As the years passed, his mental horizon widened and he understood more and more of the complicated structure of American life; and invariably as he grasped one obscure and difficult point after another he took his stand in favor of enlarging the average man's control over his own destiny.

Because his comprehension increased slowly, he was always a conservative; but because his understanding, when he did attain it, was thorough and profound, his support of democratic processes was tremendously effective.

Even at the risk of tedium it is necessary to labor the point that Ochs's conservatism was based on principle. His conservatism proved to be highly profitable, therefore suspect. When a man pursues any course that brings him millions, the world has a right to demand pretty substantial evidence before it credits him with a disinterested spirit.

In this case, however, there is ample evidence, dating from 1896, that avarice certainly was not the man's ruling passion. On the contrary, he sometimes dismayed his business associates by his apparently reckless disregard of the profit motive. His elimination of "reading notices," already mentioned, frightened some people in the business office, although it did effect an immediate saving. But he did more than that. He went through the advertising columns of the *Times* and combed them out ruthlessly. The paper, as a matter of fact, had always been more careful about its advertising than some of its rivals, but the new owner imposed ever more rigid standards. For him it was not enough to reject advertising that was obviously dirty or blatantly fraudulent; if the copy presented afforded any reasonable ground for suspicion, he ordered it held up until it could be investigated, and if the advertiser objected, then out it went.

THE MAN INCREASES IN WISDOM

It was physically impossible, of course, to make an exhaustive inquiry into every advertisement offered. The publisher was aware that a cleverly concealed fraud might slip by without blame to his advertising department; but he did demand that they refuse to pass anything that was suspicious on its face. Years afterwards, when the *Times* had grown rich and powerful, cynics sneered at this policy as being a bit of business morality that Ochs could well afford. But he could not well afford it in 1896 when he was hanging on to solvency by a thread, yet that was when it was instituted.

Even more convincing was the case of certain city advertising offered the *Times* in the autumn of 1896. This was more or less routine. The same advertising—it related to contracts which could not lawfully be awarded without public advertising—was offered to six newspapers and had been so offered for years. The total sum involved was about $200,000 and the *Times's* share would have been approximately $30,-000. At that moment no publisher in New York needed $30,000 worse than Adolph Ochs. But investigation showed that the law required advertising in one paper only, not in six; therefore the *Times* rejected its part of the money and denounced the city administration for waste. There was quite a flurry at the City Hall, but officials had to admit that the *Times* was right, and the habit of inserting such advertising in many papers was abandoned.

About a year later a somewhat smoother approach was made. Tammany was all-powerful in the city at the time and reputable newspapers were suspicious of it when they were not consistently hostile. Ochs was approached by certain politicians with a proposal that all city advertising be concentrated in the *Times*. There was nothing illegal in this and no question of extravagance. The law required the advertising to be placed somewhere and it was not proposed to give the *Times* any advance in the rate the city had been paying. More than that, the emissaries were careful to explain, indeed to insist, that Tammany did not expect the *Times* to change its editorial position by a hairsbreadth.

It was none the less a trap. If Ochs had accepted and had continued to oppose Tammany editorially, the force of his opposition would have been broken by public knowledge that he was receiving all city advertising. At the same time the money was there, he needed it and he could obtain it legally. It was a clear case of profit or influence— he could have one, but not both. Without hesitation he sacrificed the profit. He informed the politicians that under no circumstances would the *Times* accept a monopoly of city advertising. Probably his treasurer sighed, contemplating a balance still written in red ink, but the *Times* remained clear of Tammany influence and there were no sighs from the staff.

Indeed it was precisely at this point that the lower ranks of *Times* workers, who had had little personal contact with the new owner, suddenly developed the startling suspicion that he was an honest man. In those days, and for a good many years afterward, the lower ranks in any newspaper staff were slow to accuse a publisher of honesty without strongly convincing evidence. Editorial policy and ideological trends are hardly evidence in the opinion of the city room's leg men and the business office's junior clerks; but, when a man turns down money, genuine, unmistakable legal tender, merely because it is a little greasy, that is different. That is evidence. Throughout the staff the conviction was driven home that the *Times* was definitely not for sale and it had an electrifying effect. Perhaps Ochs did not lose a cent by that deal, for although he passed up the city's $30,000, the increase in enthusiasm and self-respect that his act gave the staff may have been worth much more than that.

Nevertheless, when he stuck to the gold standard and swung his paper against Bryan, there were many honest and sincere men outside the craft who believed that he had been influenced by something other than a desire to serve the public interest. So it was, indeed, all his life. The middle-of-the-road man is bound to incur the suspicion and usually the active hostility of both extremes. Ochs was too intelligent not to understand this and in general the attacks of extremists worried him not at all. Yet there were times, usually when his decision had been unusually obscure and difficult, or when he was suffering from undue fatigue, when the attacks got under his skin. The martyrdom of the fanatic is spectacular; nobody can miss it. But the idea that a moderate man also suffers for his faith, the idea that a man who becomes rich and successful also is sometimes a victim, is one that people find it hard to accept. It is nevertheless true and it sometimes accounts for things that are otherwise inexplicable in a great career.

CHAPTER VII

In Which the Man Traffics with the Mighty and Is Not Greatly Impressed.

I

THE *Times* occupied premises at 41 Park Row, but the main entrance faced Printing House Square. In a corner cubicle perhaps eight by ten feet, partitioned off from the main business office on the ground floor,[1] the new proprietor sat with a watchful eye on all that went on. Perhaps from time to time his gaze shifted to the statue of Benjamin Franklin, secular patron of American newspapermen, just outside, and perhaps he mused upon the boy munching bread in the streets of Philadelphia and the boy delivering papers in the streets of Knoxville; but if it happened at all it could not have been often. There were too many other things to watch; he could not devote many minutes to contemplating Franklin.

The theory that an executive cannot spend his time attending to detail work is sound enough in general, but there are emergencies in which general principles do not apply. In the early months of his ownership of the *Times* Adolph Ochs was facing such an emergency. He was rebuilding an organization that had been well designed originally but which, for lack of competent attention, had become ramshackle throughout.

This is why it is difficult to explain in a few words what he did when he took over the paper. He effected no spectacular cure by one brilliant stroke, for the *Times* was not suffering from a specific disease, but from general debility. Its system had to be built up, which could be accomplished only by attention to a multitude of petty matters, each trifling in itself but in sum making all the difference between increasing feebleness and economic health.

[1] So described in the Edwards M.S.

[170]

THE MAN TRAFFICS WITH THE MIGHTY

The bare narrative of what the man did would not only be intolerably tedious but might give an entirely false picture of his accomplishment. Mention any specific detail to a man of average intelligence and he is likely to say, "Why, that's nothing. I could have done that—anybody could do that, for it's only plain common sense!" So it is; but swiftly to introduce plain common sense into every department of a large organization is no small thing that anybody can do. On the contrary, it calls for a man of extraordinary endowments, both of intelligence and of character. Genius does not consist always of the power to range beyond the bounds of ordinary thought, like a Newton, a Descartes, a Galileo, to discover truth hitherto unknown; sometimes it manifests itself as a capacity to do the obviously correct thing, which others somehow had overlooked. This was Ochs; to his problems he applied nothing but common sense, but it was an inspired common sense and its effect was anything but ordinary.

This characteristic gives to his correspondence of the period a curious, almost a fantastic tone. A psychologist going through it with no knowledge of the circumstances might be excused for imagining that these letters were written by a split personality because of the impartial enthusiasm with which they treat the trivial and the immense. The question of permanent quarters for the paper was becoming acute and millions were involved; Ochs writes of it and in the next breath gives equal significance to the fact that a newsboy in Brooklyn reported that he had sold every one of his copies of the *Times* for six consecutive days. He regarded with anxiety the precarious condition of the United Press—the old one, not the modern news service of that name—on which he depended for his national and world-wide news; and he also regarded with anxiety the disposition of the news vendors to thrust the *Sun* upon customers because they could not return unsold copies of that paper; he was encouraged by the offer—although he rejected it—of a western millionaire to purchase a half interest in the *Times* and put practically unlimited financial resources behind it, and he was also encouraged by the brave show of the electric sign he had erected in Madison Square.

In short, his letters present to the uninitiated the picture of a hope-lessly scatterbrained individual who could not be expected to make a success of anything. Small wonder if some of the staff members, like the printer of later years, saw him merely as a little man who went about turning off the lights. At this period, indeed, that sort of activity absorbed a large part of his time and energy—stopping the innumer-able small leaks that were draining the financial resources of the paper without any equivalent gain.

The mystery is why this sort of thing did not absorb all his energies, or so great a part of them that he would have little left for larger en-terprises. The explanation, apparently, is a double one. In the first place, he was endowed with a tremendous store of energy—not inex-haustible, but tremendous. In Chattanooga he had never been as happy as when he was doing too much, or what to an ordinary man would have been too much. The Chattanooga paper was not big enough to absorb him completely, and that is why he became involved in count-less outside affairs, with disastrous results. The New York paper, when he took it over, offered work enough for three ordinary men, which is to say, it was just about difficult enough to keep Adolph Ochs busy and, incidentally, happy. Even so, there were times when he did too much. His energy, be it repeated for emphasis, was not inexhaustible and more than once he overdrew his physical resources, with the re-sult that he lapsed into a mood of black pessimism coming uncom-fortably close to melancholia. At this time, however, with the stimulus of a new environment and illimitable hope, he was tireless.

In the second place, he seems to have had another natural endow-ment which is easily described in words but impossible to explain analytically. An associate, but not an employee, who worked closely with him for forty years,[2] regards it as a matter of intellectual tempo. It was not that Ochs thought differently from the average man, but he thought faster. Given a certain problem a man of ordinary intelligence might mull it over for half a day and reach a certain conclusion. Given

[2] Alfred A. Cook, the lawyer, whose firm for many years was counsel for the Times.

the same problem, Adolph Ochs would reach the same conclusion, but he would reach it in half an hour. Let us not be deceived by the simplicity of that explanation. In words it seems to carry little significance; but its implications are quite enough to explain why he became rich and famous, while you and I remain poor and obscure.

Perhaps it explains also another characteristic of the man which everyone who came into contact with him observed and remembered. It was his genuine modesty. This was far too consistent to have been a pose. It was patently sincere. It is explicable if one assumes that the man never quite understood the immense advantage that mere speed of thought gave him. He did perceive that his ideas were in the main the ideas of the average man and therefore were unremarkable. He seems accordingly to have assumed that he was in reality an unremarkable person if not a downright mediocrity. In the presence of coruscating brilliance he was always a little abashed; and when people called him a genius he was puzzled and uncomfortable.

He was not without pride. On the contrary, he had it and it was very strong indeed, but it was not pride of intellectual achievement. Like his ideas, it was a pride appropriate to and understandable by the average man. All his life Adolph Ochs had worked hard and paid his debts. He knew very well that not everyone can say as much and he was intensely proud of that achievement. On the few occasions when he was thrown into a towering rage, a wrath that swept even his steady judgment from its moorings, the cause in every instance was an intimation that he owed something that he had not paid—not necessarily money, but perhaps favors, or influence, or special consideration of one kind or another which were due from him on account of his position.[3]

[3] A case in point, although it occurred many years after the period under discussion, is recalled by Mrs. L. K. Lang, Mr. Ochs's confidential secretary for a decade. A Congressional investigation of the securities market was under way and the Times had been publishing the testimony verbatim. It was pretty bad, so bad that it had spread consternation through Wall Street. One of the mightiest figures in the financial world, a great banker, wrote Ochs sharply condemning him for printing the testimony in detail and intimating that he owed it to big business, which had been friendly to the Times, to soften, if not to suppress, this scandalous news. Mrs. Lang was called in to take a letter in answer; four or five times Ochs

But industry and integrity he differentiated sharply from intellectual distinction. As the *Times* within a few months of his taking charge began to regain something of its old position in the estimation of the public—for before the advertising, and with it the money, began to come in in quantity, people realized that the *Times* was once more an exponent of dignified, reliable and responsible journalism—the city's magnificoes granted recognition to its publisher as a man of consequence and he was invited to all sorts of stately functions of a public or semipublic nature. He found himself sitting at dinner tables with statesmen, soldiers, artists and philosophers whose very names rather awed him. Businessmen, however important, he could meet on an equal footing; but who was Adolph Ochs to be sitting beside President Butler, of Columbia, Carl Schurz, soldier, statesman and scholar, Walter Damrosch, the musician, and the learned Dr. Shaw of the *Review of Reviews?* To his wife and his mother he wrote of these affairs with a naïve delight touched with bewilderment as to how he got there.

This complete inability to regard himself as a great man was one of his most attractive traits, but it was not without its disadvantages. It endeared him to his associates and helped him to strengthen and solidify his organization by intensifying the loyalty of his men, so on balance it was unquestionably an asset. But it did have the effect of erecting a barrier, slight, but perceptible, between him and the top members of his staff. In the course of time Ochs found himself the employer of some of the ablest men in journalism and the truth may be that he was a tiny bit afraid of them. The editor in chief remained to the day of his death "Mr. Miller" to Ochs, never "Charles," much less "Charlie"; the managing editor was "Mr. Van Anda," the chief editorial writer was "Dr. Finley," and even the attorney and lifelong friend was "Mr. Cook." This touch of formality was sometimes taken for coldness, but probably it was a Victorian mannerism.

A second disadvantage of the publisher's lack of appreciation of his

---

started to dictate, and each time after a sentence or two exploded into an incoherent fury that would never have done in a letter. In the end he gave it up, called the man on the telephone instead, and all but melted the wires telling him what he thought of him and where he could go with his complaint. No further effort was made to muzzle the *Times.*

own quality was more important, for it definitely affected the trend of his thinking. Ochs knew that he possessed industry and integrity and he knew that he had succeeded; how could he avoid assuming, then, that industry and integrity are guarantees of success? Had he realized clearly that in addition to these he also possessed a lightning-like mind, he would never have declared in his old age that any boy of average intelligence and willing to work could do as well as he had done. He might have perceived, also, in the complaints of the dis-possessed more merit than he was inclined to attribute to them; and that could have led him to a greater degree of political liberalism than he ever attained.

But such considerations are trifling weights indeed to throw into the scales against the solid achievements of Adolph Ochs during his first years in New York. From the little cubicle looking out upon Benjamin Franklin's statue health and vigor flowed into the *Times* organization from the very first day. Slowly at first, painfully slowly to the man operating upon a shoestring, the paper pulled itself together and began to move forward; and that movement never was halted.

II

It came appallingly close to being halted, however, only a year after the start, when the United Press collapsed in 1897. The *Sun*, the *Herald*, the *Tribune* and the *Times* were all served by this agency, and when it went down they were all at the mercy of the *World*, which held the Associated Press morning franchise and therefore had the right to veto the granting of a franchise to any other paper in the same city. If Pulitzer chose to exercise his power, the others would be brought close to ruin, for with the United gone the Associated Press was the only adequate news service left.

But Pulitzer chose not to be wholly intransigent. It was prudent not to be adamant, for although the Chicago *Inter-Ocean* case was not to be decided in the Illinois Supreme Court for nearly three years, it was already brewing. Attorneys for the *Inter-Ocean* were alleging that the

Associated Press was a monopoly and it was no time to be handing them additional evidence free of charge. So the publisher of the *World* graciously waived his veto right as regarded the *Sun*, the *Herald* and the *Tribune*, consenting to their becoming full-fledged members.

But he vetoed the application of the *Times*.

This discrimination startled the newspaper world. It seemed irrational. Of the four competitors the *Times* was obviously the weakest. Its circulation was creeping up, to be sure, but it was still small, and its advertising patronage was proportionately still smaller. Of all the newspapers in New York this one seemed least likely to offer dangerous competition to the rich and powerful *World*. Pulitzer's non-admirers—and their name was legion—therefore promptly jumped to the conclusion that his act was based on personal spite, and asked each other what Ochs had done to Pulitzer to engender such venom. But they could find no answer to the question and the mystery grew deeper.

Heavy pressure was brought to bear upon Pulitzer. By this time Ochs was no longer unknown in New York, but had many personal friends, some in fairly high places. These came to his aid, and even his competitors, the *Sun*, the *Herald* and the *Tribune*, embarrassed by the patent unfairness of the situation, did what they could to reverse the decision. After all, Ochs, as publisher of the Chattanooga *Times*, was already a member of the Associated Press and had done good service for it in the South. The southern members were all for him and the directorate was disposed to favor him. At length Pulitzer grudgingly gave way; he would not consent to full membership but at length he allowed the *Times* a Class B franchise, giving it a restricted service.

Three years later, however, the *Inter-Ocean* won its case in the Illinois Supreme Court. The veto right was judicially declared a monopolistic practice. But the court's writ ran only in the state of Illinois; the Associated Press, therefore, dissolved as an Illinois corporation and reorganized overnight in New York as a non-profit-making organization with a legal status resembling that of a social club. In the reorganization Pulitzer's veto right of course disappeared and Adolph Ochs obtained a full membership. Soon he was a director and for the rest of his life remained one of the most valuable and influential men in the organization.[4]

Joseph Pulitzer certainly had a vindictive strain in his temperament and it is possible that Ochs, without knowing it, had somehow offended him. But there is another explanation of his course of action that does not involve personal spleen, yet accounts first for what he did and second for the fact that he would offer no explanation.

Pulitzer, after all, was one of the greatest publishers of his time, shrewder by long odds than nine-tenths of his contemporaries. He had gone into sensational journalism, not because it was the limit of his capacity, but as a means of building up circulation and obtaining a sure footing in New York. Without doubt he was already sick of the roaring, expensive war with Hearst and was contemplating that change of the World which he later effected into a sedater and more responsible newspaper. That is to say, he already had his eye on precisely that part of the newspaper field into which the Times was already moving. He read the Times, he understood what it was doing, and he saw that it commanded the sort of brains that would make it a success.

But how was he to say this publicly? To proclaim aloud that this small, starveling sheet was in reality more formidable than the brilliant Sun, the cosmopolitan Herald, the stately Tribune and the howling Journal all combined would have been a tremendous endorsement of the Times. Indeed, such a confession, coming from such a man, might have been enough to put the Times on its feet overnight, franchise or no franchise. His play, then, was obviously to kill the thing quickly, while he had the chance, with no explanation. If people chose to attribute it to personal spite, so much the better; with that explanation they might not stop to consider how good the Times really was, and Pulitzer would have disposed of a dangerous competitor without advertising its quality.

[4] Forty-five years after this event and ten years after Ochs's death another case came up from Chicago, a city that seems to be the nemesis of the Associated Press. This one was brought by the Chicago Sun in the federal courts and was fought through to the Supreme Court of the United States, which ruled substantially as the Illinois court had held in 1900. Such discrimination as the World practiced against the Times in 1897 is, therefore, no longer legal.

It is true enough that this attributes to Joseph Pulitzer no scruples about using an unfair—and, as the courts now hold, an illegal—advantage against a competitor; but no one who has studied the journalistic history of the period will regard that as implausible. Hearst and Pulitzer were daily doing to each other, and to anyone else who stood in their way, things that by comparison make this treatment of Ochs look like a model of ethical conduct. In the late nineties New York journalism was a rough-and-tumble fight with no holds barred; and none survived save those who were made of durable stuff.

Even with a Class B franchise, though, Ochs survived. His circulation was 20,000 now and still slowly creeping up. It was largely composed, too, of the very class he wanted as readers, the solid, respectable citizens, who took the paper home to their families, giving it to their children with no fear of moral contamination. In the lordlier clubs it lay upon the reading-room table. Bankers, brokers, lawyers and doctors were coming to rely upon it more and more.

But advertisers were still wary. After all, 20,000 was only 20,000—pretty small, even for quality circulation. At the end of his first year the new publisher's deficit was $68,000—only half that of the previous year, but still $68,000 more than he had. His most careful calculations persuaded him that to be safe he must have a circulation of 50,000, which meant 30,000 additional readers, and where was he to get them? The year 1897 ended with the *Times* doing well, but still by no means out of the woods.

III

But in the new year a fresh calamity fell upon the struggling enterprise. The Spanish-American War broke out and the *Times* was in no position to handle it in a spectacular way.

Cynics have long asserted that this war was cooked up by the sensational press to serve its own ends. Certainly the yellow journals did nothing to promote a calm, impartial examination of the issues; but to assume that they precipitated the war singlehanded is to attribute to them a disproportionately large influence. After all, many other factors contributed to the outbreak of hostilities. The responsibility was not exclusively American and certainly it did not lie exclusively upon Messrs. Hearst and Pulitzer. This must be understood if one is to appraise correctly the course followed by Adolph Ochs and the *Times* during the next two years.

By its inept administration of the island of Cuba the Spanish royal government unquestionably was maintaining an international nuisance on the American doorstep. As far back as the days of Henry Clay the people of this country had developed a lively sentimental interest in the struggle of the Spanish colonies to win their independence. Clay's famous "American System," now usually regarded merely as the genesis of the protective tariff, was originally a grandiose, if nebulous, scheme to develop the Monroe Doctrine, a purely defensive policy, into a sort of hegemony over the Western Hemisphere. The scheme never had gone far enough for its essentially imperialistic nature to become clear; but it had set up in the mind of the average American a dim but persistent idea that we bore some sort of moral responsibility for the maintenance of common decency on this side of the Atlantic. It was felt, therefore, that notoriously bad government in Cuba was to some extent a reflection upon the United States; and this injected a moralistic element into all discussions of the situation.

Furthermore, the rapid development of this country in both population and wealth had created an enormous market for sugar and tropical fruits which Cuba was in position to supply. Accordingly a great deal of American capital and considerable numbers of American businessmen had gone to the island and were developing a large and quite legitimate trade which was continually threatened by the increasing political disorder. This injected an economic interest into the situation. Moral indignation plus the indignation of traders who have been abused and robbed can combine into a highly explosive political compound. We had in this country a situation strikingly similar to the one that drove the British into the War of Jenkins's Ear, another imperialistic adventure based largely on moral indignation; and this situation existed before the intervention of the yellow press.

Finally Madrid made its contribution to the witches' brew by sending to the island General Weyler, about as bad a choice as can be imagined. He was by no means the monster of infamy that the Americans were presently to see in him, but he was blundering, unimaginative and endowed with his full share of the obstinacy of the stupid man. Tormented by guerilla warfare, with which he was professionally unable to cope, he adopted the ruinous expedient of rounding up the entire population of certain country districts and confining them in concentration camps.

To a generation familiar with the concentration camps in Germany and Poland half a century later Weyler's worst atrocities seem relatively mild; but at the time they shocked the world. They did paralyze the economic life of Cuba and they did inflict unmerited suffering on large numbers of innocent people. With relatively little exaggeration they could be made to seem hideous beyond all precedent to people who had never heard of gas chambers and mass cremations; so the sensational newspapers fell upon them with boundless enthusiasm, playing them up for all they were worth and for a vast deal more than they were worth.

From the standpoint of Ochs and other journalists with some sense of responsibility, the damnable feature of this was that it was good for circulation. Day after day column upon column of horrors displayed under screaming headlines in varicolored inks did sell papers in enormous numbers. Circulation figures of the World and the Journal climbed to what were then regarded as astronomical heights. Eventually the United States battleship Maine was sent to Cuba for the protection of American interests; and while lying at anchor in Havana harbor she was blown up, with the loss of some hundreds of American lives. Responsibility for the explosion has never been definitely fixed, but later researches in the archives at Madrid have not produced the slightest evidence that the Spanish home government knew anything about it.

In this country, however, in the spring of 1898 there was no doubt whatever that we had been deliberately and treacherously attacked. Conservative President McKinley's control had been slipping for some time and now he lost it completely; the country plunged headlong into a brief, brisk war.

Throughout the excitement the course of the *Times* had been steady, sensible and careful—and highly unprofitable. Miller, never a startling writer, grew, if anything, even more cautious and pedantic; he urged upon the President careful investigation and the avoidance of precipitate action. He was right, but he was also dull. The *Times* was one of the papers that McKinley read; its expostulations may have had some effect in the White House, but not much anywhere else, and the White House was no longer in control.

Other considerations apart, from the professional standpoint of an American newspaperman the Spanish-American War was the most perfect in history. It was fought near by, it was brief and it was spectacularly successful. It was all over before the first wave of fervent patriotism had had time to subside. Typhoid fever and "embalmed beef" killed a great many more of our soldiers than Spanish bullets ever touched. So great was the enthusiasm that even the pacifistic William J. Bryan commanded a regiment of infantry, which never got to Cuba, while the bellicose Theodore Roosevelt led a cavalry charge near San Juan and became a national hero. All this helped to sell papers at an unbelievable rate and the yellows cashed in.

Not so the *Times*. If it had wished to be a war profiteer it couldn't for lack of resources. In the traditional metaphor, it was raining duck soup and all Ochs had was a fork. Hearst and Pulitzer flung literally millions into covering the war and the other papers spent thousands and tens of thousands. They chartered swift dispatch boats, tugs, anything that would float. They hired regiments of war correspondents. They had relays of couriers. They had platoons of artists—the news camera was still in its infancy and the main reliance for illustration was placed upon sketches. They had leased wires to Key West and Miami. Expense was simply forgotten, for if tremendous sums were being lavished, tremendous sums were pouring in from increased business.

None of this was possible for the *Times*. It had to depend on the regular news services, plus a little mail correspondence. About all that

Ochs could do was watch and take notes. To a man born for leadership it must have been gall and wormwood, but there was no help for it. Throughout the Spanish-American War, he was on the outside, looking in.

His competitors emerged from the war with gigantic circulations and enormously increased revenues from advertising. The *Times* came out with a circulation of 26,000—by contrast with the others, downright pitiable.

This is, however, not quite the full story. Such circulation as the *Times* had acquired it held firmly. Its news coverage may have been scanty and sometimes slow but it was in general reliable. The yellows with their vast expenditures had bought a great deal of stuff that was pure moonshine without a word of truth in it. As the excitement subsided, this became more and more clear to the public. In some ways the sensational papers had done a great job in 1898; their efforts unquestionably advanced the methods of news gathering and news transmission by many years. Ochs knew that, and gave them the tribute of reluctant admiration. But with part of their extravagant expenditure they had bought public distrust of their own reliability.

Pulitzer knew it and from that time on he began to change his tone. Sensationalism had served its purpose, as far as he was concerned. He ended 1898 thoroughly established in a commanding position; therefore he left extreme sensationalism to Hearst, and made the *World* steadily more and more moderate. In the end, it became a great liberal newspaper, but it never quite attained the reputation for solid reliability that the *Times* had built up, partly during the excitement of the Spanish-American War.

IV

But this was an asset with no current cash value. The *Times*, even with 26,000 circulation, was still losing money. Its revenue from circulation alone was paying the bills of no American newspaper. The *World* and the *Journal* were selling for one cent, which included the news dealer's profit; the fraction of a cent that came into the business office did not pay for the white paper used; the expense of making the paper and the profit were all derived from the advertising revenue.

As a matter of fact, the 26,000 that the *Times* possessed counted for more than the figures alone would indicate. It was recognized as "quality" circulation; that is to say, it was made up largely of people who had money to spend for an advertisers' goods and, what was even more important, it was the sort of paper that was not often discarded on the street, but was taken home where women, the usual spenders of the family income, could see it.

Even so, 26,000 was pretty small for New York. The advertising simply wasn't coming in and Ochs made up his mind that it would never come in sufficient quantity until his circulation was doubled. With 50,000 he could get it. With 50,000 his books would balance and leave him a reasonable profit. But where were the extra 24,000? Ochs decided that they were among the poor.

All the conservative papers in the city, his own included, sold at the standard price of three cents. Nobody had ever dreamed of selling anything but a yellow for less, for the superstition prevailed that anybody who would like a conservative paper would have three cents with which to pay for it. Ochs, against frantic protests from his associates, ordered the price of the *Times* reduced to one cent.

Bystanders, including his competitors, have long recognized that cutting the price from three cents to one was a stroke of genius. It jumped the circulation from 26,000 to 75,000; the increased circulation was reflected in increased advertising and increased rates for advertising; and the increased revenue put the paper on a profitable basis from which it was never afterward dislodged.

This act has been cited as proof of Adolph Ochs's keen business judgment; and the results sustain that interpretation. But the basis of that judgment included something more than the ability to calculate with rare accuracy the financial returns of an untried policy. Whence came the courage that Ochs displayed in taking this radical step? It was a terrific risk. It was staking everything on the turn of a card. If circulation had not risen promptly, the paper and the publisher would have been wiped out speedily.

[183]

Men who were absolutely honest in their advice and whose news-paper judgment ordinarily was of the soundest warned him that it couldn't be done. He was proposing to offer a quality product in a market dominated by the yellows; and it was the fixed conviction of New York newspapermen that people who could pay only one cent for a newspaper wanted such papers as the *World* and the *Journal* then were.

Ochs thought differently. He did not expect—nor did he ever attain—the mass circulations of the Hearst and Pulitzer press. But he did not need such circulations. A total of 50,000 would put the *Times* on a profitable basis and he believed the requisite number of readers could be found among those to whom the difference between three dollars a year and ten dollars a year for a newspaper was a material difference. This is the point at which he differed from his advisers, and this is another proof of his essential Americanism.

Ochs was never much interested in speculative generalization. He looked for results and when he got them he was satisfied. He formulated and expressed certain rules for the conduct of a newspaper, but beyond that he was little given to philosophic analysis. For instance, he would probably have been astonished and amused if anyone had suggested that his reduction of the price of the *Times* was one expression of an idea that distinguishes American civilization—if anything distinguishes it—from all others. This is the idea that democracy is quite capable of being civilized.

Of course there is nothing exclusively American in the idea itself. It had been adumbrated before the time of Plato, and its most powerful exponent in all history was none other than Jesus of Nazareth. But the flat truth is that it had not made much progress among men who were themselves truly civilized; and, for that matter, it is probably not accepted by a majority of them to this day. The Platonic conception of democracy has always been easier for an educated man to understand; Hamilton gave it its classical American expression in his famous outburst, "Your people, sir, is a great beast!"

No politician would make such a remark today, but plenty of them believe it. They do not give it expression, because with the passage of time the emphasis has shifted until now—and, in fact, by 1896, when

Ochs came to New York—the significant word had become the adjective, "great," rather than the noun, "beast." In 1789 democracy became formidable in the French Revolution; in 1832 it became more formidable when it took over England without firing a shot; in 1848 it jarred every country in Europe to its foundations; and in 1917, in the perverted form of Communism, it jarred the world. Today it is theoretically triumphant. It is the most powerful force in existence and statesmen of every nation have to reckon with it.

But it does not necessarily follow that they like it, or hope much from it. Even as enlightened a statesman as Winston Churchill quite frankly holds that the task of statecraft is to work out a *modus vivendi* whereby democracy can be restrained from wrecking civilization; and even in America, a nation founded on the basis of democracy, a large proportion of the most highly trained minds still agree with Fisher Ames that "Monarchy is like a splendid ship with all sails set; it moves majestically on, then it hits a rock and sinks forever. Democracy is like a raft. It never sinks, but, damn it, your feet are always in the water."

Yet it is certainly in the United States that men have most frequently developed enough faith in democracy to stake their lives and fortunes upon it. It may be true that most of the Founding Fathers believed that they were setting up an aristocracy and that the true democrats, Jefferson excluded, were such relatively minor figures as Sam Adams, Patrick Henry and Christopher Gadsden; but with the passage of time and the rise of proletarians of the stripe of Andrew Jackson, the thing began to be taken more and more seriously. It is a curious and little-noted fact that among the most effective vindicators of democratic theory were many leaders of big business, some of them men with no conscious faith in democracy at all.

What is the basis of the success of such men as John Wanamaker, John D. Rockefeller, Five-and-Dime Woolworth, Heinz of the 57 pickles, and Henry Ford? Perhaps some of them were guilty of dubious practices, but in general each of them contrived to furnish a good product at a reasonable price. Yet this would have availed them nothing had there not been a genuine appreciation of excellence in the masses. Without doubt, some rascals have made some money by foisting worthless goods upon a gullible public through fraudulent advertising; but in general a business that has made a prodigious success through many years supplies a reliable product. Many great American fortunes are monuments to the ability of the generality of mankind to prefer a good product to a bad one when the prices are approximately the same.

Yet from Plato down the philosophers who have dreaded democracy have feared it because they believed it incapable of appreciating excellence. Even today the philosopher who admits that a merchant or a manufacturer must be reliable if he is to succeed with the American public rarely has equivalent confidence in the ability of the public to discriminate in nonmaterial things. As between soaps selling at the same price, yes, buyers eventually will prefer the better; but as between ideas, oh, no!

Adolph Ochs denied this. He held that the discrimination of the American public is not confined to material things. He was no perfectionist. He never believed for a moment that all people, or even that most people, are really intelligent; but he did believe profoundly that intelligence runs in roughly the same proportion at all economic levels. He believed that in a population consisting of a hundred rich, a thousand fairly well-off, and ten thousand poor, if you find ten intelligent among the rich, you will find about a hundred among the well-off and about a thousand among the poor.

But this is of the very essence of democracy as it has been worked out in America. Even Abraham Lincoln, certainly one of the greatest exemplars of the theory, had to admit that "you can fool some of the people all of the time," but he regarded it as enough that you can't fool all of them all of the time. No social philosopher, monarchist, aristocrat or proletarian, has maintained seriously that all people are equally endowed mentally. Where American democracy diverges from other theories is in its insistence that neither heredity nor fortune is of much effect in determining worth; which means that the bulk of human value is to be found in the bulk of the population.

Ochs was publishing a newspaper designed to appeal to the intelligent, a term, by the way, not synonymous with "the intellectual."

Dana's *Sun* served the intellectual, as the *World* and the *Journal* served the emotional; the *Times* was aimed at those who were interested less in brilliance or in sensation than in facts. But it was a common delusion among newspapermen at the time—dare one deny that it is fairly common still?—that really intelligent interest in facts was concentrated almost entirely at the top of the income scale. Because the yellow press was enormously successful at the lower end of that scale, it was assumed that no other sort of paper would sell at all to the masses.

Yet every newspaperman in the city was well aware that among the so-called "upper" classes there were large numbers who surreptitiously read the *World* and the *Journal* with avidity. That is to say, they were aware that the craving for sensation is not confined to the poor, but is a human trait spread pretty evenly through all economic classes. If the sophisticated were rather ashamed of it, nevertheless they had it; the principal difference was that they did not read the yellow newspapers openly.

But these same newspapermen, willing enough to believe that the less admirable traits displayed openly at the bottom of the economic scale actually spread to the top, were not willing to believe that the more admirable traits loudly claimed at the top of the scale might actually spread down to the bottom. That stupidity exists in all classes they knew; but that intelligence may, in due measure, exist in all classes they were unwilling to concede. Therefore they told Ochs that no matter what price he put on the *Times* the poor would not read it, because the poor did not want that kind of newspaper.

Here the man's early experience came to his aid. Ochs had been poor himself and had lived in a country fought over by armies for four years and reduced to dire poverty as a result. He needed no advice about what the poor thought. He knew. Therefore he gambled everything he had on the theory that if the *Times* were offered at the same price as the yellow papers, enough of the poor would prefer it to give him the circulation he required.

This must not be confused with either altruism or the reformer's zeal. The move was not made to benefit the underprivileged or to uplift them. It was made to benefit and uplift the *Times*, and for no other purpose. It was Ochs's intention,[5] as soon as he had established a satisfactory circulation, to raise the price again; if he did not, it was because the one-cent price was so colossally successful for a dozen years that it would have been foolish to risk changing it.

But while it contained no element of altruism or piety, it was based on a profound belief in democracy, specifically American democracy. Like many of the leaders of big business who were his contemporaries, Adolph Ochs's success rests, in the last analysis, on his belief that a considerable proportion of the common people do appreciate excellence even in nonmaterial things and will choose the excellent when it is within their means.

This is a flat repudiation of the Platonic theory that the rise of demos necessarily means the subversion of every form of excellence. It is a denial of the essence of the Hamiltonian dictum. Your people, sir, may be a great beast, but necessarily so and not altogether so. Your people, sir, has within it the same leaven of reason, the same capacity to choose the better and reject the worse, that sustains your hope for your aristocracy; and if your aristocracy makes a better showing it is because its intelligent minority has freer play, due largely to its favorable economic position.

A man who holds this doctrine is a democrat. His economic theories have nothing to do with it. In the business world he may be the rankest of reactionaries, although this is not likely. Philosophically, he may believe that every word of *The Wealth of Nations* was divinely inspired and that William J. Bryan was Lucifer, and Henry George, Beelzebub, thinly disguised. He may have voted the Republican ticket straight from Grant to Harding. But if he believes, really believes with his whole heart, that the masses have just about as large a proportion of reason and virtue as the classes, then he is indubitably a democrat and the chances are ten to one that he is an American democrat, for it is in this country that such people are most frequently found.

More than that, he is a man unafraid. The most conspicuous social

---

[5] Such, at least, is the belief of his son-in-law, Arthur Hays Sulzberger, at present publisher of the *Times*.

phenomenon of this century, the common man's discovery of his political power when he combines with his fellows, the phenomenon that has paralyzed the rulers of the Old World with fright, does not terrify the genuine democrat. It may exasperate him beyond measure not only by taxing him heavily but also by compelling him to readjust many of his ideas not once but continuously. It may infuriate him by adhering to leaders he distrusts and dislikes. In fact, it may kill him outright by driving him into apoplexy with its fumbling inefficiency. But it will never drive him into whimpering allegiance to some fantastic Fuehrer, because he knows in his heart that the common man, when all is said and done, is not essentially different from the aristocrat and his rise means only that political power has shifted its base, not that it has changed its nature.

V

But if the instinctive faith in the essential intelligence of the people, the faith that the moral and mental élite are pretty evenly spread throughout the population, is evidence that Ochs was an American democrat, the phrase should be taken as a whole. He was American, thoroughly American, which is to say that he had the defects of that station in life as well as its qualities. This is clearly illustrated by his course in the Presidential election of 1900, when Bryan was again the Democratic candidate and the *Times*, which had supported Palmer and Buckner, the gold democrats, in 1896, went the whole way and backed William McKinley, candidate of the Republican party, who, as it proved, was also backed by a majority of the voters.

The issue, declared Bryan, was imperialism and it is plain enough now that it was; but a majority of Americans, including Adolph S. Ochs, didn't believe it for a moment. To him the issue was Bryan, and he had conceived for that extraordinary politician a distaste that almost amounted to a phobia. For one thing, Bryan's theory of bimetallism had been seriously damaged by events. The discovery of huge deposits of gold in South Africa and Alaska had suddenly eased the currency situation throughout the world. In addition, by 1898 the wreckage of the panic of 1893 had been largely cleared away and the country had entered another period of an expanding economy, that is to say, of good times. All opponents of Bryan were therefore convinced that in keeping him out of the White House they had delivered the country from nameless but fearsome dangers. It was obviously their duty to keep him out again.

Many of them—also including Ochs—believed that in raising the cry of imperialism Bryan had discovered another mare's-nest, even more fraudulent than bimetallism. They were serenely sure of their own good intentions and they were unable or unwilling to admit the possibility of a nation's entering upon a career of conquest by inadvertence.

Yet the physical facts are inescapable. After 1898 the United States, up to that time strictly metropolitan except for Alaska, its only non-contiguous possession, was a colony-holding nation, thrusting a thousand miles into the Atlantic and clear across the Pacific. It is true that this development was not consciously planned by Congress or the President, nor did it reflect any great expansionist enthusiasm in the people, prior to the war. Theodore Roosevelt, the assistant Secretary of the Navy who ordered Dewey, commanding the Pacific squadron, to attack Manila, may have cherished some notion of the development of an empire in the Far East, but if so he represented an extremely small group. The people of the United States found themselves in possession of Puerto Rico, Hawaii, the Philippines and assorted islands strewn across the Pacific without well understanding how it all came about.

On one point, however, their minds were quite clear. They knew beyond peradventure that a career of conquest was no part of their original program. They made war on Spain to free Cuba; and Cuba had been freed. Imperialism, in the mind of the average American, was a political philosophy asserting the right of the imperialistic nation to rule all others. Americans in general asserted no such right; and where the philosophy did not exist, imperialism could not exist. Therefore when Bryan bawled about imperialism, he must be talking nonsense.

It was all the easier for Ochs to accept this view because he had developed a high esteem for William McKinley, President of the United States. He regarded McKinley's high-tariff policy with abhorrence, but the rest of his domestic measures appealed to Ochs's conservative instincts. The *Times*, therefore, had been only mildly critical of the administration for the past four years. It was Ochs's belief, in fact, that an American administration, once elected, should always receive fair treatment from the press and, as a rule, should be supported except on measures so blatantly wrong that to support them would be self-stultification. He had therefore consistently given McKinley the benefit of the doubt where any existed; and the President was appreciative of fair treatment by a newspaper technically in the opposition.

Thus cordial relations had existed between the *Times* and the White House for four years and the publisher of the *Times* was in position to know the real attitude of the President better than the public knew it. For one thing, he knew that William McKinley had as little of the spirit of the conquistador in him as any man alive. For another, he knew that Madrid had made a large and important contribution to the difficulties that had finally exploded into war. He knew that the White House had made desperate efforts to hold back the mounting fury of the country and that it might have succeeded if the Spanish government had pursued a reasonably intelligent course. Therefore he was disgusted and indignant when the Democrats began to portray this mild citizen of Ohio as a sort of merger of Caesar, Tamerlane, Genghis Khan and Napoleon, retaining the worst features of each. More of Bryan's nonsense, as faulty in logic as sixteen to one, he decided; the issue was not imperialism because this country did not desire or intend to be imperialistic. He therefore went Republican.

It was a decision based on an error, but what a characteristically American error! More than any other nation in history we have laid stress upon the intent in judging the act—a sound doctrine in morals, but sometimes leading to disastrous results in politics. The fact that in 1900 we were already engaged in a small but exceedingly bitter war to subjugate the Filipinos was not evidence of imperialism as long as our leaders were disavowing any imperialistic ambition and the chief among them making the disavowal in perfect sincerity.

To take the will for the deed, the pronouncement for the act—this has been the besetting sin of Americans from the days when the Puritans passed laws against wearing gaudy attire and winked at their violation to the days when adoption of the prohibition amendment inaugurated the Jazz Age. The publisher of the *Times* was realistic and clear-headed in general, but, after all, he was an American and he could not wholly escape the spirit of his country and his age. He was convinced that we did not intend to be imperialistic, therefore we were not imperialistic; and the fact that at the very moment we were busily creating an empire was irrelevant.

Yet before we assume a smugly superior attitude toward those Democrats who supported McKinley in 1900, let us consider realistically the fact that the alternative they faced was Bryan. Eventually this curious genius came to be Secretary of State and his record in that office was not one to inspire confidence in his ability to hold the more difficult post of President of the United States. But it was not his radicalism that made him a bad Secretary of State; it was a certain obliquity of vision that made it impossible for him to see anything quite straight.

William Jennings Bryan was a great and good man, but he was cursed with a genius for being right in the wrong way. In 1896 he was right in his appraisal of the distress of the people, and he was right in attributing it to no divine ordinance but to the work of man in erecting a badly adjusted economic system; but he compromised his position by advocating bimetallism, a scheme that at most would have treated only one minor symptom of the disease. In 1900 he was right in asserting that the American republic was developing into a world-wide empire and he was justified in regarding that development with repugnance and dread; but in so far as he proposed a remedy at all, it was the inadmissible remedy of merely booting the Puerto Ricans, Filipinos and the rest out of American jurisdiction without protecting them against anarchy followed eventually by political slavery either to some other power or to the shrewd and grasping among their own people.

Bryan was an honest man but never did he, like Washington, erect a standard to which the wise and honest could repair. He collected the honest by millions and they followed him with fanatical devotion; but the wise and honest, when they followed him at all, followed with trepidation. To the very end, it was always possible to oppose this honest man honestly. His last years he spent crusading violently for temperance and religion, of all causes in the world the two that must most certainly command the approval of all decent men; but his way of advancing them was by prohibition and the enactment of laws forbidding the teaching of the findings of science!

Yet he had power based on solider foundations than his resounding eloquence. In spite of his slanted thinking his mind was shrewd, penetrating and, above all, tireless. In his personal contacts he had the charm that comes only from a genuine liking for and interest in people. In all practical matters involving dealing, dickering and manipulating he was one of the ablest politicians of his generation. Small wonder, then, that he imposed upon his devoted following the slant that his own mind took, in the end persuading them that no one could stand against Bryan except for sordid and probably dishonest reasons.

Adolph Ochs was a big man, but he wasn't so big that he could work the political miracle of charting a precise course between the unplanned and almost involuntary imperialism of William McKinley and the genuine but blind and clumsy idealism of Bryan. Nobody else could chart such a course. Had we had a strong leader capable of doing so, he might have steered this country into the happiest century of its existence, instead of into the bloodiest and most sorrowful. But lacking an ideal leader to follow, Ochs swung to McKinley.

There is not a shred of evidence that his decision was influenced by hope of personal advantage except as his personal advantage was bound up with the welfare of the country. Nevertheless, in the eyes of the extreme Bryanites, it damned him utterly. They wrote him down as a tool of big business, the mouthpiece of Wall Street, ally of all the predatory forces against whom the Peerless Leader was waging the people's battle.[6]

Within a few years, of course, the more sensible among them realized that this was nonsense. Nevertheless, a certain distrust of the *Times* continued to smolder among the die-hards, always ready to break into flame whenever the paper said so much as a polite word about a millionaire or an Old Guard Republican. It was one of the trials of Ochs's life. He understood that it was inevitable and he never permitted it to influence his course; but he was sensitive enough to feel it keenly when honest men, even stupid ones, regarded him with distrust.

VI

It was from the standpoint of outsiders only, however, that the political direction of the *Times* constituted the chief, or even the major, interest of these years. Ochs's head was teeming with projects, which in itself was merely his normal condition, certainly nothing new; but now they were more and more becoming possible of realization, which was something new.

He had been correct in his calculation that with 50,000 circulation enough advertising would come in to balance the *Times's* books and show a profit, but he had underestimated what cutting the price would do. Within less than a year he had a circulation of 76,000 and it was still rising; and the advertisers had not merely come in, they had fairly stampeded toward the paper. By 1900 the *Times* was not merely making money, it was beginning to make big money.

But if his income rose, his plans soared. Before the end of 1899 he had fulfilled the condition of the purchase contract; the paper was on a paying basis, the stock held in escrow was released to him and he thenceforth held absolute control. Thus he was able to plow back into

---

[6] The fact that this was the only occasion on which Ochs bolted the Democratic party should be sufficient answer to the accusation. He frequently disagreed with some of its leaders, but he chose to regard his position as that of a moderating influence in a radical party; and to maintain it he had sometimes to accept men and measures that he disliked.

the business by far the greater part of the paper's earnings and to undertake large and expensive innovations that would have been retarded and perhaps prevented had a majority of the stock been in other hands.

His brother George had been brought up from Chattanooga and in 1900 Adolph hit upon a scheme precisely to George's taste and for which he was admirably equipped. It was the publication of a special Paris edition of the *Times* during the great exposition of 1900, which was drawing thousands of American visitors to the French capital. George had always been tremendously energetic, if somewhat impatient of conventional restraints, and he flung himself into this job with furious industry. After a long, heartbreaking struggle with official red tape, he set up a complete printing plant on the exposition grounds and with the aid of a hastily recruited staff [7] plus inside-page matrices sent over from New York he turned out twelve to eighteen pages daily during the exposition. It was all the more impressive as the Paris newspapers at that time were customarily printing six to eight pages only.

As an advertising stunt it was brilliantly successful and it brought George the decoration of the Legion of Honor from the French government—ironically, Adolph, who had devised and paid for the scheme, received no official recognition at all. But it introduced the *Times* to Europe, as well as to vast numbers of Americans not residents of New York. More than that, to an important extent it introduced Europe to Adolph S. Ochs, for he took his family to the exposition and at Paris entered a wider world than he had ever known.

The episode of the Paris edition has usually been dismissed as no more than an interesting chapter in the history of the New York *Times*, but it was more than that. Here was the point at which the man who had already emerged from provincialism into regionalism and then into nationalism first began to look attentively at the world beyond the boundaries of his own country. Because he was the publisher of a large and increasingly influential newspaper his development was far more than a personal matter. For as Ochs thought, so thought the

[7] According to the Edwards MS. he had, in addition to his New York squad, men from Johannesburg, South Africa, Manitoba, Canada, Hong Kong, China, and Australia, as well as Parisians.

New York *Times*, and as the *Times* thought, so began to think an increasing number of Americans largely of the most influential class.

It was nothing new, of course, for an American newspaperman to come into intimate contact with Europe. Benjamin Franklin himself had been minister to France, and a long line of ambassadors and ministers since had been drawn from newspaper offices. Among them James Russell Lowell and Whitelaw Reid had come from New York. But their contacts were official, restricted by protocol, and concerned strictly with diplomacy, that is to say, with political relations.

Up to this time only one publisher of a great American newspaper had concerned himself with Europe to any marked extent. This exception was the second James Gordon Bennett, who was essentially light-minded, more interested in sporting events and society than in economic and cultural relations. The New York *Herald* was authoritative on the new sport of automobile racing and life at the European spas, but beyond that its European service gave Americans little real information as to what Europe was thinking or even what it was doing.

Had there never been a Paris exposition the restless, searching intelligence of Ochs must soon have penetrated the European field, but the visit of 1900 undoubtedly speeded the development of his interest. He toyed for awhile with the idea of establishing a permanent Paris edition of the *Times*, but eventually decided against it. He was determined, however, that his paper must develop a far better European service than it then possessed. In the course of his visit he made many contacts and eventually came into touch with the Walter family, who then controlled the *Times* of London. The next year he returned and made a deal with the Walters, who were not satisfied with their American service. Ochs swapped them the New York *Times*'s American special correspondence in exchange for the London *Times*'s continental correspondence, which was then incomparably the best in London. This arrangement was continued for a dozen years, immensely strengthening both papers.

The arrangement was never altogether satisfactory to the New York publisher, however. The quality of the service was excellent; he had no qualms about that. But it was necessarily British, written from the

British point of view and designed to appeal primarily to British readers. Although no man was more completely free of chauvinism, Ochs was too thoroughly American to be quite satisfied with British news. The reciprocal agreement with London served well enough for a time, but he always regarded it as a stopgap, to be ended as soon as he had the resources in both money and men to set up his own service in Europe. Eventually he did it and by great good fortune it was done just before the outbreak of the First World War.

But this is getting somewhat ahead of the story, and in fact it is a part of the history of the paper rather than that of the man. The significance of the visit to Paris in 1900 is what the visitor brought back. It is an interesting facet of Ochs's character that while he nearly always traveled as a tourist, he always came back laden, not with the junk that ordinary tourists collect, but with ideas that he made fruitful.

To see him on one of his jaunts abroad no one would have suspected how keenly he was observing and how accurately he was remembering the important things around him. Outwardly he seemed completely absorbed in whatever holidaymaking was afoot. Probably not an American in Paris that year missed less of the amusement side of the show than he did. Sideshows always delighted him, the more absurd the better; Ochs at the Paris exposition might have sung with Riley's hired man at the county fair,

> There was some balls 'at ye throwed, an' I throwed,
> An' a thingumajig 'at ye rode, an' I rode.
> There was a game 'at ye played, an' I played,
> An' a catch in the same where ye paid—an' I paid.

But what he brought home was an idea, which he promptly translated into action. It was an idea that perhaps transcended in importance any other contribution he made to American journalism—the idea that American thinking about Europe was based much too largely on misconceptions and misinformation and that the swift and orderly progress of civilization, if not its safety—it is too much to assume that he foresaw in 1900 the holocaust of fourteen years later—would be facilitated by more adequate and more accurate information, not about the speed of automobiles and the doings of the lords and gentry, but about the people, their ideas and their work.

As far as the paper was concerned this idea was excellent without qualification; but as regards Adolph Ochs's personal life it, like his political stand, acted both to his comfort and to his malaise. The foreign service increased the prosperity and power of the *Times*, but in later years, when war broke, that connection with London, although it had been severed, brought down upon its publisher the abuse of all enemies of Britain. They accused him now of being a tool not of Wall Street only but of Lombard Street also, and the very act by which he had contributed most to the national welfare and, as it proved, the national safety, was denounced as despicable if not downright traitorous subservience to the British crown. Well, no man can please everybody.

VII

During these same years another and mightier project was taking shape in Ochs's mind. It was the question of providing permanent quarters for the paper. His downtown facilities were rapidly becoming intolerably overcrowded. When the circulation jumped in less than a year from 26,000 to 76,000 he had to borrow the use of presses from a friendly contemporary in order to get enough copies printed to supply the news dealers. It was clear that the *Times* must have greater working space and the publisher was determined that it should have a building of its own.

In its function as a newspaper plant the *Times* building belongs to the history of the paper and it is enough to say of it here that it was as efficient in every detail as ingenuity could make it. But its efficiency was the work of dozens and scores of specialists, not of Adolph Ochs. The mechanical and engineering wonders of the building reveal nothing about the personality of the man, but its architecture and its location do. The significance of both has been somewhat obscured by the development of the city in the last forty years, yet enough remains to throw much light upon the man responsible.

From the day he took over the paper it was clear to the publisher that the building on Park Row was too cramped for production of the sort of newspaper he planned, but there was nothing he could do about it then—except think. But in 1899 the paper that had been losing $2500 a week made a clear profit of $50,252[8] and that was obviously a mere beginning, so by 1900 the publisher was beginning to lay his plans. He moved with what was for him unusual deliberation, although that was not the impression New York received; for not until January 18, 1904, was the cornerstone laid, and construction took approximately a year. Even so, the city, staring at the new building, regarded it as proof of meteor speed shown by a man who had come to town nine years before practically unknown and some hundreds of thousands of dollars worse than penniless. The rapidity and especially the certainty with which Ochs moved, the clarity and firmness of his purpose and the dexterity with which he side-stepped innumerable pitfalls that might have trapped him, gave him a reputation for almost supernatural acumen. A feat that wiseacres had declared impossible he undertook and achieved with apparent ease; a scheme that they deemed insane he carried through and it proved to be high wisdom. It is small wonder that some began to credit him with second sight and all agreed that he was far and away the luckiest man in the publishing business.

The sardonic Leopold Wallach fairly represented the New York attitude. As Ochs was discussing his plans for the new building one day he suddenly realized that Wallach was not, according to his custom, raising objections, but was agreeing with everything. Ochs wanted to know why. "Well, Adolph," said Wallach, "if you must know, I approve because you are never happy except when you are in hot water, and this project will keep you in hot water for the rest of your life."

What New York forgot, or chose to ignore, was Chattanooga. In New York Ochs was making his second career, not his first, and there was hardly a problem facing him in the big city that he had not strug-

---

[8] Adolph S. Ochs in the *Times* of August 18, 1921, the twenty-fifth anniversary of his acquisition of the paper.

gled with and somehow solved in the small one. When he was in position to move he moved surely and rapidly because he was treading familiar ground. True, the problems in New York were magnified by ten diameters, but they were the same sort of problems and would yield to the same sort of handling.

In the matter of securing adequate quarters, for example, he faced a situation in its essentials identical with the one he had faced in Chattanooga ten years earlier. In that case he had attacked the problem on the principle of what military men call "the calculated risk," which demands extreme daring, resolution and energy but, if it succeeds at all, succeeds brilliantly. He was not content to erect a weatherproof shelter large enough for his purposes; he determined to have nothing less than the handsomest building in town placed on a commanding site. He built it, and although it strained all his resources, moral as well as financial, in the end it paid handsomely.

Taking into consideration his youth, his poverty and his environment, it may be argued with great plausibility that the building he started in 1892, costing $100,000, was a more remarkable proof of his courage and ability than the one he started in 1904, although its cost ran into the millions.

Of course there were prophets of disaster on both occasions who were certain the man had lost his wits; but they had sounder reason for thinking so in Tennessee, where he really was breaking a new path, than they had in New York, where he was merely repeating on a grander scale what he had done before.

Another reason that blinded many to the basic common sense in what seemed superficially to be an extravagant project was the incredulity with which the mediocre commonly receive the utterances of an extraordinary man. In his salutatory, in conversation and in letters, and in practically every public utterance he made with reference to his paper he tried to pound into the heads of his hearers that he was building an institution, as well as a profit-making enterprise, and an institution quasi-public in its nature.

People heard him, but they didn't believe him, any more than they believed John D. Rockefeller and Andrew Carnegie when they referred in comparable terms to their oil and steel companies. Unfortunately, it was not the Titans only who talked like that. It had become the prevailing cant of the business world, until every peanut-vendor, to hear him tell it, was only mildly interested in profit and at heart devoted to public service.

But it took a man with something like Ochs's own range of vision to perceive that when he spoke of the *Times* as a quasi-public institution he was not talking cant but merely pointing the way to the long-term profit. A newspaper of the kind he envisaged, a newspaper that would command the respect of all reputable citizens, a newspaper that would add to the honor of its city and to the pride of its residents, might make less money in any specific year than a cheap and nasty sheet, but it would last a great many years longer and its income would be a great deal steadier.

Furthermore, while Ochs was exceptionally free of petty vanity, he cherished a frank and honorable ambition to be recognized by his fellowmen as a man of worth and dignity, and he could achieve this only through his enterprise. Therefore his pecuniary interest and his personal ambition combined to persuade him that the permanent home of the *Times* ought to symbolize his conception of the paper. It should be not merely a business structure, but monumental in the true sense—a dignified adornment to the city, so placed that it could be pointed out with pride by citizens to visitors.

For such purposes Park Row wouldn't do. Newspaperdom had established itself there long ago when the city virtually ended at Fifty-ninth street and the Brooklyn Bridge was close to the center of things. But by 1900 the vast northward movement had carried the bulk of New York miles away from Park Row. The magnates of the newspaper world assured him that it was impractical to attempt to produce a newspaper uptown. It never had been done, therefore it obviously couldn't be done. But by this time Ochs had had dealings enough with the mighty to discover that they are generally far better experts on what can't be done than on what can. He discarded the advice of the great and relied on his own good sense.

He would therefore move uptown, but where could he place a truly monumental structure in that checkerboard pattern? A monument to be effective must be seen and a big one must be seen at a distance; but in New York the utmost distance at which most buildings can be seen is the width of one of the avenues.

The only places where the pattern is interrupted are the four points where Broadway, reeling drunkenly across the checkerboard, intersects Fifth, Sixth, Seventh and Eighth avenues. To these, then, Ochs turned his attention and fixed at first upon Twenty-third Street and Fifth Avenue.

He did not know who controlled the property, so he went, as was his wont, to consult his friend Henry Morgenthau, Sr. His relation to this man was an interesting one. When Ochs first came to New York he asked a friend to name three men of fine judgment who would not object to giving a newcomer friendly advice. All the rest of the city, Ochs added with a grin, he reserved as prospects from whom to borrow money; but with these three he would never have business dealings of any kind. The friend obliged and named Morgenthau as one; he then introduced the pair with an explanation. Morgenthau, much amused, accepted the condition and a friendship resulted that was broken only by Ochs's death.

But when the publisher asked who controlled the Twenty-third Street property, Morgenthau's unexpected answer was, "I do." He was acting as broker for the owners, who wished to sell. Yet with a customer in his office and a commission—a big one, too, for the property was among the most valuable in the city at that time—his for the taking, he refused to sell to Ochs.

He told the publisher that he had chosen the wrong site; that the business center had already passed Twenty-third Street and was moving north and that the site he needed was where Broadway crossed Seventh Avenue at Forty-second Street, then known as Longacre Square. Besides, he added smilingly, there were to be no business dealings between them and he had no interest in the Longacre Square property.

To make a long story short, Henry Morgenthau assembled the various parcels of real estate—then partly occupied by a hotel in trouble with the city because its structure violated the building code—secured options on them all and gave the publisher invaluable help in financing the project, all without a fee. When Ochs, embarrassed by such generosity, went himself to Morgenthau's office and handed him a check for $25,000, Morgenthau tore up the check and smilingly reminded him that no money was to pass between them. None ever did; but it is not surprising that Morgenthau, in his later diplomatic career, had a stout and devoted champion in the *Times*.

Having secured his site, Ochs presented his architects, Cyrus L. W. Eidlitz and Andrew C. McKenzie, with a problem refractory in the extreme. In the first place, the site was a trapezoid, twenty feet wide at the north, fifty-eight at the south and a hundred and thirty-one feet long, with only two right angles. In the second place, the building was isolated, visible from all sides, requiring all four to be treated with equal care.

The irregularity of the site eliminated at once any thought of a classical or Renaissance design, so the architects fell back on Gothic. The columnar treatment of tall buildings had not yet been developed and the final outcome was the idea of a tower supported by a base. The records do not make clear who first thought of Giotto's tower at Florence as the inspiration of the building, but there is a tradition that it was Ochs himself. Certainly he had seen and admired the famous campanile and he approved, if he did not originate, the suggestion.

The engineers also had their troubles. The only subway then in existence—in fact, it was still under construction—came from Brooklyn Bridge up Fourth Avenue to Forty-second Street, swung west to Broadway and then northwest, curving through one corner of the *Times's* basement. This complicated the construction job at the very beginning and it continued difficult to the end. Everything happened to the building. There were strikes, there were storms and floods and freezes, there were a few accidents, there were delays in obtaining materials, there were unexpected costs. Still the work went on. The excavation was finished and braced, the foundations were solidly laid and the day came when the cornerstone hung poised by what was to be the entrance at the Broadway side, and after a prayer by Bishop

Potter and a speech by Mr. Miller, the publisher's eleven-year-old daughter stepped forward and declared, "I dedicate this building to the uses of the New York *Times*. May those who labor herein see the right and serve it with courage and intelligence for the welfare of mankind, the best interests of the United States and its people, and for decent and dignified journalism; and may the blessing of God rest ever upon them." Then as the great stone settled into place she struck it three times with a trowel, saying, "I declare this stone to be laid plumb, level and square."

After that, things moved more rapidly, but Ochs had to move faster than the building. The usual fate of the aspiring houseowner befell him. The construction work proved costlier than had been estimated. He was urged to abandon the tower altogether or at least to strip off the ornate and expensive decoration, but he clung stubbornly to his original idea. Somehow the money was found and the building went ahead precisely as it had been planned. Within a year it soared into the air three hundred and sixty-two feet above Forty-second Street, dazzling in its terra-cotta and cream-colored brick, with more than a suggestion of the flower-like grace of its great original. It was the second tallest building in New York and by long odds the most beautiful.

A delighted Board of Aldermen promptly changed the name of Longacre to Times Square. Ochs had achieved his end. For more than forty years the Times building has been pointed out by citizens to visitors as one of the truly monumental structures of the city; and although it was long ago surpassed in height, in size and in magnificence, it still retains its dignity and still remains, in the eyes of New Yorkers, the center of things.

Indeed, he built better than he knew. This symbol of his aspirations has become inextricably interwoven with the life of the city. It is the Areopagus, the forum, the market place into which the people rush under stress of any great emotion. Serene and high it has looked down upon the people as they wept and as they rejoiced. Let a great President die suddenly and the people for no apparent reason pour into Times Square to plod there, sober and downcast. Let news of victory come winging across the world and they rush into Times Square to dance and sing the whole night through. There every four years they gather a million strong to hear the news of their own decision as to their own government. There on the last night of each year they gather again, straining their eyes toward the luminous white ball at the top of the flagstaff to catch the first hint of its movement as it starts to slide down at the tick of midnight; each wishing to be first to hail his neighbor with greetings for the New Year that is always to be happier than the last.

Yes, he achieved his purpose. He built an institution, not merely a commercial enterprise. He built it in the heart of New York and into the heart of New York.

CHAPTER VIII

In Which the Man Works Wonders That Amaze All Beholders and Slightly Startle Himself.

I

THE decade following occupation of the new building probably covers the period of Adolph S. Ochs's most complete fulfillment as a human being, yet it is precisely at this point that he eludes the biographer's grasp and disappears into the institution he had created. For these years it is flatly impossible to draw any clear line of demarcation between the life of its publisher and the history of the New York *Times*. The man from Tennessee at last had found a job big enough to swallow him, and he was content to be swallowed.

They were years of prodigious labor—in fact, he ended by working himself into a nervous collapse that momentarily converted him into a black-browed misanthrope—but they were also years of vast achievement. He had his discouragements, his disappointments and frustrations, but they were all relatively minor ones, irritations, not calamities, and they were heavily outweighed by his successes.

Within a year after moving into the new building he had completed the team to which, on his twenty-fifth anniversary as publisher, he was to attribute the success of the *Times*. Miller had been his editor from the beginning. In 1906 Louis Wiley achieved the ambition with which he had entered Ochs's service—he was made business manager. In the same year Ochs made another of the best trades of his life when he employed Carr V. Van Anda as managing editor.

These four working together constituted one of the strongest teams in American journalism, and it was characteristic of Ochs that at the twenty-fifth anniversary celebration he insisted that the success of the paper was the work of the team, not of any one man. He ignored the probability that all America could not have produced another driver capable of handling that team without a runaway and a grand smash. All these men had worked for other employers with but moderate success and Miller, as publisher of the *Times*, had been a flat failure. Only under the leadership of Ochs did all of them develop their full powers.

Like all strong men they were difficult to handle—all opinionated, all bold, all resolute, all born fighters, and to prevent them from fighting each other to the peril of the common endeavor was no light task. Each had the defects of his qualities. As an editorial writer Miller was scholarly, sound and cogent, but at times he could achieve a stuffiness without parallel. As a newsman Van Anda had no superior and few equals in America, but he tended to go too fast and had to be restrained from overworking himself and his staff. As a business manager Wiley was superb, but the very exuberance of his personality threatened constantly to involve the paper in embarrassing entanglements. The basis of Ochs's greatness as a publisher was his skill in stimulating and developing the strength of each man and at the same time balancing and compensating his weakness.

This was a far more remarkable achievement than the Paris edition, or the new building, or even the purchase of the paper itself, but it never struck Ochs as remarkable at all. He protested that he only applied common sense when the opinions of able men came into violent collision and he was called on to adjudicate the dispute. Basically, this was true. It is the testimony of every man who participated in the editorial councils of those days that when the publisher had listened to all sides of an argument—and he invariably listened patiently to all —and had made his decision the dispute evaporated. A particular disputant may not have been convinced that the decision against his side was altogether right, but it was always so lucid and reasonable that he could not claim that it was altogether wrong. In other words, it did embody common sense.

But there were two factors entering into those decisions that apparently were hidden from the man who made them, one a factor of intelligence, the other of character. The first was the speed of the man's thinking, that quality, already mentioned, that enabled him to pierce through a fog of obscurities and irrelevancies and see the main point instantly. This commanded respect.

The other, the factor of character, was the man's obvious desire to be fair. Despite that touch of aloofness Ochs liked and respected his men and they knew it. They were accordingly convinced that no decision, however much they disliked it, was based upon personal jealousy, or petty resentment, or anything else except his impartial judgment of the evidence in the case. Therefore they left the meeting frequently disappointed, but never resentful; and they applied the decision loyally and with a will.

Yet it is far from true that in these years the publisher's sole function was that of the flywheel, keeping the power of the machine balanced and smooth. He did perform that function, but with that the metaphor breaks down, for he also supplied the steam.

It would be fatuous to suggest that he, or he in combination with his three chief associates, originated all the ideas that made the Times what it eventually became. The paper in the course of its history has been served by enough brilliant men to make up an infantry regiment, each of whom made some contribution, many of them highly important contributions, to its success. But it was Ochs who was behind them, Ochs who released their energies and allowed them scope to show what they could do.

For instance, it was the publisher and no other who decreed that the Times should become the newspaper of record, the one to whose files future historians would refer when it became necessary to settle some obscure point. Other men carried out the decree, exhibiting boundless energy and ingenuity and sometimes making great names for themselves in so doing; but Ochs was the man who decided to do it.

It had to be the publisher in this particular case, for the decision involved throwing away a fortune and none but the man who held control could do that. When it was determined that the Times would thenceforth publish in full every important document and every important speech in the transactions of the day, Louis Wiley may well have groaned, for it meant woe to his department. In the first place, it entailed tremendous expenditure for the mere typesetting, paper and ink; and in the second place it frequently meant crowding out profitable advertising. The *Times* has spent literally millions publishing matter that nobody on the staff expected a single purchaser of the paper to read through.

The immediate cost was stupendous and it is not possible to trace to this policy even an ultimate profit in dollars and cents. The profit came in enhanced prestige, an addition to the institutional, rather than the commercial, side of the paper. A hundred years earlier another American journalist, Hezekiah Niles, of Maryland, had adopted for his *Register* the motto, "The past, and the present—for the future," and he succeeded in making his paper an authoritative original source for modern historians. How much, if at all, Ochs was influenced by the example of Niles is uncertain; but it is quite certain that the files of the *Times* today stand in the estimation of historians alongside those of *Niles's Register* as records of the life of the nation for the period they cover. But Ochs went his predecessor one better in publishing the *Times Index* to make the information in the files readily available to scholars.

The debt that American historical scholarship owes to the man is sufficiently obvious; but the *Times Index* has served another purpose less obvious but equally important. In scores of newspaper offices where no file of the *Times* is kept, the *Index* is in constant use to ascertain the exact date of an event which can then be looked up in the paper's own files. It has therefore played no small part in making contemporary journalism richer, more exact and more accurate.

II

Another feature of the paper's development that reflected the owner's personality was the part it played in technological advancement, especially in the fields of transportation and communication. At the moment when the *Times* began to prosper both aviation and wireless telegraphy were born. Ochs was fascinated by them and was not content only to keep his readers informed of their progress. In addition to space he gave money, time and energy to help both through the critical early years.

To some extent this represented commercial shrewdness, for the development of rapid and easy communication is advantageous to newspapers even more directly than to most business enterprises. But there was more to it than that, much more. When he heard of these new things Ochs was not merely alert to their utilitarian value but really excited. Here was something in the grand style, two steps toward the conquest of time and distance, and there was something in the man that responded instantly to a lordly concept in any field. Small matters he might pass with a shrug, but if anything really big was going on Adolph Ochs had to be in it or die, not necessarily as an actor, but as a close-range spectator. The consuming desire always to be among those present when anything important happens is, of course, what makes a newspaperman and few, even in that inquisitive fraternity, had a larger share of it than Ochs.

Once it was verified that the Wright brothers actually had made their heavier-than-air machine lift itself from a North Carolina sand dune the *Times* lavished attention upon every phase of the new art. Men of the *Times* still remember with rueful amusement that incredulity cost the paper a beat on that night in 1903 when an unknown Coast Guard telegrapher sent in a query—that is, an announcement that the flight had taken place with an inquiry as to how many words the paper could use on the story. Like nearly all the rest of the country's newspapers, the *Times* declined to be caught by what the editors regarded as an obvious hoax; but when the truth of the story had to be admitted by the most skeptical a few days later, the paper proceeded to make up for its original doubts with an interest so vigorous that eventually it came to be the leading purveyor of aviation news. Not only did it report what was going on, but it offered prizes for successful flights and employed aviators to take part in various promotion schemes.

In all of this the publisher was a leading spirit, even though the specific plans were usually devised and executed by others.

Even stronger, if anything, was his interest in the work of Guglielmo Marconi in wireless telegraphy. When that curious genius succeeded in flashing the Morse code signal for the letter S across the Atlantic on December 14, 1901, the *Times* was not caught napping. It carried the story under a display head.

But it did far more than that. Under the direct order of its publisher the *Times* became an early and one of the most important patrons of Marconi's company. Breaking his own rule against holding industrial securities, Ochs bought stock in the American Marconi Company— for his personal account, of course, not for the paper—and he saw to it that more and more business was given to Marconi as fast as wireless facilities were able to handle it.

Indeed, there is reason to believe that Ochs advanced the thorough establishment of radio communication by some years by an analysis of its service from the newspaper standpoint. Studying the elapsed time of transmission of London dispatches to the *Times* he discovered that wireless messages commonly fell behind because of the poor transmission system at each end, when the messages were transferred to land wires. The company officials knew this, of course, but didn't know quite what to do about it. But Ochs knew and had the power. He brought pressure upon the Western Union Telegraph Company at this end and, through his London connections, upon the British post office, operator of telegraph lines in England, and kept it up until he had induced both to reconstruct the land lines.[1] At the same time, he stimulated the wireless people by promising them the entire business of the *Times* on a certain date. He gave it, too, and the Marconi Company handled it successfully. Dispatches thousands of words long appeared every day under the notation, "By Marconi Wireless Telegraph to the New York *Times*," the finest possible demonstration of the commercial practicability of the system.

Incidentally, the purchase of that stock turned out to be a bad idea. In the first place, it cost money; Ochs eventually sold the shares at a considerable loss. What was worse, when the English Marconi Company, an entirely distinct corporation, became involved in a smelly

[1] Davis, *op. cit.*, pp. 280–282.

stock-market scandal a few years later Ochs's critics used his ownership of some of the American company's stock as basis for insinuations
that he was somehow mixed up in the scandal. He had nothing whatever to do with the English company, but the very words "Marconi
stock" were enough to give the scandalmongers a running start and
Ochs blamed himself for affording them even that much of an opportunity.

The incident of the Marconi stock was a trifling episode in itself,
but it illustrates vividly the difference between Adolph Ochs and his
peers in the Imperial Age of American business. He has been compared
to Rockefeller, Morgan and Carnegie, but the comparison is ridiculous
if it is measured in terms of money. Ochs became a rich man, but he
never amassed a tithe of the fortune piled up by the least of these
others. He never made as much money as some other newspaper publishers, Frank Munsey, for example.

But the reason was that he didn't try, and he didn't try because it
was unnecessary. What all the Titans thirsted for was power and prestige, that is, for success. But in the case of a merchant or manufacturer,
and to a lesser extent in the case of a banker, the only generally recognized measure of success is money. The ownership of money is somewhat less important to a banker, because he can attain power and
prestige merely by controlling it. It is not without significance that
of Rockefeller, Morgan and Carnegie, each a top-ranking man in his
line, the smallest personal fortune was that of Morgan, the banker.
It was unnecessary for him to own a billion, or even Carnegie's
three hundred millions, in order to hold first place in the banking
world.

This is even more strikingly true of a newspaper publisher. Money
is only a secondary measure of his importance in the world as the public
rates importance; the first measure is the influence of his paper. He
must be solvent, of course, in order to be independent; but once he
has enough to pay his bills, additional money adds little to his power
and prestige, so why spend time and energy amassing it when the real
object can be better achieved by other means? Will the President of
the United States and Congress sit up and take notice when his news-

paper speaks? Will historians, sociologists, economists base their arguments on the news that his journal presents? Will actors, musicians, writers and painters grow hysterical when his paper criticizes them and purr when it lauds their work? If the answer is in the affirmative in all these cases, then people regard him as an important and powerful man, even though his income may be small by comparison with that of a Henry Ford.

No man alive understood this better than Adolph Ochs. To have those questions answered affirmatively with respect to the *Times* he cheerfully spent money, time, energy and every other resource available. It is not enough, therefore, merely to say that he was not greedy in explaining his failure to accumulate a much larger fortune. True, he was not greedy, but perhaps he would have been had money been the only measure of success in his world; fortunately, his was a somewhat wider world in which he could climb to the place of his desire by other means than first building up a pyramid of gold on which to mount.

III

It was during these years, too, that he toyed for awhile with the idea of altering his whole attitude toward newspaper publishing. American journalism has produced two distinct types of successful publishers— the one-newspaper man, Greeley, Bennett, Pulitzer, and the chain-newspaper man, Hearst, Scripps, Munsey and their like. Pulitzer owned the St. Louis *Post-Dispatch* and Ochs the Chattanooga *Times*, but they were essentially one-newspaper men for the bases of their renown were the *World* and the *Times* of New York.

Back in Tennessee Ochs had considered the idea of a chain of southern newspapers, and when he was negotiating for the Nashville *American* it seems to have been his plan not to stop with that, but to use it and his Chattanooga paper as the foundation of a chain. In 1901 he apparently thought for awhile of reviving the project on a national scale.

His brother George had just returned from Paris full of steam and fairly spouting ideas. In Paris George had done a highly creditable job under difficult circumstances and he was looking for new worlds to conquer. Adolph, fair-minded even to his family, admitted that George had a claim to consideration. At first there was talk of his going back to Paris to establish a permanent edition of the *Times* there, but careful investigation revealed the impracticality of that idea. After Paris George had not much taste for Chattanooga and besides the situation there was being satisfactorily handled by Milton Ochs and a brother-in-law, Henry C. Adler.

As to why he did not include George in the New York staff, he kept his own counsel. Incidentally, Harry C. Adler contributed to the *Times* organization more than his own services. Thirty years later his son, Julius Ochs Adler, was to become general manager of the New York paper and to figure largely in its later history, not to mention such incidentals as serving with distinction in two wars and picking up a general's stars in the South Pacific. At any rate, he bought a collapsing Philadelphia newspaper, also called the *Times*, and put George in chief command. This was in 1901 and a little over a year later, July 21, 1902, he acquired the *Public Ledger* of the same city, combining the *Times* with it. Some time later Milton Ochs was brought up to join George and the *Public Ledger* continued under Ochs's ownership for eleven years.

Here was obviously the beginning of a newspaper chain, and newspaper men in general confidently expected Ochs, established in New York and Philadelphia, to proceed to Baltimore and Washington, then to Richmond and Louisville, giving him what on paper at least looked like a relatively compact and logical chain of newspapers from Tennessee to New England.

But he never developed it. On the contrary, in 1913 when Cyrus H. K. Curtis offered for the *Public Ledger* a price that would enable Ochs to get out with a profit, the offer was accepted and Ochs reverted to the ownership of two newspapers only. Indeed, there is hardly a doubt that his retention of the Chattanooga paper was due more to his affection for the town than to strictly business reasons, although it was always a good property.

Possibly George exerted some influence toward turning Adolph away from the chain idea. George had a pretty thunderous career in Philadelphia. In justice it should be added that it was, on the whole, a pretty good career, too; but it was not soothing. George got himself involved in a series of resounding battles that shook up Philadelphia and Pennsylvania politics very thoroughly, which was probably good for them. But he shook up his brother in New York, too, and the shaking did Adolph no perceptible good at all. Figuring what George was going to do next must have been one of his most difficult—and anxious— intellectual operations during those eleven years. He must have given some consideration to what he would do as a chain publisher with not one but five or six editors like George to hold in line; and it could not have been a reassuring thought.

It is unlikely, however, that the dominant consideration was George or anything else but the *Times* itself. Ochs could and did manage three newspapers profitably, and there is no convincing evidence that he could not have managed thirty and made them pay. But the *Times* was becoming vastly more than solely a profit-making enterprise. It was becoming a power in the land, and its political, social, literary and other noncommercial relations were becoming steadily more complicated.

The details of all these things were in competent hands, but their over-all supervision the publisher retained. He was too good an executive to interfere unnecessarily with any department, once he had found a first-rate man to run it, but he watched them all like a hawk, and when real necessity arose his interference was prompt and effective. Staff men were constantly being startled by having their attention called to slips in the most obscure corners of the paper.[3]

[3] Edwin L. James, now managing editor of the *Times*, declares roundly that an error in a one-line head over a one-inch item at the bottom of page 37 would bring a telephone call from the publisher. "He would usually begin," says Mr. James, "not with a complaint but with a compliment on the handling of some important story on the front page and of course I would be elated. Then he would

But no human being, not even one with Ochs's extraordinary capacity for rapid work, could give such unremitting attention to each of a whole chain of newspapers. It is, in fact, unnecessary to assure their commercial success and a fair measure of professional success. Ochs unquestionably was capable of handling a large number of profitable and respectable journals. The choice lay between a number of respectable newspapers and one great one. The larger profit lay in numbers. It is possible, although not certain, that the greater political power also lay in numbers. But every other sort of power and true professional supremacy lay in the other direction. No human being has ever yet built simultaneously two newspapers each of which had a serious claim to the title of the greatest newspaper in the world. This was not clear to Ochs from the beginning. He hesitated long between the two courses; but in the end his decision was to play for the championship and let the big money go.

It was a decision characteristic of the true Titans as distinguished from the merely acquisitive. Many of them played for their positions *through* big money because they had no other avenue of approach; but whereas the merely greedy never looked beyond money, the really big men of that period always grasped at something beyond money and the biggest accepted blithely the responsibility that goes with power.

This was conspicuously true of Adolph Ochs. In the opening decade of the century the *Times* was succeeding beyond his utmost expectations in every way. To begin with, it was bringing in more money than he had ever expected to have; but beyond that it was increasing in power and influence in a fashion that was positively startling. After the big jump when the price was cut in 1898 circulation never took

---

add, as if it were an afterthought, 'By the way, there is a head on page 37 that I think is hardly adequate.' I would look at it," continued the editor, "and it would be awful. But the previous compliment would have cushioned the shock so that I wouldn't be downcast, merely determined not to let it happen again." The story throws a great light upon Ochs's remarkable success in keeping good men and keeping them at the top of their form.

any spectacular bounds, but every year showed a substantial increase. It crossed 100,000 in 1900 and 200,000 ten years later—four times what the new owner had set as his goal in 1896.

More satisfactory than the size of the circulation was its quality. Business leaders read it almost to a man and that gave cynics the impression that it was distinctively a rich man's paper. But it wasn't. Bringing its price within reach of the poor was what had made it in the first place and a vast proportion of its readers still were people of relatively small income. College professors read it. Schoolteachers read it. Clergymen read it. These are all notoriously below the big-income brackets, but they count prodigiously in the formation of public opinion. Politicians, labor leaders and professional men read it. What it said was noted in Washington sometimes more carefully than in New York.

Adolph Ochs had created an engine of publicity vastly greater than he had calculated. He was proud of it, of course, but an intelligent and conscientious man could not overlook the fact that its potentialities for evil were terrifying. If he refused to turn his back upon it while he busied himself with other enterprises, one strong reason was that he was afraid to. He had built this thing and it was his responsibility to see that it did not turn into something socially destructive. Authority he could delegate, but the final responsibility was his and he could not pass it on to Miller, or Van Anda, or anybody else. To assume comparable responsibility for a dozen or a score of newspapers was enough to appall even Ochs. He refused to do it.

The profits he made from the *Times* he consistently plowed back into the business. On his twenty-fifth anniversary he calculated that during the quarter century the paper had earned a total of $100,000,-000, of which less than 4 per cent had been paid out as dividends to stockholders, all the rest having been used to strengthen and improve the paper. Fifteen years later, when he died, he owned nothing except his newspaper, some real estate and a few government bonds. Plowing back the profits into an expanding enterprise was good business, of course, but in addition to that it had the negative virtue of preventing distraction of his attention. He anticipated Woodrow Wilson's dictum: "Put all your eggs in one basket—and then watch the basket."

But he watched the basket not only because it held all his own eggs, but those of a great many other people for whom he felt responsible. These included first the employees of the *Times*, already numbering hundreds and soon to number thousands, whose living depended on the paper; but secondarily, yet importantly, they included many thousands of readers who were relying on the *Times* for accurate news and intelligent, disinterested comment. To let these people down he would have regarded as the worst of failures; and to let them down for no better reason than to pile up millions that he did not need, he would have regarded as personal disgrace.

Needless to say he, being human, fell short of his ideal. Sometimes he was misinformed, sometimes his judgment slipped, sometimes his inferences were inaccurate and errors and failures resulted. But these were invariably attributable to faulty execution, not to any defect in his concept of the duty, public and private, of a newspaper publisher.

During his later years especially there were many who saw in the man little more than one of the country's stoutest defenders of the rights of private property. These may be disinclined to accept the assertion that he regarded his own property as very definitely affected with a public interest. That has a socialistic ring, and the very idea of connecting Adolph Ochs and socialism, even in the slightest degree, is ridiculous on the face of it.

But the evidence is incontrovertible. In all sorts of public statements, written and spoken, he said over and over again that a newspaper is, or ought to be, a public institution. But talk is cheap. Many a man has professed lofty ideals in all his speeches and never adhered to one in any act. Dismiss what this one said altogether and consider only what he did. At great cost—in money—he made the *Times* a newspaper of record because the public interest called for such a newspaper. At great cost, through many years, he threw out advertising because the public interest requires presentation of all the news that's fit to print. At great cost he supported historical and scientific research, exploration and experimentation from which the public would benefit far more than the *Times*. Men may profess an idea with tongue in cheek, but they don't spend money for it unless they believe in it.

There was one incident in these early years that gives rise to a suspicion even more startling. There is some evidence that Ochs cherished an idea too radical for the wildest Socialist to propound publicly, to wit, the idea that there are some men, as well as some businesses, who are affected with a public interest, men whose right even to possess property is limited by the public interest.

Hill and Harriman, two railroad Titans, fell to battling for control of transportation in the northwestern states. Certain short railroad lines were vital to the plans of either and both rushed into the stock market to secure control of those lines. The result was bedlam in the market. The stock of one obscure railroad shot up to sixteen times its price a week earlier, and speculators went mad. After the din had subsided and the dust was beginning to settle, Ochs remarked to a friend that he could have made a million that week, for he had had a reliable tip on what was going to happen. Asked why he didn't act, he replied that it came home to him that if he did make that money taking care of it would distract his attention from the *Times* and he had no right to be distracted.

It may be argued that he meant he could make more by attending strictly to his own business, but that is hardly sound. He couldn't make more and he didn't. A man in his position in New York was constantly coming into possession, entirely legitimately, of information that could be turned into money. Ochs was arguing that a man in his position ought not to possess much outside property because it distracts his attention; and regardless of his own interest the public interest requires that he attend strictly to the business that serves the public. It is a principle well recognized as regards certain officers of state; the Secretary of the Treasury, for example, is forbidden by law to engage in private business or to hold certain forms of property during his term of office; but when Ochs applied it to a private citizen holding no office, he went well beyond socialism, to the extreme border of ethics where it begins to merge into religion.

IV

Although it is true, broadly speaking, that he had no private life during these years, it is not true that he spent all day and every day in his office. For one thing, he was too capable an executive to do that. As a mere matter of policy it was advisable for him to absent himself occasionally, if only to keep his subordinates confident of their own ability to run things. He liked to visit Chattanooga as often as he could. He had become a director of the Associated Press, and he was never a dummy director in his life; to this position he gave increasing time and attention.

But the most important innovation in his way of living was the habit he developed of going to Europe nearly every summer. These trips usually had their business aspects, for Ochs rarely went anywhere without espying something he could use somehow for the *Times*; yet in the main they were not business, but jauntings in an extraordinarily high, wide and handsome manner. To this day the tales told about them in New York reveal one of the most amusing, and at the same time one of the pleasantest, aspects of the man.

He never went alone, and rarely with no companions other than his wife and daughter. His great delight was to assemble a group of young relatives, nieces, nephews, cousins and what not, and take them all along. If they had little or no money, so much the better—they would enjoy it all the more. But if the youngsters thought that they were embarked on a staid and stodgy family party in traveling with Uncle Adolph they were badly deceived. He played as hard as he worked, and in a European capital he could run the legs off all but the most sinewy of them and come in at the end of the day fresh, debonair and all in favor of dancing at least until midnight. He tipped lavishly and therefore got swift and obsequious service; and when he trailed his caravan through theaters and museums, restaurants and night clubs, to race tracks and spas and beaches, he brought with him such an atmosphere of laughter and gaiety and youthful high spirits as would make the dullest of places sparkle and glow. Those who went on such trips as adolescents are all mature men and women now; but even yet their eyes light up when they speak of them and they always laugh, but a little wistfully. They were marvelous trips for boys and girls and Adolph Ochs did much more than pay for them—he engineered them, giving them his time and careful attention as well as his money, putting drive and zest and sparkle into them. So these men and women, some of them well into middle age now, never see him quite clearly, but always in the light of their own lives' springtime, touched with a glint of their golden days; and a man cannot be more delightfully remembered.

Unfortunately, it is by no means as easy to describe the effect of his European travels upon the man himself. It is not that he was inarticulate; on the contrary, he wrote countless letters to his family and friends in which he described his experiences minutely, especially the odd and amusing events and characters he encountered. They describe his own response to such encounters and occasionally record his moods. They are always readable and sometimes charming, yet withal singularly unrevealing to one seeking to identify the forces that shaped his thinking.

That his journeys did influence him is obvious, for it was in these years that Ochs became the internationalist. It is safe to assert that in 1900 Europe to him was pretty vague and distant, a geographical expression, making no urgent demands upon an American's attention. But by the time the First World War began, in 1914, he knew better. In the meantime Europe had come within the range of his personal experience, and he had the type of mind that made every experience fruitful.

Now that the United States has been constantly embroiled with Europe for more than thirty years, it is hard to understand how any informed and intelligent man could have taken any position other than the one Ochs took; yet it brought him under sharper and heavier attack than anything else he ever did. Internationalism was familiar enough to Americans, but not this kind, and being novel it inevitably came under suspicion.

Long before 1900 we had internationalists, but most of them were of the kind satirized by Mark Train in *Innocents Abroad*, that is to say, pretty cheap, or of the kind typified by Henry James, that is to say, intellectually rarefied. Neither type greatly impressed the ordinary American and it was the difficulty of identifying the publisher of the *Times* with either type that gave rise to suspicion and recrimination.

Americans knew all about the esthetes and pseudo esthetes who claimed Europe as their spiritual home. From Benjamin West to Whistler and Sargent, American artists had been withdrawing to Europe to do their best work and after them flocked droves of persons who may have been artistic but were hardly artists. Musicians and the musical-but-not-musicians, certain types of writers and some who only thought they were writers followed. Among these expatriates the genuine were greatly outnumbered by the fraudulent and the country knew it. The exodus therefore was lamented with much restraint.

There was also the mighty race of snobs, as a rule not exiles except for a few months of the year, but people whose idea of the height of earthly bliss was telling the neighbors in America how they had consorted with royalty and nobility at Nice or Biarritz or Cowes. The pattern had been set a hundred years before by Betsy Patterson, whose marriage to Jerome Bonaparte, briefly King of Westphalia, had been briskly annulled by Napoleon; she wailed, not for loss of husband and country, but over the necessity of returning "to my Baltimore obscurity." The country found Betsy and her spiritual kindred amusing but not important.

Yet here was a man, obviously international-minded, but who did not fit into any of these categories. In 1914 there were not many such in the country, but they were a most disturbing element because they could not be dismissed as either temperamental or silly. The great dread of the isolationists—and we were nearly all more or less isolationist in 1914—was that they might be forced to admit that there was common sense in the international point of view. This is, at least, a plausible accounting for the fact that Ochs and men of his way of thinking were assailed with a vindictiveness otherwise inexplicable.

But it was certainly common sense that brought the publisher of the *Times* to this point of view. It could not have been anything else. An artist or a novelist might be enthralled by the richness and variety of European culture, but Adolph Ochs's esthetic sensibilities, while strong and sincere, were anything but subtle. In the early years he dutifully made the rounds of the museums, the concert halls and other spots that all visitors are supposed to see, but there is no evidence that his response to them was more than mildly pleasurable. In music, for example, he always liked Stephen Foster more than Beethoven and frankly admitted it. In painting and sculpture his taste was erratic, to put it delicately. With the history of Europe he had only the acquaintance of an intelligent but largely self-educated man—certainly not that of, say, a Henry Adams. His internationalism was plainly not due to the cultural pull of the old continent.

On the other hand, while he always exhibited a childlike delight in associating with celebrities, it was too naïve to bear any taint of true snobbery. He would go to a great deal of trouble to meet any famous man; but he would go to as much trouble to meet a champion prize fighter as to meet a duke. This is evidence, not that he was essentially a snob, but that he was essentially a newspaper reporter, who likes to meet the famous, but is about as well content if he can meet the genuinely infamous, for they, too, are news.

What made Ochs an internationalist was not his admiration of European culture, or his adoration of European pomp, but his realization of the inevitability of American-European contact. It must be remembered that he was intensely interested in wireless telegraphy and in aviation. He knew not only what they were doing but, with his characteristic foresight, he was about five years ahead of the average man in his realization of what they were going to do. He saw the Atlantic steadily narrowing as a barrier and he had the courage to face the implications of that narrowing. He observed that there were forces in Europe inimical to what he regarded as the spirit of Americanism and other forces agreeable to that spirit. He drew the inference that we should stand ready to support the latter if they came into conflict with the former. It was plain common sense.

But when war broke out in 1914 and the *Times* promptly spoke up for Great Britain and France, the policy was attributed to every motive save that one. In Germanophiles this was understandable; but many Americans with no liking for Germany were quite as reluctant to credit Ochs with common honesty and common sense. To do so meant to impugn their own sapience, and a man can confess heinous crimes more easily than he can admit that he lacks common sense.

V

Years before the outbreak of war, however, events had proved that sometimes Adolph Ochs's own sense could be a little too common. The greatest material triumph of his career, the magnificent building with which he had adorned the city and proclaimed before the world his soaring faith in the institution he had created, had hardly been occupied before it proved to be, ironically, evidence of a faith all too limited. It wasn't big enough.

In 1904, when the cornerstone was laid, the builder was satisfied that he had provided all the room for expansion that could possibly be needed in his lifetime, if not forever. But by the time it was occupied, January 1, 1905, he may already have begun to cherish some doubt that he had built well enough and within a couple of years there was no doubt at all. The paper was plainly outgrowing the building.

That building remained the home of the *Times* for just eight years and for the last year or two of that period various departments had to be stuck away in such holes and corners as could be found, to the detriment of the general efficiency of the whole organization. So Ochs set himself to the task of building again.

This time, however, he felt no call to do anything except provide adequate working space. He had already erected his monumental structure and he intended that to remain the Times Building, as it has. The new one, half a block west on Forty-third Street, he did not even dignify with the name of building, calling it merely the Times Annex. He secured a street frontage of 147 feet with a depth of 100 feet and on it erected a building of 11 stories, to which production of the newspaper was removed February 1, 1913. When this in turn proved inadequate a decade later he added 100 feet frontage and 3 additional stories

making a building with something over three times the floor space of
the original one. This, one of the great newspaper plants of the world,
has held the *Times* for thirty years, but it remained the Annex as long
as Ochs lived. Giotto's tower was the Times Building, and appro-
priately so, for its grace and dignity symbolized a great ideal better
than either the massiveness or the brisk efficiency of the structure in
which the paper is actually produced.

It was in this new building that the *Times* achieved most of the technical and professional triumphs that gave it its commanding position
in American journalism. But while they constitute an important part
of the history of the craft as it has been practiced in this country, they
were usually triumphs of the organization, rather than of any individual. Yet, while writing the story of Ochs apart from the story of
the *Times* in this period is rather like writing about Napoleon without
mentioning the *Grande Armée*, there is always a distinction between
the commander in chief and the general staff. It can be illustrated by
mention of two feats, both celebrated in journalistic annals, but only
one revealing much about the man.

In 1910 Theodore Roosevelt, returning from a hunting trip in Africa,
made a speech at the Guildhall in London which the *Times* had cabled
word for word and printed in full the next morning. This was Ochs's
doing.

In 1912 the White Star liner *Titanic*, biggest ship in the world,
struck an iceberg on her maiden voyage and for many hours there was
uncertainty as to what had happened to her. The company finally announced that she was safe and limping into port under her own power,
which satisfied most newspapers. But the *Times* kept its staff on duty
and made all preparations to handle a huge story, so when news finally
came that the ship had sunk with the loss of sixteen hundred lives it
beat the city in covering the story. This was largely, if not altogether,
Van Anda's doing.

The difference was the difference between policy and technique. In
the case of the Roosevelt speech no technical difficulties were involved.
It was purely a matter of judging how much the speech was worth.
Roosevelt had been out of office and out of the country for two years,

but he was still the most influential American in private life and it was expected that his Guildhall speech would give some indication of his attitude toward his successor. Ochs perceived that in the existing situation the speech was worth everything the *Times* could give it. He was right.

In the case of the *Titanic* disaster, the technical difficulties were everything. There was no question that it was the biggest story the century had provided—if it had happened. The keen appreciation of the significance of apparently unimportant details, the delicate and accurate balancing of probabilities, and the encyclopedic knowledge that convinced Van Anda that the thing had happened were part of the equipment of a great newsman, not necessarily of a great policy maker. Indirectly, of course, credit for the *Titanic* feat does come back to Ochs, but it is the credit, not of handling the story, but of having seen Van Anda's quality years before when he put him on the job.

There is one characteristic of the *Times*, however, that is unquestionably attributable to Ochs directly and exclusively, but that is open to various interpretations. This is its policy with regard to features.

The *Times* has never run a comic strip in the daily, nor a comic section in the Sunday issue. This was not Van Anda's doing or that of any other member of the staff. The publisher would not have it. He knew that the things were tremendously popular. He knew that they were circulation builders. He knew that there were available comics that were morally irreproachable and that the outcry against them on that score was largely balderdash. Finally, although he was not a wit, neither was he humorless. But he would have no comics. On the point he was adamant.

In the end the staff adopted his attitude. Probably it was not very hard to bring them around, for a large proportion of newspapermen regard comics as an unfortunate necessity, at best. When it was demonstrated that the *Times* could succeed without them, no tears were shed.

But it is interesting to speculate on why from the very beginning Adolph Ochs set his face like flint against this particular innovation. Every other idea suggested to him he seized with avidity if it offered any promise of interesting a new reader. Neither technical difficulty nor large expense daunted him. In the early days he squandered money like a drunken sailor on radio, on aviation, on the magazine section, on the book review section, and on a dozen other new, untried things. He ran his mechanical force half crazy with his demands for better printing, better pictures, better matrices and stereotype plates, faster and smoother press work, and he did not hesitate to go across half the world for such an item as rotogravure.

But comics he would not have. It has been generally assumed that this was simply a violent reaction against triviality and vulgarity. As far as the second count, the vulgarity, is concerned, this is doubtless true enough, but was that he simply could not believe that anything so far removed from news had a legitimate place in a newspaper, and the *Times* was strictly a newspaper.

There is, however, another obvious reason for his objection to comics—obvious, that is, if one remembers Chattanooga. Among the things that Adolph Ochs had learned down in Tennessee was the trade of the printer. More than that, he had been not only a practical printer, but an all-round one. He knew more than how to set type; he knew how to lay out a page, how to make up a form, and enough about press work to distinguish the good from the bad.

Well, it is a safe assertion that from Gutenberg to Warren G. Harding there never was a practical, all-round printer who did not delight in what he calls a "well-dressed" newspaper, that is to say, one that is not only clearly and cleanly printed, but with its headlines, body type, pictures and advertisements arranged in logical designs pleasing to the eye. But in this respect, there is nothing to be done with comics. In the first place, they are usually crudely drawn and each has its own arrangement of white space and heavy masses of black or color. There is nothing the printer can do to make them balance the rest of his page. Even the political cartoon is a trial to the spirit of a master craftsman because it frequently spoils the dress of his page and he is helpless to correct it.

Triviality and vulgarity Ochs heartily disapproved as a rule, but he realized that there may be times and circumstances making both not inappropriate. But most comics offend the taste of a good printer, and it may be that this outrage to his eye underlay all the other reasons that the printer-publisher of the *Times* had for keeping them out of his paper. Certainly he had one of the best-dressed newspapers in the world. If occasionally some genius of make-up on a rival sheet excelled it in grace or liveliness, none ever beat it for suave dignity.

There is no such facile explanation, however, for another characteristic of the paper under Ochs's management. This was its decided and uncompromising masculinity.

Misogyny may be dismissed instantly. Notorious amorists aside, it is hard to think of a man less open to the charge of woman-hating. Not only did he like them, but he respected their intelligence. The two with whom he was most intimately associated, his mother and his wife, were both women of exceptional intelligence. Although he was chary of accepting advice, on more than one occasion he accepted theirs on matters connected with the newspaper and found it excellent. Yet the *Times*, alert to seize and exploit without limit every imaginable interest of men, hardly admitted the existence of any special interest of women beyond the conventional society page. A certain amount of fashion news it admitted, and when women broke into the front page —Carry A. Nation by smashing a saloon, or Emmeline Pankhurst the House of Lords—it carried full accounts, of course. Under Ochs's management, however, it made no sustained, vigorous effort to build up a distinctively feminine clientele.

Perhaps this was due merely to the publisher's recognition of the fact that intelligence is not a sexual characteristic, from which he reasoned that any story that appealed to intelligent men would be equally attractive to intelligent women. But here again, it may be, was old Tennessee peeping out. Ochs was a southerner, and southern chivalry by setting woman upon a pedestal very neatly kept her out of the way when serious business was afoot. This suggestion would have scandalized him and he would have volubly pointed out that his own mother, his sisters and his wife had all taken an active part in the most serious business of his life, the establishment of the Chattanooga *Times*.

This is true enough, but it is also true that Ochs was reared in the

South during the last third of the nineteenth century; and in that region at that time it was the accepted convention that a woman's identity was, or should be, pretty well submerged in that of the male
members of her household—father, husband or brothers. Add to this
the fact that Ochs himself was emphatically masculine and the sum
may be an explanation of why an obvious opportunity was overlooked
by a man who ordinarily overlooked none.

VI

By 1913, when the Annex was occupied, the Imperial Age of American business was ending. It had been twenty years since the Census
Bureau had officially declared the frontier closed and the Titans who
had subdued three-quarters of a continent within a generation were
for the most part dead or in retirement. Harriman was dead. The elder
Morgan was dead. Jim Hill was to die soon. Rockefeller and Carnegie
survived but busied themselves largely with philanthropy. Collis
Huntington, Leland Stanford, the second Vanderbilt, all were gone.
John Wanamaker remained and a few others, but for the most part
a new generation had come up and Pharaohs reigned who knew not
Joseph.

To put it more precisely, new Pharaohs occupied the thrones but
they did not reign. They had no lack of brains, no lack of energy, no
lack of courage, but something was missing that the old boys had, and
it was precisely this missing factor that worked the magic. The big
businessmen of the first decade of this century were bigger, in some
dimensions, than their fathers had been. Their companies were bigger,
their output was bigger, their payrolls were bigger, their fortunes were
bigger; but for all that, they were not themselves the Titans that the
old men were. They could strengthen and extend their control of the
nation's economy, but they could not grip the imaginations of their
countrymen in the old style. The second J. Pierpont Morgan was as
able a banker as his father, perhaps abler; but the populace never believed of him, as it had believed of his father, that his tread rattled the
windows as he walked down the street. The second Rockefeller's range

of interests was much wider than that of the first and he has played a much more distinguished part in public affairs, but he has never terrified any large part of the population. His father did. The railroads today are better run than they ever were before; but no railroad man is as vivid a personality in men's minds as was Harriman, or Hill.

It is the fashion to assume that the imperial regime first cracked under the assault of a group of writers whom Theodore Roosevelt, then President of the United States, called "muckrakers,"[4] but the assumption is doubtful. When Theodore Roosevelt was a schoolboy people were calling the Titans names that make the most violent muckraking seem mere badinage, but to no perceptible effect. The glamour that once surrounded American big business was not destroyed by the muckrakers. It faded for other reasons.

To Ochs, however, it seemed in the beginning that the President was right and that muckraking was simply irresponsible journalism in a peculiarly vicious form. Some of it, indeed much of it, was exactly that; but some of it was factually as accurate as it was strident, and to offset it there was no longer the old belief that the Captains of Industry were captains indeed, as conscious of their responsibility as they were of their power.

Naturally a man cut out of the same cloth as the big businessmen of his youth was loath to surrender this belief. He knew he had never shirked his own responsibility and he was unwilling to concede that the practice was becoming general among men at the top of the economic scale. His initial response to muckraking was one of violent distaste. He had done enough crusading in his Chattanooga days to learn the perils of the practice. Possibly the time when he had turned MacGowan loose on McAdoo in an irresponsible way recurred to his mind. At any rate, he knew that a headlong assault is practically always unfair and at least in part untrue, and he was assiduous in his efforts to keep the *Times* clear of that sort of thing.

But his personal and professional dislike of the methods of the muck-

---

[4] He took it from the story in *Pilgrim's Progress* of the man who ignored the crown being offered him because he was intent on raking together the muck on the ground.

rakers of course provided cynics with an opportunity to charge him with disliking their objectives. What was in reality a defense of responsible journalism was construed as a defense of crooked business and crooked politics. To such charges the one effective answer is to pursue a rigidly upright course until time disposes of suspicion.

This answer the *Times* made and in the end it was effective; but there was one horrible moment when the enemies of the paper came nearer than they ever knew to acquiring a really knobby club to use upon it. Not all that was agitating the business world in these days was mere irresponsible journalism. The courts and legislative bodies were beginning to take a hand. For some time evil odors had been hanging around the insurance business and at length the state of New York undertook an investigation, intrusting it to a young and at that time little-known attorney named Hughes.

The results were terrific. On an adequate stage for the first time Charles E. Hughes demonstrated the ability and character that were to establish him in later years as one of the greatest Americans of his generation. Shocking revelations of mismanagement, incompetence and outright criminality poured from the investigation. Some insurance executives were prosecuted, many were expelled from their jobs and some fled the country barely a step ahead of officers of the law. Naturally, there was a stampede of businessmen to get clear of the explosion, for anyone who had the slightest connection with an insurance company was in an embarrassing position.

In the midst of the uproar word came to Ochs that within a couple of days the Equitable Life was to come in its turn under Hughes's piercing spotlight. This was the company that had made him the original loan when he purchased the *Times* and although most of it had long been repaid, he still had a note for $300,000 in the company's vaults. He knew nothing of conditions within the company, but he knew that if anything wrong were discovered—and plenty was—his enemies and rivals would howl with delight to learn that the dignified and conservative *Times* was entangled in the net. At the moment Ochs had nothing like $300,000 available and to borrow from a bank might precipitate the very publicity he desired to avoid. The fact that the transaction had been perfectly legitimate would not stop the scandal-mongers.

His capacity for friendship drew him out of the scrape. In his per-plexity he told the story to a man with whom he had no business rela-tions whatever and on whom he had no claim save that of a pleasant acquaintance of some years' standing. At the end of the recital the man's response was a roar of laughter and a check for $300,000. So when the investigators went into the Equitable they found not a scrap of Ochs's paper there.[5]

Little by little, however, Ochs was driven to the admission that an era had ended. In 1904 he could conscientiously support the estimable, but hopeless, Judge Parker as the Democratic candidate for President, but in 1908 the appalling Bryan surged up again and Ochs still had no doubt that he was a fraud. By 1912, however, it was clear that whatever Bryan might be the political movement that he had led so long was based on genuine grievances and inspired by a genuine philosophy. As the date of the Democratic National Convention approached there was some vigorous soul-searching in the office of the *Times*; and the convention had not only assembled, but was deadlocked before the paper made up its mind. Eventually, however, it came out for Wood-row Wilson and Ochs and Bryan found themselves shoulder to shoul-der at last.

It is possible by reading only the superficial aspects of this course to construe it to the discredit of the publisher and the more violent liberals were not slow to do so. They declared that Ochs had waited for the bandwagon and had climbed on at the last possible moment; his ostensible liberalism, therefore, was nothing more than a desire to be on the winning side.

But at the moment when the *Times* declared for Wilson he was anything but a winner. On the contrary, Champ Clark had a clear majority of the delegates and only the two-thirds rule prevented his

---

[5] This man, still living, smilingly refused to permit his identity to be divulged. If any obligation existed, he said, it was canceled a few years later when Ochs learned from other sources that he was caught in a jam in the market and without solicitation marched into his office bearing securities worth much more than $300,000 and offering to raise yet more if necessary.

nomination; a bandwagon-jumper would have plumped for Clark, especially as Wilson's fight was being led by the detested Bryan.

The declaration for Wilson is interesting because it illuminates the state of mind not of Adolph Ochs only but of the group that he represented—his colleagues on the *Times*, first, but in addition to them an extremely important element in American life, namely, the honest conservatives. In recent years there has been an increasing tendency to deny that there is any such animal and to identify all conservatism with self-interest, but the facts invalidate this extremist view.

To be sure, in the broader sense a man is serving his own self-interest whenever he works and votes for just and efficient government, but that isn't what the extremists meant. They had in mind the narrow self-interest that impels many men to seek a position of special advantage regardless of the general welfare. In 1912 this narrow self-interest certainly did not dictate support of Wilson. He was proposing a program of social reform that would certainly cost a great deal of money and that would sharply restrict some business activities, particularly as regards great corporations and market operators.

But this program was on the whole intelligently conceived. It did not include any such blatant fallacy as sixteen to one and it did include certain measures that Ochs and other honest conservatives had, reluctantly perhaps, decided were necessary to the general welfare. Clark was also proposing reforms, but Clark's record was simply that of an old-line politician, while that of Wilson was the record of a reformer who had actually done a great deal of reforming as governor of New Jersey. Wilson was supported by Bryan but, on the other hand, Clark was supported by Tammany and Hearst, who were no more to Ochs's taste than Bryan.

The truth is that Ochs had never believed Bryan capable of reforming anything and he did regard him as capable of making a mess of everything. Therefore he consistently opposed Bryan. But when a man appeared who seemed to have the ability and the will to give the country an intelligently liberal administration, the publisher supported him. Yet he was unquestionably conservative. The liberals who denounced him erred in drawing no clear line of distinction between a conservative and a reactionary, the sort of man who is for everything that is old simply because it is old, brushing aside the possibility that it may be rotten, too.

This does not imply that Ochs was temperamentally the ideal citizen of a democratic republic. There is plenty to be said against the conservative temperament, not the least of its defects being the fact that it sometimes holds back for so long that reform, when it does arrive, comes with explosive violence that may do more harm than good. But the best type of American conservatism has always had the judgment to yield at the right moment. It will firmly refuse a Bryan, for twenty years if need be, but it will accept a Wilson; and the history of this country as compared to that of more ebullient democracies is the best possible evidence of the value of a brake that can cut down dangerous speed without locking the wheels.

It is plain enough now that for all purposes except the calendar's the election of Woodrow Wilson in 1912 was really the end of the nineteenth century in the United States. Even in 1912 the more enthusiastic liberals were proclaiming the beginning of a new era, but no man alive realized how true—how appallingly true—was their proclamation. Certainly Adolph Ochs, although he was uncommonly farsighted, had little suspicion that the world was on the point of turning upside down. The bulk of the Wilsonian program he endorsed, especially the establishment of the Federal Reserve System and other financial reforms, and such items as he criticized he questioned mildly and with carefully reasoned argument, not with wild denunciation. His own relations with the President were not particularly close, but whose were? The World had beaten the Times to support of the winning candidate, and the President plainly regarded the World as his chief journalistic mouthpiece, but on the whole the Times was a sound Democratic newspaper.

So when the old order blew up with the rending crash that is still resounding after thirty years, the explosion found the Times marching sturdily under the banner of the New Freedom.

VII

It was in these same busy and fruitful years that the Tennesseean gradually became the New Yorker. It may be that Adolph Ochs would have resented that statement. To the end of his life he regarded himself as only a resident of New York and essentially a son of Chattanooga. But that was not quite the true relationship; in time he came to be more like Chattanooga's rich uncle, always coming down with handsome and delightful presents for the old home, but identified with the great northern city.

For one thing, he corrected his illusions about family life. Nothing spectacular happened to change his views, but they changed, and it is easy to believe that the slight and quiet but persistent influence of his wife did it. In any event, the family were soon established in an apartment of their own and then a house and, finally, a still better house, the really impressive establishment on West Seventy-fifth Street which remained their home until late in Ochs's life when he purchased the beautiful home at White Plains which was his last residence.

There was one feature of the Seventy-fifth Street house that contradicts the impression that the man's esthetic sense was undeveloped. This was the room peculiarly his own, the library in which he did much of his work. It was a large room, extending across the whole width of the house on the second floor. At one end was a fireplace big enough to take a three-foot log and the room was paneled in oak, rather simply but flawlessly. The charm of the room depends, however, upon its excellent proportions—precisely the right length and height for its breadth.

Here, after dinner, it was the owner's habit to receive visitors who came for something more than a mere social call—men from the *Times* with office problems, citizens having affairs other than financial dealings to discuss with the publisher and old, intimate friends with whom he wished to chat privately. Here, too, he used to take the young people of his wide acquaintance, boys and girls in their moments of triumph or defeat. There in the subdued lamplight glowing in the serene and

mellow room Adolph Ochs must have done some of the best talking
in his life, and he always talked well. What he said had nothing to do
with the *Times* or any other newspaper, and it was all completely off
the record. It cannot be recovered except by inference, but hints and
suggestions are still to be found around New York—small stories of a
young man who had landed in a college scrape and who with the exaggeration of youth was almost desperate when he went into that room,
but came out steady and sane again; of a young wife who had lost her
child and found the relief of tears there; of another youth dumfounded
to learn that his small triumph had not passed unnoted and who
emerged intent upon greater ones; of many, mostly people of little influence in the world, who at some crisis in their lives found in that
room genial tolerance, sympathy and sure, penetrating wisdom.

It was all off the record and the substance of what he said is gone;
but those talks account for the singular vehemence with which today
certain gray-haired men and women maintain that this was a great man.

In any event he was a happy man in that first decade and a half of the
new century, perhaps happier than at any other period. Why not?
It is possible that he had not yet attained the full development of his
powers and it is certain that he was still to grow in wisdom and understanding of men and events. But these were the years in which he
grasped not merely success, but success in a large way. His newspaper
with 250,000 circulation was immensely profitable and in prestige was
approaching the level of its namesake in London; indeed, if the American *Times* never quite became The Thunderer it is easy to explain by
the fact that in a continent-wide domain metropolitan journalism cannot exert the power it does in as small a country as England. It simply
cannot reach as large a proportion of the people as quickly.

All this meant that Adolph Ochs's labors were justified. The ideas
he had cherished since youth were proved sound. His years and his
brains he had invested wisely and the usufruct included much besides
money; professionally he had won his way to the top and in the estimation of the world outside the craft his position was honorable and dignified.

Nor was his content marred by domestic strife. Effie, indeed, irritated him somewhat by a bland refusal to take her duties as hostess seriously, and irritated other members of the family still more. She simply declined to charge herself with the details of entertaining and at important dinners would leave even such things as the arrangement of the place cards to her husband. Then at the last moment she would appear, serene and gracious, to give the guests the impression of a perfect hostess and to fill her female relatives with wrath.

Yet there is a possibility that she was wiser than they knew. Her husband, after all, was a managing man and she knew it. Indeed, the only criticism brought against him by those who frequented the house as boys and girls was a tendency to manage too much, to leave no detail, no initiative to them. Occasionally he would explode over some such thing as the necessity of his seating the guests at dinner, but it may be that secretly he liked it and that Effie knew he liked it.

In any event, it wasn't enough to impair his affection for her or to shake his confidence in her loyalty and good judgment. His daughter was blossoming into a young woman in whom he took increasing delight and pride. They were more than merely companionable; as his only child he treated her somewhat as a son as well as a daughter. For one thing, he explained to her carefully and seriously every important innovation in the development of the *Times*. She had followed him not once but repeatedly through every part of the plant from the reel room in the basement to the very roof, precisely as he would have conducted a son to whom he expected eventually to leave the conduct of the paper. He coveted her understanding and was fortunate in receiving it.

It was a world much to his liking that Adolph Ochs inhabited as the year 1914 began. Times were changing, yes, but in an orderly and manageable fashion. The clamor against economic tyranny had proved to have more in it than merely the gabble of self-seeking demagogues, as Ochs had once regarded it, but the Wilsonian program was eliminating the worst abuses and there was every reason to assume that democratic processes could be relied on to ease the stresses and strains before they became destructive.

A world much to his liking—and to that of other men of good will, but without the fatal gift of prophecy. Better than most Americans of his type Ochs knew that there was trouble brewing in Europe, but he shared the common belief of his countrymen that to the extent that we were affected at all, it would be more in the nature of a nuisance than a menace. Better than most Americans he understood who were our real friends in the Old World, but he had at that time no conception of the mortal peril in which our friends stood. Who had?

So the old era, tranquil and reasonably contented, walked on the crust of the volcano straight into the explosion.

CHAPTER IX

In Which the Twilight of an Era Begins to Darken and the Man Is Sore Afraid.

I

NONE but the elderly or those in later middle age can understand without an effort what happened to Americans of the type of Adolph Ochs when a shot fired at Sarajevo exploded their world.

For this generation has never known a solid and stable world comparable to that in which its grandfathers lived and into which its fathers were born. In 1914 Europe had had no general war for ninety-nine years, both the Crimean and Franco-Prussian clashes having been limited wars for limited objectives. It was a peace unprecedented in the history of the continent and while it lasted Europe developed amazingly; among other things it developed was an impression upon the minds of other peoples, especially Americans, of invulnerable strength and stability.

It was a false impression, of course, but it was real enough. The *Pax Britannica,* like the *Pax Romana,* was a peace imposed from without, not built up from within and so it was bound to end when the control began to slip. But few Americans knew this. To the vast majority such a catastrophe as the war of 1914–1918 was in the most literal sense unthinkable. Even after mobilization had begun they didn't believe it and of the 300,000 American tourists in Europe that summer vast numbers at first refused to interrupt their vacations. After the first battle of the Marne half America was sure that the thing was practically ended, and when the months of fighting had stretched into years as astute an American as Henry Ford could still believe that only a little persuasion was needed to "get the boys out of the trenches by Christmas." He took a shipload of misguided enthusiasts to Europe to do it.

Adolph Ochs was better informed than Ford, it is true. He regarded the voyage of the peace ship as fantastic, and he was convinced from the beginning that unless the democracies represented by Great Britain and France triumphed, tyranny must engulf the world; but even he was by no means prepared for the extent of the disaster.

This point deserves sharp emphasis, for without making some effort to comprehend the magnitude of the shock no one can hope to understand the attitude, not of Ochs alone, but of most of his contemporaries in the years after 1914. It is the fashion among the moderns to dismiss their conduct as flatly insane, but it was nothing of the sort. On the contrary, it was logical and shrewd, granting the original premise. The trouble was with the premise. They were men facing what according to their philosophy simply couldn't be. It was an article of faith with them that the world had progressed beyond the level of tribal butchery and wars of extermination, and sane and well-poised men do not abandon their basic faith at the first apparently contradictory suggestion.

If this was true of Ochs, it was even more conspicuously true of the official chiefly responsible for our national course, Woodrow Wilson, President of the United States. Before entering public life he had won distinction as a historian and an expert on constitutional law; and he was faced with a situation that seemed to imply that much, perhaps most, of the history he had learned was a lie and that constitutional law did not exist except locally. Naturally, he refused to believe it and did not believe it until events rammed the distasteful truth down his throat. William J. Bryan, Secretary of State, in whose mind an article of faith could not be shattered by any fact, never believed it and resigned his office rather than base his course upon facts that he hated.

Ochs accepted the situation long before Wilson did, yet he refrained from denouncing the administration as a whole. It is probable that two factors account for this. In the first place, Wilson was the responsible official and Ochs was too fair to indulge in vituperation of a man whose responsibility he could not lift or even share. But there is also the fact that Ochs was of Wilson's generation, he had been bred in the same atmosphere, he had absorbed the same philosophy. As compared to Wilson he knew little history or constitutional law; but all that generation shared the faith that civilization had become too strong to tolerate more than sporadic, local outbreaks of barbarism. The solid earth was blown from under Ochs's feet, as well as from under Wilson's, and the publisher had a clear comprehension, based on experience, of how the President felt. This sympathy undoubtedly operated to stay his hand; so the *Times*, while strongly advocating support of the Allies, yet always spoke of the President moderately and courteously.

It is a curious fact that this did not apply to many of Wilson's original supporters. The liberals were badly split. Such men as Bryan, in the Democratic party, and George W. Norris, in the Republican, were belligerently pacifist, while certain other liberals, if not actually Germanophile, were certainly Anglophobe. On the other hand, a great many were as ardently pro-Ally as Theodore Roosevelt and Henry Cabot Lodge, both opponents of Wilson. The result was that for two and a half years the President was bitterly denounced by one wing of the liberals for baiting Germany and by another wing for baiting the Allies. Thus it came about that the *Times*, regarded by many as ultra-conservative, became a better Wilsonian than a good many original Wilson men.

Yet from the very beginning there was no doubt where it stood nor was there any doubt that its stand represented the fixed conviction of its publisher. It represented the conviction of the staff, also, for in this case there was no division of opinion at all in the *Times* office; without exception the chief men were in thorough agreement with the publisher.

In the case of Ochs there were two strong reasons for his attitude. In the first place, he had gained a considerable familiarity with Europe by his visits there, for he had been seeing vastly more than the youngsters with whom he surrounded himself. He had the good newspaperman's ability to sense a situation by means that he could not himself have explained—by hints here, by innuendoes there, by emphases and inflections rather than by words themselves and, especially, by what was not said. Try to explain these things and they dissolve and vanish; but every newspaperman knows that they constitute the "feel" of a situation that frequently brings him to the truth that is never expressed in words.

In the second place, for several years prior to the outbreak of the war he had been working hard to develop his own foreign service. His method was to depend not so much upon roving correspondents as upon the development of well-organized bureaus in a few great centers. Before 1914 the *Times* offices in London and Paris were functioning so efficiently that when a dispute arose with Lord Northcliffe, who had acquired the London *Times* from the Walters, Ochs had no hesitation in breaking off the arrangement with that paper. He was now getting European news written by Americans for American readers, and while its factual content did not differ appreciably from the British service the shift in emphasis and the difference in idiomatic structure made it clearer and therefore more informative to Americans than the best British news writing.

Undoubtedly the first person informed by the *Times*'s foreign service was the publisher of the *Times* himself. When he found his own observation supported by the observations of his men, Americans like himself, he no longer had room for doubt. From the outbreak of hostilities, therefore, he was certain that this was no mere squabble over territory or trade but a genuine ideological war, a desperate attempt to put down "government of the people, by the people, for the people" before that ideal was accepted by all mankind. In such a quarrel Ochs had no doubt on which side the United States must take its stand. Neither had any other American—in such a quarrel. The difficulty was that vast numbers of Americans did not believe it was that sort of quarrel at all, because they cherished the comfortable illusion that all serious support of tyranny had disappeared with the flintlock musket. The history of the last ninety-nine years was all against it. Was not Germany leading the world in technological progress and making vast advances in social amelioration? To assume that such a nation took seriously all that declamation about the master race was nonsense; no, it was a collision of imperialisms disputing over trade. Nobody was actually a mortal foe of the democratic theory.

So the *Times* inevitably came under suspicion. As early as December 15, 1914, Miller turned loose a blast two columns long that definitely placed the *Times*. The gist of the argument was that the defeat of Germany was inevitable, because Germany was making a deliberate attack on civilization—a magnificent *non sequitur*, but one accepted by a generation that believed civilization many times stronger than it actually was. This brought upon the paper a storm of denunciation, not from the friends of Germany only, but also from those who did not wish to have their faith in human progress disturbed. For if civilization were under attack, it was the obvious duty of every civilized nation to defend it. Therefore, it could not be civilization; it must be, it should be, something else, British imperialism for preference.

It followed, therefore, that those who were making such statements as that contained in the *Times* editorial were lying, and there must be some motive, presumably a sinister one, for lying. Innumerable persons were prompt to suggest the motive. The favorite one was bribery; the *Times* had accepted British gold. The second was secret control by alien owners. A third was snobbery and from that they ran the gamut of everything discreditable that slander could imagine.

Ochs and his paper were not the only victims, of course. Practically the entire New York press came under the bombardment to some extent, for it was almost solidly pro-Ally, the Hearst papers excepted. But the *Times* was a particularly shining target for the very reason that it had built up a reputation for restrained and responsible journalism. The more reputable the witness, the more damaging is his adverse testimony, and the greater the necessity of breaking it down if possible. The *Times* was a reputable witness, not only on account of its previous reputation, but because it was making tremendous efforts to print all the news from both sides. In the very beginning, in August, 1914, it had published the British White Paper and on the next morning had followed it with the German White Paper, both published in full, although it had taken some heroic labor to get the German document translated in time. It was carrying every day innumerable letters from defenders of Germany. It was moving heaven and earth to plant its correspondents at every strategic news point and was demanding of them all that they write the truth as nearly as they could without bias of any sort.

So the effort to discredit it was particularly vigorous and determined.

Part of it, of course, was the work of German propagandists, but by far the more venomous and disturbing assault was that of American isolationism, then strong throughout the country and well represented in Congress. In the end this influence actually precipitated a senatorial investigation of the *Times*. The ostensible cause was the paper's opposition to a bill for the purchase of interned ships, but once the Senators got Miller on the stand before the committee they forgot all about ships. They proceeded to demand information on the most intimate details of Och's private business.

It was an indefensible attempt at official browbeating. If freedom of speech means anything, any man, even a newspaper editor, has a right to oppose any bill pending in Congress for any reason or none, without molestation by a Senate committee. But although the principle of the thing was bad, as a practical matter it afforded Ochs an excuse to set the record straight. The Senators got the information they asked for. They got it in detail. They got it with all the emphasis that Miller could give it. On oath the editor declared that the *Times* had no business interests of any kind in England save that of maintaining its correspondents there. He swore that the publisher had received no financial support of any kind from England or from any Englishman.

The incident justified the *Times* in declaring editorially the next day,

That there may be no cause to believe that Mr. Miller's answer to the impertinent inquiry about Mr. Ochs's private affairs does not fully and satisfactorily end the inquiry, Mr. Ochs wishes to make the assertion as broad and as sweeping as language will permit that he is in possession, free and unencumbered, of the controlling and majority interest of the stock of The New York Times Company, and has no associate in that possession, and is not beholden or accountable to any person or interest in England or anywhere else in the world, nor has he ever been beholden or accountable in any form, shape, or fashion, financial or otherwise, for the conduct of The New York Times, except to his own conscience and to the respect and confidence of the newspaper-reading public, and particularly to the readers of The New York Times —and more particularly to the respect and confidence of those who are associated with him in producing The New York Times and expressing its opinions.[1]

[1] The *Times*, March 17, 1915.

The closing words of this statement are significant. What Senators might believe of him did not greatly worry the publisher, nor did he care at all what isolationists, not to mention pro-Germans, believed. But he was very much disturbed by the possibility that some of his own men might accept some of the slanders floating about. The statement was really addressed less to the general public than to the staff of the *Times*; for it was always Ochs's belief that a paper produced by honest men who were confident of the honesty of their enterprise could not long be misjudged by the public. As long as the staff had no doubt of the paper's integrity, slander could cause it nothing worse than temporary annoyance, not permanent damage.

This, of course, was the mark of the good executive. Ochs retained the respect of his men because he sincerely respected their opinions. He never regarded it as beneath his dignity to explain to any employee affected his reasons for any of his acts. It made no difference whether the employee concerned was the editor in chief or an elevator man; if he had a just claim to know what was going on, and why, Ochs always had time to explain. Sometimes he annoyed associates with important business to discuss by stopping to talk over some triviality with a lowly and perhaps stupid worker. One of his chief executives recalls his frequent exasperation with the publisher because, he said, "Whenever I started anywhere with Mr. Ochs it took him from ten minutes to half an hour to get out of the building—somebody was always stopping him to talk over some picayune problem, and he always stopped, listened carefully and gave a considered answer."

Annoying it may have been, but it built morale and morale is no triviality.

II

Then came the spring of 1917 and with it the declaration of unrestricted submarine warfare, warfare upon everybody, belligerents and neutrals alike, who happened to stand in Germany's way. With that the least bellicose of Presidents had to acknowledge that the concept of "civilized" was was overboard and he advised Congress to draw the sword.

The *Times* had long believed it was inevitable, but it had approved Wilson's reluctance to precipitate the country into the holocaust. Even after the *Lusitania* was sunk it knew—it had good reason to know—that the country was not yet united, and it refused to join in the denunciation of Wilson's "poltroonery" in exhausting all the resources of diplomacy by filing protests instead of instantly resorting to force. Thus when the declaration of war did come, it was in the fortunate position of having nothing to retract when it urged its readers to advance boldly with all confidence in their leadership.

But the Olympian calm of the paper did not extend to cover all phases of the publisher's private life. Adolph Ochs was a man of unusual poise, but he was human, after all, and there were things capable of upsetting even his equanimity. One of them came shortly after our entry into the war when his daughter, Iphigene, announced her intention of marrying a soldier.

No incident in his career is more revelatory of the man than this. Ochs, in the expressive if inelegant vernacular, hit the ceiling. It was not that there was anything objectionable in the young man himself—that is, any further than every affectionate father finds any young man objectionable who wishes to carry off a cherished daughter. Still less was there any objection to his momentary status. He was young and healthy and the country was at war; therefore, according to the Ochs family tradition, in the army was where he ought to be. That was all right.

The objection was that his family was engaged in the silk-importing business—a perfectly respectable occupation, no doubt, but having nothing to do with newspapers. He was still too young to have become very well established, but the presumption was that he would follow the family line after the war, and if Iphigene's husband were a silk importer, what would happen to the *Times*?

Here, perhaps, was old Tennessee peeping out again. Ochs had every confidence in his daughter's intelligence and he had taken pains to develop in her an informed interest in the newspaper, going so far as to make her a director of the company; but she was a woman, and no southerner of his generation could quite convince himself that a woman is capable of maintaining a highly important interest apart from that of her husband. A son might have married the daughter of a silk importer without causing him a moment's worry; but when it was the other way about, he was dismally certain that the silk business would take precedence, even in his daughter's mind.

Viewed in retrospect, the situation has its amusing aspect, but there was nothing amusing about it at the time. Here, in fact, was conclusive proof, if more were needed, that in the mind of the publisher his newspaper was more, very much more, than simply a means of support. It was his life's work, indeed, his life, his return to the world for having burdened the earth for so many years, his justification for having lived. He believed it was a worthy return, a strong justification. He felt that if it were to die with him, he would be to a considerable extent a defeated man. He had counted on Iphigene's marrying a newspaperman who would carry on after his death. Perhaps he envisioned a dynasty comparable to that of the Walter family, who held the London *Times* for a hundred years. In any event the prospect that his descendants were to be anything but newspapermen left him disconsolate.

On the other hand, Iphigene was not his daughter for nothing. She had her father's clear and definite understanding of what she wanted. Nor was she a modern American woman for nothing. She loved and respected her father, but she was quite definitely emancipated from the old European concept of paternal authority. Her mind was made up, and that was that. The situation was becoming difficult, to put it mildly.

It was saved by the soldier. Lieutenant Arthur Hays Sulzberger had not won his commission without learning the first duty of the officer on the spot when things are snarled up. It is to assume command and act promptly on his own responsibility. He appeared in New York and in an interview with the publisher explained that he was a free agent, and while what he wanted to marry was the daughter, not the *Times*, still if it would remove all obstacles to the marriage he would undertake to devote himself to newspaper work as soon as he got out of the army at the end of the war. On these terms an agreement was reached;

and nearly a dozen years after his death the *Times* is still flourishing under control of a man trained by Ochs for the job. Even under stress of profound emotion, he remained a good trader.

III

But his personal worries connected with the war were not yet ended. The bitterest—and the greatest—moment of his professional career was still to come.

It arrived on September 16, 1918, when the *Times* made a frightful blunder. At the moment when military victory was almost at hand, it published an editorial that could be and instantly was construed as advocating a negotiated peace. There are a dozen explanations of what happened, all of them containing some truth, but none explaining away the fact that the *Times* blundered.

Ever since the war had settled into a war of attrition Germany and her allies had been frantically endeavoring to secure peace by negotiation, hoping, as all the world knows now, to preserve their military power intact for a second attempt at world domination. Every pro-German in this country and many who were not pro-German but simply not resolute enough to endure the strain of war had been clamoring for a negotiated peace, so that in the minds of those who were bearing the heat and burden of the conflict the very words "negotiated peace" had become synonymous with partial surrender. The *Times* itself had been adamant against any such suggestion.

Late in the afternoon of September 15, 1918, a Saturday, the *Times* received word that the Austrian government had made proposals to Washington for a conference on peace terms. An hour or so later the State Department sternly and definitely rejected the suggestion. Both stories, the proposal and its rejection, appeared on the front page the next day.

As it was Saturday both Ochs and Miller had left the city for their summer homes, Ochs's at Lake George and Miller's at Great Neck, Long Island. The man on the news desk, recognizing the importance of the first story, telephoned them both. Ochs suggested an editorial and was informed that Miller was writing one, whereupon he dropped the matter.

The event proved that this was a mistake, but it is difficult to sustain any charge of negligence against the publisher. True, the subject was one of great importance, but policy with regard to it had been long established and Miller was a competent man. Once policy is determined, a publisher has a right to assume that a competent man will follow it, especially in matters of great importance, so when he has made certain that such a man is on the job he has exercised reasonable caution. This Ochs did. He felt, and he continued to feel, that when he had made sure that Miller was preparing the editorial he had done his duty.

What got into Miller it is impossible to say. He not only understood the policy of the *Times*, he had played a large part in determining it. He was the most honorable of men, so the idea that he would consciously alter policy without consultation with any of his colleagues— which would have been an act of sabotage—is preposterous. It follows that he must have believed that he was following policy.

Yet his editorial suggested that it might be a good idea to entertain the Austrian proposal seriously. He advanced the curious argument that to do so might speed up the collapse of morale within Germany; and this in face of the fact that the *Times* itself had long been insisting that the slightest sign of wavering on our part would certainly encourage Germany's hope of escaping her impending defeat. Something clouded the man's judgment. It may have been the tremendous tension under which he had been laboring for a year and a half, it may have been the butchery of the Meuse-Argonne drive then in progress, it may even have been the intensive study which he had been giving for some weeks to postwar problems; but whatever it was, he produced an editorial that seemed to indicate a sensational change of policy.

Van Anda, ranking man in the office, had before him not only the editorial, but the later story announcing the State Department's rejection of the Austrian proposal. Ordinarily, no man would have been quicker to perceive that the two were incompatible. He should by all means have prevented the appearance of so blatant a contradiction. But his judgment also slipped. He ran the editorial as it was, accompanied by both stories.

The result was appalling. The *Times* appeared the next morning apparently urging the government to entertain a proposal it had already contemptuously refused to entertain, the very sort of proposal that the *Times* itself had been contemptuously rejecting throughout the war. As a matter of fact, it was not that bad. But public opinion, raised to white heat by the passions of war, was in no state to make fine distinctions. The prevalent belief was that the *Times*, the *Times* of all papers, had deliberately hoisted the white flag!

When Ochs got to New York the next morning there were three thousand telegrams on his desk denouncing him with unbridled fury. Letters were pouring in canceling subscriptions. Advertisers were indignantly snatching their business out of the paper. The next day the Union League Club held an indignation meeting at which it was proposed to bar the *Times* from the club reading room (it wasn't barred, however). Patriots all over the country were making perfervid speeches denouncing the paper and everyone connected with it. The unblemished record of loyalty of all the years was forgotten in a moment— except by the New York *Sun*, which pointed out that to accuse the *Times* of wavering was arrant nonsense—and the storm of abuse raged unchecked.

Ochs was literally, physically, stunned. A friend who visited his office that morning found him sitting behind his big desk inches deep in abusive telegrams with the dazed look of a man who has been hit on the head with a club; and Edwards reports seeing him later wandering through the composing room uncertainly, as if to make sure that the machinery was still intact. Nothing comparable to this had ever happened to him before, and so badly was he shaken that he actually suggested to his friend Morgenthau that perhaps in view of his unpopularity he ought to retire and transfer management of the paper to a trustee.

The worst of it was that there was absolutely nothing for him to do or say. The position of the paper was clarified, of course, by an editorial in the next day's issue, but the damage had been done. It was simply one of those incredible happenings, known and dreaded in every newspaper shop in the world, that follow when vigilance slips for an instant. Miller and Van Anda were two of the ablest newspapermen alive; neither of them made a major mistake on an average of once in ten years. The chance that one of them would make such a mistake on a given date was therefore remote; the chance that both would make a mistake on the same day in handling the same story was so extremely remote that it approached the impossible. But it had happened.

There were, of course, certain partial explanations. They were tired men. They had been working under heavy and increasing pressure for a year and a half. By September, 1918, the work of getting out a newspaper in wartime, hard enough in itself, was complicated by the necessity of looking ahead to the cessation of hostilities and they had been giving increasing attention to the problems of the peace, which may have had the effect of clouding their judgment as to the actualities of the war. But all this doesn't explain away the fact that each of them had made a blunder, not in the estimation of the public only, but in his own estimation also. Ochs, on his part, was conscious of the purity of his intentions, but nevertheless he was the publisher of a newspaper that had made a gross blunder. There was no getting away from that fact and it was gall and wormwood to the man whose pride in his institution had reached such heights. Indeed, when the excitement had died down a little he collapsed and spent some time in the hands of the doctors.

Yet it was precisely at this moment of humiliation so deep that it almost reached despair that he showed the moral stature that gave him the right to be publisher of a great newspaper. Not for an instant did he repudiate his men.

In any business it is usually easy for the boss to pass the blame to subordinates when things go wrong. In the newspaper business it is especially easy. In this case it would have been exceptionally easy even for the newspaper business, because there was some color of truth to sustain the act. Miller had slipped; there is no doubt about it. Van Anda had slipped. If Ochs had been a small-souled man he would have tried to exculpate himself by throwing all the blame on them, as he had the power to do.

Instead, he stood by them through the storm and since he couldn't stop it he simply hunched his shoulders and took it until it had exhausted itself.

To the public this meant little, but within the craft it had an effect greater perhaps than Ochs himself ever knew. Once the initial shock had passed newspapermen had little difficulty in guessing what had happened, for they all stand in the same danger. The terror that haunts the life of every editor and publisher is fear of a momentary lapse of vigilance on the part of some good man. Obviously, that was the fate that had overtaken the *Times*. When such a lapse puts the publisher in an embarrassing position it is assumed as a matter of course that it will be followed by the swift ejection of some scapegoat, and in the country at large the only matter of conjecture was as to who would be thrown out of the *Times* to save Ochs's face.

But when day after day passed and nobody was thrown out, when no underling was even publicly blamed for the worst break in the paper's history, the original somewhat derisive sympathy that newspapermen outside the *Times* staff felt for the publisher changed into a towering respect. Here was a chief who stood by his men even when their errors exposed him to contumely—a chief who was fit to be chief! The public may have paid no heed, but newspapermen noted it, not in New York only, but everywhere. In the most obscure newspaper office in the country down to the lowest ranks they talked about it, and at the very moment when Ochs in his bitter humiliation was saying to his intimate friends that he ought to quit, newspaper workers he had never seen nor heard of were saying, "What a man!"

IV

Two months after the catastrophe that made him a hero to the craft the armistice was signed and Adolph Ochs, like the rest of America, accepted the delusion that the war was over. But he never accepted the other delusion, almost as widespread, that American responsibility ended with the fighting.

In the early part of 1918, with the artillery still thundering, the *Times* had undertaken at his direction an extensive effort to examine the problems that were bound to follow the war. Even while dispatches from the front still had the right of way its correspondents were at work collecting the best opinions available as to making and securing the peace. The *Times* devoted far more space to such discussions than any other newspaper and its publisher had a much clearer comprehension than most Americans of the complexity and difficulty of the task ahead.

At that he was not the seventh son of a seventh son, and like all his generation he walked into the new world completely blind to a great many of the changes that had occurred. As regards Russia, for example, he had no adequate conception of the significance of the Soviet revolution, misjudging it as an outburst of extremists which would subside after a relatively brief period and be followed by a return, not indeed to czarism, but to some regime fairly comparable to those existing in the rest of Europe. He was therefore inclined to treat the Bolsheviki somewhat cavalierly and the *Times* advocated an expedition to Siberia, not for conquest, but to create a diversion that would discourage the Russians from joining the Germans, as the Allies feared they would do.

But he was keenly aware that the very fabric of civilization had sustained a profound shock and he inferred that repairing it would require some radical departures from the old system. So the League of Nations program of Woodrow Wilson never struck him as a reckless and dangerous innovation. He was for it, and he was for it as a conservative. The house of mankind had been wrecked and extensive repairs were essential; more than that, the collapse was attributable in part to structural defects, and any man of sense would take the opportunity of remedying those defects during the process of reconstruction.

He was never an idolater of Woodrow Wilson. On the contrary, he had found the war President somewhat cold and stiff and to the warmhearted, agile Ochs men of that type were never congenial. He therefore examined the League of Nations with no emotional bias in its favor. He did not regard it as perfect, by any means, but something had to be done and this scheme was at least intelligible; no other then before the public seemed to make any sense at all.

So the *Times* rallied to the League motivated not by any flaming utopianism or fuzzy and indefinite brotherly love, but by the common-sense realization that in a crisis it is better to do any intelligent thing promptly than to waste time casting about for the ideal. But since it made its original decision out of cold realism, there was nothing to cool off when the fight proved long and bitter. Months later when liberals were deserting right and left, the conservative *Times* never wavered; it stuck to the League and it went down with the League, beaten, but never convinced. It supported Wilson through the incredible battles in the Senate; and when James M. Cox, as the Democratic nominee of 1920, put himself squarely back of the League, the *Times* supported him with everything it had.

Indeed, the fury of the fight seems to have warmed Ochs's emotions toward the end; for on the day of Wilson's death in 1924 he called the staff into his office for a curious ceremony. In their presence he pledged himself, and he called on them to join him in the pledge, to support the Wilsonian ideal as long as he had breath.

So although he did not clearly understand the new world, he is free of any complicity in the defeat of its one hope.

The years had taken their toll of Miller, especially the terrific ones since 1914, and by 1920 it was evident that the burden of directing the editorial page was becoming too heavy for him to carry alone. To afford him some relief in that year Rollo Ogden was appointed associate editor of the *Times*.

The significance of this statement as regards Adolph Ochs is comprehensible only by knowing who Rollo Ogden was, or, rather, what he was. He was at that time the embodiment of the impeccable in American journalism. Educated for the Presbyterian ministry, in which he served for a time as a missionary in Mexico, he did not turn to journalism until his fortieth year, when he entered the service of the *Evening Post* and worked with the famous Godkin, to become one of the most distinguished products of a paper that turned out many distinguished journalists. Not in morals alone did he adhere to austerely high standards; he was intellectually as well as personally fastidious. Spare, reserved, even aloof, he was not a companionable man; but his powerful intelligence rejected shoddiness of every kind, mental or material. As a precise logician he was superb, and he was above all the very model of moral and intellectual probity.

Such a man is never in the market place for sale to the highest bidder. No sort of salary could induce him to accept a position unless it was one of dignity and worth—not Rollo Ogden. Thus it says much for the position in the world attained by Adolph Ochs that Mr. Ogden, then in his sixty-fourth year, would entertain favorably a proposal that he become associate editor of Ochs's newspaper. No more conclusive evidence of the *Times's* high prestige could possibly be offered.

The next year another remarkable character became a second associate editor. This was John H. Finley, former college president, former Commissioner of Education of New York, immensely learned, immensely eloquent, and always called by his academic title, Dr. Finley. It may be that Dr. Finley was really an investment in grace and dignity on Ochs's part, for he was not a trained newspaperman. But, in contradistinction to Ogden, he was the most companionable of men, witty, charming and a prince of after-dinner speakers. He had Louis Wiley's social competence and added to it an impressiveness that the short and merry Wiley lacked. As a matter of fact, Finley was an exceptionally gifted writer, but if he had never written a line he would have been a valuable addition to the staff by reason of his ability to represent the *Times* with grace and dignity on state occasions.

Both men were to hold the position of editor in chief, but Finley attained it after Ochs's time. In 1922 the end came for Miller and Ogden was elevated to chief command of the editorial page. He outlived the publisher.

The years following the armistice of 1918 were years of larger and more spectacular journalistic achievement than any that Adolph Ochs had managed before. These were the days in which he attained his greatest reputation as a publisher; the *Times* marched from journalistic triumph to triumph and in each Ochs took a boyish delight, for he never grew old at heart. But the events that attracted most attention—such things as the publication word for word of the Treaty of Versailles, eight pages of it, on the same day it appeared in the *Congressional Record*, the stunt of getting news of the Democratic convention of 1920 through Canada so fast that the *Times* took to New York breakfast tables news of night sessions that had hardly adjourned in San Francisco, the sponsorship of exploration and discovery, sometimes geographical, sometimes scientific, and a dozen others—belong to the history of the newspaper rather than to the personal life of the man. Ochs was now in control of one of the most powerful newspaper organizations that had ever existed, one commanding enormous resources both in money and in talent; so his accomplishments with that gigantic machine frequently tell less about the man, indeed, were frequently less remarkable, than some things he did when he worked single-handed. The great feats made much more noise in the world, but they are not necessarily more important in a study of the personality, than some of the minor ones.

For example, the institution of the Hundred Neediest Cases was not an outstanding journalistic feat, but it explains much about the man who devised it. This was nothing but the publication, as the Christmas holidays approached, of selected cases from the records of New York charitable organizations with an appeal to the public to relieve them. All names and other means of identification were carefully deleted and the money that came in was not administered by the *Times* but turned over to the appropriate agency. But the stories were told, as simply and as eloquently as the *Times* could tell them, and the response was immense.

It is curious to note how this scheme has been persistently misunderstood. Even the charitable organizations were at first suspicious;[2] they regarded it as an invasion of their field, for the newspaper's own purposes, and it took some time to persuade all of them to co-operate. As for the public, it has always assumed that the sole purpose of the publication was to raise money for these unfortunates. One generous

[2] Cf. Davis, op. cit., p. 304.

donor, indeed, offered a million dollars to endow the Hundred Neediest Cases permanently.

But this would have defeated the main purpose of the campaign, which was to inform the people of New York of certain conditions existing in their own city and to stimulate widespread thinking about the problem of poverty. Incidentally, but only incidentally, it was designed to arouse the spirit of benevolence and for that reason the approach of the festival of the Nativity was chosen as the time to present the appeal, for if ever a man can be moved by the charitable impulse, Christmas is the time.

This reasoning was based on a tenet that Ochs held as strongly as anything in his philosophy. He was profoundly convinced that it is more blessed to give than to receive. He never doubted that the relief afforded the Hundred Neediest Cases was far outweighed by the spiritual benefit accruing to those who relieved them. The purpose of the campaign was only secondarily to help the poor; primarily, it was to help the generous by affording a fine and gracious outlet for their charitable impulses. A permanent endowment would have blocked this, so the prospective donor was gratefully but firmly urged to turn his money to some other form of benevolence.

Ochs's personal generosity was affected by the same thought. A decent display of gratitude made him think more highly of the recipient, but for himself he did not want it. Many times he turned it away with the remark, "Don't thank me; think of how fortunate I am to be able to do it." When he didn't get it—which was all too often—he was unperturbed. His charity could never be soured by human baseness, for he found his real reward in the joy of giving; and he thought that was where everyone should look for it.

Another enterprise that he undertook during these years was completely characteristic, although it was out of the field of journalism altogether. This was the *Dictionary of American Biography*, a project that had long been cherished by the American Council of Learned Societies, but that had never been undertaken because the mammoth proportions of the work and the huge financial risk intimidated commercial publishers. The idea that the *Times* might be interested seems to have occurred first to Dr. J. Franklin Jameson, of the Manuscript Division of the Congressional Library, who discussed it with Dr. Finley, a friend since their days together at Johns Hopkins University.

Finley, a man of learning himself, had no difficulty in seeing the immense value of such a work to scholarship and he took it up with Ochs immediately, but found him noncommittal. He did consent to see Jameson, but the interview left Jameson completely discouraged. The Council, however, had appointed a committee to see what could be done and Finley invited the committee to meet in the editorial conference room of the *Times* just off Ochs's office. The meeting lasted all day and in the late afternoon Finley went to see Ochs and persuaded him, after some demur, to come out and greet the scholars, merely as a matter of courtesy. He came out and stayed for half an hour, saying nothing but listening carefully and becoming impressed with the earnestness of these men in promoting a project from which none hoped to receive any personal advantage.

Some time passed and then the committee was invited to lunch with Ochs and his chief executives in the private dining room in the Times Annex. Conversation during the meal revolved around the project and then Ochs, to the surprise of the executives, whom he had not consulted, suddenly announced that the *Times* would advance $50,000 a year for ten years for the preparation of the manuscript, taking a chance on recouping its investment from royalties. Part of the money was charged to the account of the *Times* and part of it the publisher took from his own pocket; together they advanced a total of $532,000, little of which they ever got back.

But the work appeared, originally in twenty-one volumes, later supplemented by other arrangements. An editorial council of seven, four representing the learned societies, two representing the *Times* and the seventh to be elected by the other six, was put in charge. The committee as finally organized included Dr. Jameson, Professor Allen Johnson, Professor Paxton, Carl Van Doren and Charles Warren, representing the societies, with Dr. Finley and Mrs. Arthur Hays Sulzberger representing the *Times*. Allen Johnson was made editor in chief, and after his death Dumas Malone, of the University of Virginia, finished the work.

Once he had agreed to furnish the money, Ochs stepped aside. He studiously refrained from offering even a suggestion about the contents of the work and he influenced it in no way whatever; yet he must be credited with a great contribution to American historical scholarship, for the *Dictionary* has facilitated the work of historians in every college and university, and in almost every public library in America.

Yet this project, far as it was from newspaper work, was thoroughly consistent with the character of the *Times*. It had already made itself the newspaper of record by printing all important documents in full. During the war it had taken the further step of setting up the monthly magazine, *Current History*, to publish comment and exposition rather too detailed for a daily newspaper. Now it assisted in making easily available a part of the American story running far back of its own existence. To record the events of the day was the paper's primary function, but that was included in the larger purpose of furnishing accurate information about the world, and specifically about America, to Americans. "The past, and the present—for the future," old Hezekiah Niles's motto, was being nobly applied by Ochs.

V

But the years were taking their toll of him, as they had of Miller. Probably it was not altogether time that did the damage; probably it was the strangeness of this new world into which he had been projected after he had reached maturity. The psychological displacement suffered by Ochs's generation has received singularly little attention from students of the era, but its effects were profound. Today the world knows only too much about the problem of physically displaced persons and the horrible, fantastic results that flow from it. But we incline to ignore the possibility that when all a man's preconceived ideas are torn up by the roots, when he has to set to work in middle life to build himself a new intellectual home, it is reasonable to assume that he may develop mental and temperamental quirks as bewildering as the physical maladies that afflict the physically displaced. Perhaps the most considerable achievement of the men of Ochs's time is that they came through the ordeal as steady and sane as they did.

The yelling guns fell silent in November, 1918, but all around him Ochs was hearing new and strident voices screaming sinister things. He had been bred to believe absolutely in the final triumph of reason and justice as inevitable; and now he found himself in a world that believed nothing of the sort and a large part of which seemed not even to wish for anything of the sort.

Among those in the fellowship of his own faith, in particular, a movement was taking shape which he could not comprehend. It was a reaction to a way of life of which Adolph Ochs was happily ignorant. In the small southern town in which he had spent his formative years the age-old hatreds of Europe were almost, if not quite, extinct. The only handicapped minority in Chattanooga were the Negroes. Catholics and Jews were merely people, subject to no more derision and contumely than Methodists heaped upon Baptists and vice versa. Tolerance bred tolerance, and in New York Ochs had been happy to contribute $10,000 in cash and a pair of magnificent altar candlesticks to the Cathedral of St. John the Divine. It was Episcopal, but what of that? It was also an adornment to the city and a place of worship. Why shouldn't he contribute?

He was accordingly disturbed when in talking with a prominent Englishwoman in Jerusalem one day he discovered that she, a member of the faith herself, regarded him as a very dubious Jew because he did not consider the religious difference alone an obstacle to marriage between Christians and Jews. Ochs had believed that sort of thing had gone out long ago among intelligent people; yet here was a woman of title, a member of the aristocracy, genuinely shocked by the idea of intermarriage. The interview rang ominously in his ears.

The rise of Zionism seemed to him to be a manifestation of the same spirit. "I know Judaism only upon one question," he cried. "I have nothing of Judaism in me that does not spell religion. Religion is all that I stand for as a Jew. I know nothing else, no other definition for a Jew except religion."[3] The talk of a national home for all Jewry impressed him not at all. He had a national home. Politically, he was American, simon-pure American, and the notion that he needed or desired any other national home seemed to him to impugn his Americanism.

He was aware of the distressed condition of the Jews in many countries of Europe, and he admitted his obligation to relieve that distress as far as he could; but he flatly denied that the obligation rested upon him as a Jew. In sending his subscription of $25,000 to the Jewish fund for the relief of distressed Jews, he filed a protest against the policy of calling it a Jewish fund and of confining subscriptions to Jews; it was the cause of common humanity, he said, and the appeal ought to be made to all human beings.

But the sinister voices continued and increased rather than diminished in volume. The war had been won, but the world was anything but safe for democracy. The old order was collapsing and the new included many features that were strange and, to Ochs, not a little horrible. For years he had been working hard and thinking harder. Even his prodigious energy was beginning to run low. The day came in 1922 when the family physician put his foot down. Ochs had to slow his pace. There was nothing much wrong with him organically, but nervously he was at the end of his rope, and no four or even six weeks' summer trip to Europe, or elsewhere, would suffice. They bundled him on a ship for a long winter's cruise in the Mediterranean.

The doctor was a good physician, but he was only a physician, not a wizard, and it would have taken a practitioner of magic to make Adolph Ochs really slow down. When he went aboard he was in fact in pretty bad shape, and had been for months—depressed, anxious and nervous. But the ship was hardly twenty-four hours out of port before it ran into rough weather and nearly everybody became seasick. Ochs, however, didn't suffer a qualm, and that circumstance cheered him up immensely; when he had triumphantly survived for two or three days while all around him were laid low, he took a new lease on life and by

[3] Address at the laying of the cornerstone of Temple Beth El, Glens Falls, N.Y., August 3, 1925.

the time the ship touched at Funchal, in the Azores, nothing would do but that he must be drawn to the top of a near-by mountain in a sort of stoneboat and come tobogganing down, not over snow, but over cobblestones! Ochs was himself again.

As usual, he had taken a crowd along. His wife and daughter were with him and, of course, Jules, his valet, and Rose. Mrs. Ochs's maid. But Mrs. Squier, wife of an eminent surgeon and old friend, was also with him and Mrs. Milton Ochs, as well as the customary young relative or two. In addition to that, he had found two or three charming people among his fellow passengers on the cruise ship and he promptly gathered them into his entourage for much of the time.

But this was not to be one of the gay and carefree tours of the old days. Too much had happened, too much had changed in recent years. Ochs, indeed, was the same man—a little older, perhaps a trifle less buoyant, but not much. Essentially he was the same, kindly, generous, merry-hearted, ready for any sort of frolic that might be proposed; but his position in the eyes of the world was far different from the one he had occupied in the old days.

A great war had been fought and in the course of that war the Atlantic had narrowed to a mere channel, a means of communication rather than a military barrier. In the course of the war the *Times* had emerged as one of the most powerful newspapers in America, and a newspaper powerful in America could not now be ignored by Europe. The publisher of the *Times* was no longer a mere tourist; he was a personage in every capital in the world, and his good will was henceforth sought by statesmen as ardently as it had formerly been sought by reporters out of a job.

The change became apparent at Gibraltar, when the British governor sent an aide to meet the ship and insisted on extending official courtesies to Mr. Ochs and his party. Ochs was pleased and flattered, and at the same time faintly annoyed. It was pleasant to be sought out by the great, and he had a wonderful time inspecting the fortifications under official auspices, but it played hob with his own plans and he loved to make his own plans.

At Paris he was genuinely delighted when Georges Clemenceau, in retirement now, but still the one and only Tiger of France, received him and talked for a long time with his characteristic wit and malice; and he was gratified when Lord Northcliffe, happening to arrive in Paris on other business, rushed to Ochs's hotel and demanded an interview. But when a procession of lesser notables insisted on calling and on entertaining him, he found that it cut heavily into his time for the theaters, restaurants and race tracks and he was not altogether content.

At Rome when an embassy official offered to try to arrange a private audience with the Pope, Ochs vetoed the suggestion as being too much like business when he was on holiday. But at the insistence of some of the ladies in his party he accepted an offer to include his group in a public audience; so at eleven in the morning he donned white tie and tails and "felt like a fool" as he wrote home; but just the same he was impressed by the ritual of the court and the dignity of the pontiff.

At Cairo he had an interview with the sultan. At Constantinople he was the guest of the American high commissioner. At Jerusalem he was seized upon by the Zionists and shown their work in great detail; he had to admit that their accomplishment was admirable, but was unshaken in his belief that it was aimed in the wrong direction. Throughout the tour realization was forced upon him that he was no longer a simple private citizen, but was recognized everywhere as a power, unofficial, but none the less a true potentate to be courted and if possible won over by all sorts and conditions of men.

Ochs was in two minds about it. As a good reporter he liked to be on familiar terms with men who were themselves news and makers of news; and it was agreeable to have them seeking him out instead of having to seek them out. In addition to that, he was intensely human; and no man who is not either more or less than human is going to hate it when the great, the near great and the would-be great are all competing for his attention. On the other hand, he had no personal ambition to serve and a sincere dislike of personal adulation; further-more, he was keenly aware that not a few of the persons who were courting him were hoping to use him for their own ends. The result was that he was at the same time pleased and made a little uncomfortable by finding his holiday trip turned into something closely resembling a tour by some royal highness.

It wasn't at all what the doctor had had in mind and toward the end it pretty nearly finished him physically. At Paris, on the way back, he took to his bed—too much rich food, too much exertion, too many late hours, too little rest. However, a few days of complete quiet restored his body and his mind was already refreshed. While it had been incessantly active, it had been dealing with something other than the newspaper business, and the complete change of ideas had straightened out his jangled nervous system. The voyage back also happened to be stormy and once again Adolph Ochs found himself hale and hearty while all around him were green and moaning. Perhaps that helped tone him up no little. At any rate, he landed in April, 1923, extremely fit and plunged into work with all his old vigor and eagerness.

VI

But the old optimism was somewhat dimmed. This was no longer the brave new world of Chattanooga days, the world in which sobriety, industry and honesty could not fail to achieve success. It was a strange world, in which strange, unheard-of forces were moving to incomprehensible ends, in which strange voices were urging unintelligible philosophies.

It is not enough to point out that Adolph Ochs was now sixty-five years old. The change had come too suddenly for that. As late as 1918, on his sixtieth birthday, he was saying,

Success . . . is won simply by practicing the ordinary virtues—hard work, intelligence, enthusiasm, self-reliance, honesty. The resources of this country are so illimitable, the opportunities so innumerable, and the means for educating and equipping oneself so plentiful, waste and neglect so prevalent, that there is really little excuse for any healthy young man born of self-respecting parents failing to attain not only dollars-and-cents success, but success in the fullest sense of the term.[4]

Nevertheless, three years later, on the twenty-fifth anniversary of his

[4] Interview in *Forbes Magazine*, June 29, 1918.

obtaining control of the *Times*, he announced the creation of a system of old-age and service pensions for employees of the paper. Doubtless there was a charitable impulse behind this, but that it was not altogether charity is shown by the fact that the pensions were directly related both to the length and to the salary earned. A man who had served for many years drew more than one who had served few; a man who had held a responsible position drew more than one who had never made himself particularly valuable. This was recognition of the principle that long and valuable service to an institution establishes a claim that is not entirely met by salary payments. What becomes, then, of the theory that industry, honesty and sobriety will inevitably receive their full reward?

On the same occasion—August 18, 1921—he published a long review of his twenty-five years in control of the *Times*. It was interesting in its factual content, but more interesting in its tone and, indeed, in its appearance. He had built the paper up from a bankrupt enterprise losing $2500 a week to one whose gross income for the preceding year had been $18,000,000; from a paid circulation of 9000 copies a day to a paid circulation of more than a third of a million. He was careful to avoid claiming all the credit for himself. He paid sincere and moving tribute to the men, living and dead, who had shared in the labor. It was at this time that he mentioned by name a number of distinguished men who had died in the service of the *Times* and three who were still living—Miller, Van Anda and Wiley.

But why did he feel it necessary to make the statement at all? He knew that a question might be raised, for he began with an apology for what might seem to be boasting; he said that he owed an account of his stewardship to the people who, in the final analysis, had made the paper, that is, its readers. But the heart of the statement was his reference to the gross income; "not one dollar was a gift or gratuity, but every cent a legitimate newspaper income."

Yet nobody, or at least nobody whose opinion was worth considering, was accusing the *Times* of dishonesty. Why this strong, almost defiant, repudiation? The wicked flee when no man pursueth, but Ochs had no need to defend his honesty.

The fact is, it was not a defense. It was rather a proclamation that honesty, industry and sobriety do succeed. It was a reaffirmation of the faith of his young manhood, a call—could it have been a slightly despairing call?—to young men to have faith in the old verities, to adhere to the old moralities.

It is easy to believe that even as early as 1919 Ochs was badly shaken. He was a farsighted man. Although he was no Old Testament prophet, able to look down generations and centuries, his perceptions were keener than those of most of his contemporaries; where they could see a year ahead, he could see several years ahead, and in 1921 an adherent of the old order who could see several years ahead had reason to be shaken.

In Europe in the latter part of 1922 and the beginning of 1923 he saw and heard things that did nothing to reassure him; and by the next year he had no need to go abroad to realize that the blithe philosophy of Chattanooga in his boyhood—which was basically the philosophy of the Imperial Age of business—was no longer adequate in the postwar world. For 1924 was the year of the great battle in the Democratic National Convention that tore the rose-colored glasses from the eyes of the most determined optimist and compelled him to see a pretty drab and dreary reality.

Ochs's man won that battle, but it was a Pyrrhic victory in the most dismal sense. Ochs's man was John W. Davis, a lawyer of high attainments and irreproachable character, but about as adequate to the situation as a Sunday-school superintendent would be to manage a prize fight. Ochs had admired Davis for years and had urged his nomination by the Democrats in 1920. He was a gentleman of the old school and in the prewar world would have made a good candidate and an excellent President. Even in 1924 he would have been a good candidate for the Republican party, the static party, the party that was holding back. But for the dynamic, mobile Democratic party he was hopeless.

Davis was nominated, indeed, as a compromise after the two leading candidates had slaughtered each other in a fight that raged through a hundred and one roll calls. By that time the democracy was no longer a party, it was a charnel house, and what poor Davis led was not a fighting force but a political burial party.

What had happened was the seepage into American politics of one of the old hatreds that were poisoning Europe. Of the two leading candidates one, Alfred E. Smith, was a Catholic, and his religion was made an issue. The primary responsibility for this rested upon his opponents, including the noisome Ku Klux Klan; but some of his unwise friends made the error of defending him on religious grounds. Thus the issue was squarely joined and the combat that ensued had the characteristic savagery of religious wars. It wrecked the party and made the nomination of Davis a hollow mockery.

Ochs had been happily certain that America was immune to that sort of thing and at first he wouldn't believe it even after it had happened. He supported Davis vigorously really thinking, in the beginning, that he could be elected. Davis conducted a strong, dignified, intelligent campaign, to which nobody paid any attention. Those who believed in maintaining the existing status were going to vote for Coolidge, the Republican, anyhow; those who believed in change wanted much more radical changes than the mild reforms Davis advocated. Davis was badly beaten.

For awhile the conservatives, and probably Ochs among them, were still able to convince themselves that no profound change had occurred. After all, in the 1924 convention the Protestant candidate, McAdoo, had also been beaten. It was possible to regard the whole business as due to the machinations of reckless and unscrupulous politicians, who had succeeded only in disgusting the public with the whole Democratic party.

But in 1928 that comfortable illusion was torn away. There was no great battle in the convention that year. Smith, the Catholic, was nominated in a more or less routine fashion; but at the polls in November he received such a blasting repudiation that even the Solid South was shattered, five of its states going Republican for the first time in half a century. It hadn't been political trickery in 1924. It had been a real intrusion into American life of an ancient evil that our idealists had believed expelled for good many years before.

This was more than politics. This was a shrewd blow at the very basis of the blithe philosophy of the old regime. Al Smith was a conspicuous exponent of those old verities and old moralities that Adolph Ochs had said were guarantees of a man's success. But all Smith's honesty, industry and sobriety could not bring him success with the Ku Klux Klan on the rampage. Obviously, the calculations of Ochs's generation were badly out, somewhere. If there was nothing wrong with the country, there must be something wrong with the philosophy. Both could not be right.

Confronted with these alternatives, the group split into two divisions. The smaller men among them promptly decided that the country was all wrong and retired into a shell of bitterness that hardened with the passage of the years. Every new movement that appeared in those turbulent years, political, economic, social or religious, served only to confirm them in their opinion that all was lost, particularly honor. They became the die-hard reactionaries, never attempting to understand the new world, content with hating it and fighting everything it tried to do.

But some were big enough to accept Cromwell's advice to the Scotch Presbyterians—to bethink themselves that it was possible for them to be mistaken. Of this kind was Ochs. He was as bewildered as the rest. He was apprehensive and as the long armistice floundered toward the new catastrophe his apprehension mounted into positive terror. But there was no drop of deserter's blood in the son of Captain Julius of the volunteers; he was in America and of America, and where the country went he would go too. His business was not to condemn this new world, but to understand it; he might never succeed entirely, but his life would be spent in the effort.

Arrogance—social, professional or intellectual—simply was not in the man. If many of the certainties that he had once held were being torn from his grasp by the logic of events, then the fault was his for having accepted them in the first place. Let the die-hard cry, "I am Sir Oracle," if he would. As for Ochs, he would say, "There are so many wonderful things that I do not know, that I do not understand, that I am willing to believe the things that give peace, plenty and hope, and cause me to be a better neighbor and co-operate in good work."[5]

Old Rabbi Wise would have approved. Hearing that credo, he might have commented, out of the Book, "What doth the Lord require of thee but to do justly, and to love mercy, and to walk humbly with thy God?"

Humility is not irresolution. Ochs knew his mind, and his decisions were always prompt and clear-cut. But he knew that he was not infallible and when events rather than argument showed that it was time to move he could move with the utmost agility. Thus it happened that when the new forces in the world became irresistible and the reactionaries, by refusing to recognize them, led the Republican party into disaster even more overwhelming than the Democrats had encountered in 1924, Ochs was not caught under the wreckage. A conservative he had always been, and a conservative he remained, but when the political atomic bomb hit the Republican fortress in 1932, he was elsewhere and so was able to repair to the spot and inspect the damage, grimly, but without surprise.

VII

The successive steps by which a man widely regarded as the chief spokesman of conservative thought moved into a position in which he was logically bound to support Franklin D. Roosevelt, standard-bearer of liberalism, for President in 1932, represented more than the intellectual development of an individual. In this, as in other things, Adolph S. Ochs is interesting, not because he was a psychological curiosity, but precisely because he wasn't. There were a great many like him, and his case is especially worth examining merely because he was an unusually able man and unusually influential, not because he was odd. Far from being odd, he portrayed with singular clarity that body of American opinion that has been more potent than any other in shaping the course of our national history, what we are accustomed to call the solid citizen.

[5] At the laying of the cornerstone of Temple Beth El, August 3, 1925.

It is a good term. He is profoundly democratic, is this solid American, but the very word "solid" suggests mass, and massiveness suggests slow movement, unspectacular movement that passes unnoted while attention is centered on the gymnastics of the intellectual acrobats.

The solid citizen has ever in mind a dictum of Thomas Jefferson that radicals in a hurry and reactionaries in a rut both customarily brush aside. While the will of the majority is in all cases to prevail, said Jefferson, that will "to be right must be reasonable." If it is not reasonable, it is not right; and for wrong to prevail is disaster under any form of government.

The period between the two great wars—that is, so much of it as he was permitted to see—Adolph Ochs spent in a search for the reasonable. Restricted to the field of human government it is not a particularly hopeful search at any time, but during these years its hopelessness was accentuated beyond all precedent. That information we owe, however, to the advantage of hindsight; it was withheld from the men of the period and the more resolute among them clung to some hope to the end.

In this country it began as a period of tremendous exhilaration. The Old Serpent had been chained for a thousand years; only a minority perceived that the chains, none too strong to begin with, had been slipped at the last moment in the Senate fight against the League of Nations. Most of America, tremendously busy with the peaceful work of material reconstruction, accepted the assurances of the public idols of the moment that we had entered a new economic era in which poverty was to be abolished and the economic causes of war eliminated.

Ochs had his doubts but "willing to believe the things that give peace, plenty and hope," he went along. Harding had died before the scandals of his administration were revealed. When the corruption became common knowledge Calvin Coolidge, a man of a very different type, was already President. Ochs liked Coolidge. He regarded the President as a man who worked and paid his debts, and a man who had himself come up the hard way never lost his confidence in men of that type. The difference in politics did not matter enough to keep the publisher from ardently desiring to assist the President in every possible way. Relations between the *Times* and the White House were cordial, even when the *Times* was supporting Davis in the campaign of 1924, and they remained cordial until the end of the administration. Coolidge expected opposition in the election and because it was clean, open and aboveboard he felt no resentment; while he warmly appreciated the support of the *Times* at many critical moments between elections.

But Ochs in these years was doing far more than merely speaking up for the President through the columns of the paper. He was making a desperate effort to attain true understanding of the situation.

At first the question of the reparations to be paid by Germany to the victorious Allies and of the war debts owed by the various Allies to each other overshadowed all else. Ochs was prodigal of time and energy in trying to comprehend this situation and owing to his international prestige he was able to reach the best sources of information. At the time of the French invasion of the Ruhr, for example, he had a long conversation with Raymond Poincaré, Premier of France, and another with Ramsay MacDonald, Prime Minister of Great Britain. The President of the United States talked to him with the utmost frankness, and he even went as far afield as to have a private interview with Alfonso XIII, King of Spain, trying to obtain some light on the subject.

He never understood it and only toward the end did he realize that his failure sprang from the same cause as Jefferson's failure to understand some of the followers of Plato—the fact that a rational man can never understand nonsense. In all the world nobody was disposed to discuss the problem of reparations reasonably. Ochs himself proposed to Poincaré a scheme—later adopted in part, but too late—for pooling all claims against Germany and funding them to relieve the immediate necessities of the claimants without exacting impossible payments from Germany. The Frenchman replied coldly that France was not interested in "idealistic" programs. It was something new to Ochs to hear a scheme devised to get as much money as possible as quickly as possible described as "idealistic," and he perceived at once that there was a great gap between his thinking and that of the premier. He left discouraged.

Ramsay MacDonald made a much more favorable impression upon him. Indeed, he was enchanted by the splendid façade of that pseudo statesman. MacDonald talked with the utmost reasonableness, and although he informed Ochs during the interview that he might remain in office even if his Labour government were defeated in the House of Commons, the significance of this avowal escaped the American. Ochs came away unsuspecting that the intentions of the Frenchman and the Briton were identical.

The Spaniard also rather took him in. Alfonso seemed to be discussing the problem of reparations in a forthright and impartial manner; but it is easy to see now that the true aim of his proposals was not to dispose of the financial problem, but to weaken France. Ochs did not miss this entirely,[6] but intent on the financial question, he did not give it its due weight.

Coolidge was of no practical help. "They hired the money, didn't they?" his most celebrated contribution to the discussion, had a certain point as Ochs was bound to admit. He believed, however, that Coolidge would have entertained any reasonable offer; where the New Englander was unreasonable was in adhering to the New England trader's theory that it is not the business of the lender to make a proposition. Here was a deal that could not be handled by New England trading rules, yet Coolidge had nothing else to offer.

The Young Plan, the Dawes Plan, innumerable other plans, notes, memoranda, agreements, as they came up Ochs examined with care and usually supported with enthusiasm, always hoping that at last the world was about to apply the rule of reason. Explosions of irritation in this country he deprecated, but they became more and more frequent, culminating in the Johnson Act, as unreasonable a measure as any country had taken, which forbade further loans to any country in default in its payments. No reasonable lender, anxious to get his money

[6] His notes, in the Ochs MSS. of this conversation show that he perceived the king's dislike of the French army.

back, absolutely cuts off all hope of further accommodation; but that is what this country did.

In the hope that light would bring wisdom Ochs had rebuilt his foreign service on a new plan. Instead of separate and independent bureaus in many capitals, he now centered the European service in Paris, with Edwin L. James in supreme command. He continued to maintain correspondents in many places, but now they reported to Paris and looked to James for assignments. This tightened and co-ordinated the whole system, allowing the *Times* to present a far more coherent picture of the situation than it had ever had before.

For a time he contemplated going further. He had discovered that if American understanding of Europe was woefully inadequate, European understanding of America was even worse. He was doing all he could to interpret Europe to his own country; could he not double his value by undertaking to interpret America to Europe? Why not set up an edition of the *Times* in London or Paris and devote it to that purpose?

James was enthusiastic over the idea, and started work on it with a will. He hired the ablest men he could find to survey the field and give him exact information. Their reports showed that the edition would probably lose money, but that did not deter Ochs. He was willing to accept a reasonable loss. However, when further investigation made it seem likely that the loss would run to $300,000 annually, he was given pause. That was more than he had calculated.

It was Van Anda, however, who dynamited the scheme.[7] He pointed out that the *Times*, as an independent newspaper, was frequently in opposition to the government. In this country that was necessary and desirable; but in a foreign country might it not be misunderstood, especially if the *Times* set itself up as an exponent and interpreter of the United States? Suppose some foreign government should accept the *Times*'s advice in regard to an international affair, only to find that Washington thought otherwise—would not the resultant embarrassment adversely affect the prestige of the paper? To oppose one's gov-

[7] His shattering memorandum is preserved among the Ochs MSS.

ernment on foreign soil is a delicate and doubtful undertaking. Van Anda was against it.

After reading the memorandum, so was Ochs. He canceled all arrangements by cable. After all, he was American, first and last; for no consideration would he do anything that would allow any doubt of that. James was disappointed, but he acquiesced cheerfully and when Julius Ochs Adler, coming a few days after the cable, brought a long letter from Ochs and his own interpretation of the situation, James himself agreed that the decision was probably correct.

But to a man of the nineteenth century the job of interpreting Europe was becoming steadily more difficult, for there was steadily less reason in it. Nor indeed was it Europe only. This whole new world was taking on insensate phases, the United States included. The new economic era, for example, had an aura of doubt about it that he could not overlook. By 1928 the financial pages of the *Times* were drawing protests from exponents of the new era on account of their Cassandra-like tone, and once the election was passed they grew even more ominous. This was actually the work of Alexander Noyes, financial editor; but Ochs stood behind him until the day when his predictions were dreadfully justified.

The election of 1928 made Herbert Hoover President of the United States; for the new President himself Ochs had a high admiration, but the manner of his elevation could not be regarded with satisfaction by any man who believed in the rule of reason in public affairs. Mr. Hoover himself had been perfectly correct throughout the campaign and so had his chief supporters. There is no evidence that they had any hand in the dirty work that went on, and plenty of evidence that they deplored it. Nevertheless, the religious issue was injected, and in any campaign when religious hatred comes in reason goes out. If that was the sort of politics that was to prevail henceforth in the United States such men as Ochs must regard the future with deep anxiety.

But Hoover had been in office little over half a year when bigotry itself was swept into the background of men's thinking by the panic of 1929, which was no mere stock-market flurry but the collapse of an entire economic system.

THE MAN IS SORE AFRAID

For all his growing doubt of the new economic era, and for all that Alexander Noyes had been writing in the *Times*, to say that Ochs was prepared for this catastrophe would be fatuous. Nobody was prepared for it, least of all the great officers of state and the great industrialists and financiers. Yet it was the perfectly logical culmination of a decade of unreasonable refusal to face the plain facts, not in this country only but throughout the world. The economy of every nation involved in the war had suffered a fearful battering and no intelligent measures of repair and renovation had been taken, unless, indeed, the Russian process of complete demolition be regarded as intelligent.

Ochs knew this, and it was the cause of his increasing uneasiness from 1919 to 1929; but although he had looked for trouble, he had no idea of the fearful extent of the disaster. His first impulse was to minimize it, and he approved the President's efforts to reassure the country. Events proved that he was wrong, but they do not prove that he was as absurdly wrong as some critics have asserted. After all, what was to be gained by increasing the terror that was already flailing the country? In a crisis it is the duty of a leader to put on the appearance of a confidence he may not feel. He risks being made to look silly, of course, but it is a risk that must be assumed; and there is nothing absurd in a man's doing what at the time seems to be his plain duty. To go back to the files and read today some of the statements made by the *Times* immediately after the crash is to receive an impressive lesson in the fallibility of human foresight; yet it is a question whether they really represent more folly than courage and devotion.

But the crash of 1929 and its aftermath dragged down more than the economic structure. It also demolished the common man's confidence in his political, financial, industrial and social leadership and brutally unmasked passions so long decently veiled in the trappings of the social order that most people had believed them smothered long ago. True, there had been an outbreak of these things in Italy seven years earlier; but it was the economic depression following 1929 that loosed them elsewhere. Anti-Semitism, religious hatred, crazy nationalism, every form of obscurantism including hatred of learning and fear of liberty, surged across the world in a hideous tide that was to mount and mount until it broke against the last bastions of civilization when the Mikado surrendered in 1945.

It was here that Adolph Ochs's gift of foresight proved to be something less than a personal blessing. About 1930 a man who could look ahead a few years was not made any happier by that ability for there was not much to see that was pleasant to look upon. This was conspicuously true if the man in question happened to be, in the first place, a democrat, in the second place, a conservative, and in the third place, a Jew, for democracy, conservatism and Judaism were all to be subjected to increasingly ferocious attacks within the next decade.

In the dreary years following the panic of 1929 it is small wonder that his bright spirit began to be somewhat dimmed. Even Adolph Ochs could not be jocund with the world falling to pieces about his ears, especially since he had a bleak certainty that worse was to come. He made the best he could of it. His faith in the integrity and patriotism of President Hoover never wavered; but his faith in the President's political philosophy was shattered by the impact of hard facts. Forces were abroad in the world that had somehow to be brought under control, forces that were only remotely related to economic theory, yet too strong to be successfully handled by any one man or group of men.

Adolph Ochs was still firmly convinced that a man's personal destiny depended upon his exercise of the old virtues, honesty, sobriety, industry; but he was beginning to be aware that without equality of opportunity their exercise is fruitless, and that the forces of evil bent upon restricting that equality included more than mere greed. The love of money was not the root of all evil. There were evils whose roots went back beyond the invention of money, back into the dark hours before the dawn of history, when men butchered each other out of hatred arising from a difference in superstitions. There were evils arising from a perversion of as admirable an emotion as patriotism. There were evils arising from pride of caste, that had little to do with money. And all these evils were being shrewdly manipulated by men imbued with bitter hatred of the very idea of government of the people, by the people, for the people.

The President, and especially his principal advisers, held sturdily to the idea that, given a little time, the old controls would reassert themselves. Mr. Hoover was not, as his critics have loudly asserted, impassive in the face of disaster. The Reconstruction Finance Corporation alone is sufficient proof that he was willing to act and did act vigorously; but he acted strictly within the framework of the old conception of government as the impartial umpire between men who were created equal. Ochs became more and more strongly convinced that this was not enough. He edged more and more toward the view that government is not merely an umpire, but an instrument in the hands of the people to effect their happiness, and a weapon with which to protect themselves against their enemies.

Yet in his own mind, at least, he was never more genuinely conservative than at the time when he was making up his mind to demand abandonment of the old attitudes and the substitution of a new and more dynamic policy. He believed that the function of a conservative is to conserve, and he believed that the methods by which that function is discharged are of secondary importance. If new dangers were confronting democracy, he did not think that a conservative changed character when he adopted new defenses against them. He would change character only if he abandoned his determination to conserve everything that the past had proved to be sound and useful. As a conservative, therefore, he supported Franklin D. Roosevelt for President in 1932.

Whether his reasoning was correct or erroneous, whether he would have changed his mind had he lived more than three years longer, are matters of secondary importance in a study of the man. Pragmatically, his decision was sound. When Roosevelt won overwhelmingly, the *Times* found itself in an excellent position. It could give effective support to everything it approved in the administration program, and it could criticize what it did not approve without suspicion of being animated by partisan prejudice. As a matter of fact, in the years that followed it was a powerful influence, either as supporter or as critic of the New Deal program. Mr. Roosevelt was not the man to be much influenced by newspaper opinion, either friendly or adverse; but it is certain that there was no newspaper whose opinion he respected more than that of the *Times*.

As regards Adolph S. Ochs, however, what shows his quality is the fact that at seventy-three he was still capable of making such a decision. The years were heavy upon him and worse than the years was the weight of anxiety that had oppressed him since the end of the First World War and that had doubled and redoubled in the last four years. In his youth he had believed, as all his generation believed, that the enemies of the people were merely the greedy and unscrupulous seeking their own advantage regardless of means; he had come to late middle age without seeing any valid reason to modify that point of view. Not until he was elderly and while he was growing old was it revealed to him—and to the rest of the world—that there are enemies of the people whose greed is only a secondary motive and whose primary urge is bitter, implacable hatred of the principle of democracy. Bonds sufficient to restrain the greedy were ropes of sand to these, for they had a devilish ingenuity in employing the baser passions of the people themselves to work the people's ruin.

So violent a disruption of fundamental beliefs is enough to daunt a man in the prime of life, enough to paralyze an old man. But Ochs survived it—not without loss, for his old optimism ebbed away and he was frankly very much afraid of what lay ahead. But he survived, and his last important decision as to policy was made with the same clear, resolute application of inspired common sense as was his first. He had fairly earned the extraordinary compliment that Theodore Roosevelt, in his life of Benton, pays to Old Bullion—he came to the end of his active life still rising.

CHAPTER X

A Gleam at Sunset.

I

THE year 1932 was the last of Adolph Ochs's active career as a newspaperman. Before the end of 1933 he began to feel the first approaches of the illness from which he was never fully to recover. His heart was failing, and the term may be accepted in both the medical and the figurative sense.

Nearly seventy-five crowded years had taken their toll of the sturdy physical organism and the dismal years of the great depression, together with the storm clouds, ever thicker and blacker, hanging over the horizon of the future combined to drain away the optimism that had once been as sturdy as his body.

Two years earlier he had definitely moved out of New York City to a suburban home at White Plains, a great, rambling house, somewhat formless, but notably tranquil, set upon a hill with gracious lawns sloping down, here to tennis courts, there to a formal garden, yonder to a pool overhung with willows. It was the very model of a seat for a country gentleman withdrawn from the bustle of affairs and with nothing on his mind other than to spin out the days through a serene old age; but it was incongruous as the residence of such an embodiment of energy and driving power as Ochs. Yet he loved it. For the most part its many acres were tended with the care given the park around an English country home. But there was one corner that the gardeners had not reached when he bought it, a tangle of scrub and bramble with trees never touched by a pruning hook, but growing as they would—especially a titanic wild cherry overhanging a bit of rough country lane. Ochs would not allow this spot to be touched. The cool, well-ordered peace of the White Plains place soothed his perturbed spirit, but apparently there were moods in which the rough, uncombed patch of woods, so like the woods near Chattanooga when he was a boy, appealed to him when close-clipped sward and formal garden moved him not at all.

For the first two years after the purchase he continued to rule the *Times* much as he had ruled it from the Seventy-fifth Street house. At White Plains, too, he had an oak-paneled library—oak and books seem to have had in his mind a sort of association that many another mind has understood—but his working space was a large attic room with a gable window looking down a grassy slope to the pool and its overhanging willows. His massive desk was planted in front of this window and Ochs sat with his back to the light in one of the articles old John Adams scornfully described as "Mr. Jefferson's whirligig chair," able with a single movement to turn from papers on the desk and rest his tired eyes on green grass and placid water. The telephone at his elbow put him into instant communication with the office and in the evening the chief executives frequently came out from town to talk with the master of the enterprise undistracted by the noise and confusion of the city.

It was an ideal setting for spacious and gracious living, for a gentle, unruffled descent toward sunset and the end of the long day. But it lasted only a year or two. In 1933, after Ochs suffered a sharp attack, the doctors ruled against further presentation of the vexations of the office and the executives came out from town no more.

But it meant only partial surcease. The patient accepted apathetically the ruling that he must no longer concern himself with the newspaper's affairs, but the tired mind then conjured up vexations of its own. It was the time of the wave of kidnapings, culminating in the terrible Lindbergh case, and the sick man developed a pathological anxiety over the safety of his grandchildren. He could not be quieted until they had been taken to England. As the financial depression dragged down to its nadir that, too, plunged him into a depth of gloom that he never knew when he was actually hanging over the edge of bankruptcy, first in Chattanooga, and then in New York. The most solemn assurances of his business associates, backed by the testimony of the best accountants, could not quite convince him of the truth, that the position of the *Times* was so strong that there was not the least occasion for worry. He who had been chipper, even gay, when he had not a dollar in the world, now with millions available saw ruin threatening around every corner.

All this, of course, was simply evidence that the machine was wearing out. It was not the heart alone; more than seventy years of intense living, of hard work and hard play, seventy years of battle with intermingled triumph and defeat, seventy years of burden-bearing for others as well as for himself, had exhausted, tremendous as they were, all his energies of mind as well as of body. He was simply meeting the decree from which none is exempt: "Man goeth to his long home."

In these days when his medical advisers forbade him to concern himself with the problems of the present, and when the aspect of the world made him shudder to think of the future, his mind turned inevitably to the past and especially to Chattanooga. There, at least, was something on which he could dwell with pleasure.

The relation of the man and the town that had been the scene of his early struggles is a sort of American idyll, honorable to both sides. The philanthropy of Adolph Ochs was widespread. He had been a moving force in securing an adequate endowment for Hebrew Union College, chief theological seminary of the branch of Judaism once led by Isaac M. Wise; he had not only given large sums of money to the college, but he had contributed to the campaign time and energy that were worth more than his money to the fledgling institution. He had contributed to the erection of a dozen temples of his faith and to the shrines of other faiths, as in the instance of the Cathedral of St. John. He had never refused a subscription to any campaign for the amelioration of human suffering or the relief of human destitution, whether the victims were Jewish, Christian, heathen or atheist, or whether they were around the corner in New York or in some flood-swept Chinese river valley.

Yet there is good reason to believe that the existing record of his charities omits the most beautiful of them all. He had an extraordinary capacity for finding out quietly who was in trouble, and again and again he came to the rescue stealthily, one might say—except that it was good work—furtively, forbidding the beneficiary to say anything about it. His death revealed a startling list of pensioners, some of whom he had been carrying for many years.

It is a fine thing to build temples and endow colleges and write five-figure checks for relief funds; but it is finer, because it is very much more laborious, to make one's gift with a human sympathy and understanding that extracts from it all the flavor of the bitter bread of charity. When asked for it, Adolph Ochs would always give his check to any worthy cause, which won him great, but deserved, credit in the eyes of men. But before he was asked for anything, over and over again, he spent time and energy and ingenuity finding out where help was needed and what form it had best take; which is to say, he gave his heart with his check. So it has come about that among those who knew him best some look at the list of his public benefactions with a sort of impatience, as making a wholly inadequate impression of the richness of his giving. Perhaps it is unreasonable to regard a twenty-dollar bill, secretly placed where the donor had laboriously learned that it was needed, as a lovelier thing than a twenty-five thousand dollar check given to a college or great relief fund. But some people are just that unreasonable.

A man has his preferences, in good works as in any other, and it was when he could do something for somebody in Chattanooga that Ochs obtained a satisfaction not quite equaled by giving anywhere else in the world. What is known of his personal benefactions there is impressive, yet there is reason to believe that of the vastly greater number no record remains. Many of the recipients of his bounty died long ago, and others were under a strict injunction never to tell. So nobody knows the whole story, but enough is known to give rise to a generous suspicion that makes his name a little radiant in the town to this day.

But his public benefactions were perforce exposed to the sight of all the world and they make an interesting study. One, indeed, was only quasi-public, primarily a work of religious and filial piety. He spent some $300,000 erecting a beautiful temple to the glory of God and to the memory of his father and mother.

Even the strictly secular and public works reflect the personality of the man. His generosity was never thoughtless. In Chattanooga he considered every project before he supported it as carefully as he had considered, say, the *Dictionary of American Biography* before he supported that. In the matter of the library of the University of Chattanooga, for example, he devoted much thought to the needs of the town, as well as of the school, and devised a plan whereby the two together could support a more adequate joint library than either could maintain alone. Then he was ready to contribute handsomely.

There were other projects, too, not charitable at all, but which made a powerful impression upon Chattanooga. On several occasions he learned of an industrial enterprise in the town that was in difficulties, not because it was basically unsound, but for lack of sufficient working capital. By advancing money he saved to the town more than one enterprise that was on the verge of collapse and enabled others to expand, thereby creating jobs and adding to the general prosperity of the place.

These advances were neither investments nor gifts. They were loans made on a strict commercial basis except for the all-important feature —for collateral, he accepted the character and ability of the management, which banks and other lending agencies could not do. When he made up his mind that the city needed a modern, new hotel he summoned to New York his friend Sam Read, proprietor of the ancient and somewhat dilapidated Read House. When Read arrived he found that Ochs had already gone to one of the great insurance companies and arranged for a loan of a size that took the proprietor's breath. The Chattanoogan was under no illusions. He was aware that the insurance officials had never heard of him, but they knew Adolph Ochs and therefore were certain that the loan would be repaid. It was, and by the borrower, not by Ochs; but without him the town might have had to wait for years for its new hotel, and well Chattanooga knew it.

The striking thing about all these activities was not so much that the man was willing to give money for the benefit of Chattanooga as that he was willing to give time and thought and care. His purse benefited Chattanooga, but his mind benefited it more; and the gift of his interest drew a response that money alone could never have brought.

This interest was never more evident than in the greatest work he did for the city, the preservation for the use of the public of its historic sites. Adolph Ochs worked at this task for fifty years and put into it more than a quarter of a million dollars; but the money was inconsiderable by comparison with the stimulation of his leadership.

Back in 1887, when the Army of the Cumberland held a reunion in Chattanooga, he took the lead in establishing the organization that succeeded in having Chickamauga battlefield taken over by the government as a national monument in 1890. His newspaper fought constantly and in the main successfully to have other scenes of great battles taken over or at least marked by suitable memorials.

But the great glory of Chattanooga, the mountain that looms over the town and on whose crest the armies came into collision in "the battle above the clouds," was in private hands. The top of Lookout is more than a famous battlefield; the Point, that is, the end nearest the city, also affords one of the most magnificent views in eastern America. For years during Ochs's early days in Chattanooga the owner, one James Whiteside, put no obstacle in the way of anyone wishing to visit the place; but after his death his heirs, lacking his public spirit, fenced off the Point and charged admission; then they charged a toll for use of the road up the mountain; then they compelled every visitor to use one of their own carriages for hire, not one supplied by any of the city livery stables. The thing was fast developing into an unconscionable racket.

The Chattanooga *Times* battled for years to rescue the mountain. Eventually Ochs took part in forming a corporation to buy the Whiteside interests, after the courts had intervened to break up the monopoly. The Point and thirty acres surrounding it were promptly converted into a public park. This occurred before Ochs left for New York.

However, he was still unsatisfied. The top of the mountain is a narrow but fairly level plateau, which had been largely sold off as dwelling sites on which Chattanoogans built their summer residences. These, with the development of the automobile, have largely become year-round residences. This was not too bad, for the place has become a handsome suburb, well designed and well kept. But there was a tendency to develop on the slopes what have come to be known as "string slums," decorated with hot-dog stands, cheap amusement places and eyesores of every imaginable type.

To Ochs that was desecration. Lookout Mountain was unique. There were countless miles of land available for all the hot-dog stands, soda-pop counters and dance halls that heart could desire, without planting them on the only slope that could be converted into such a public park as would make the Hanging Gardens of Babylon insignificant by comparison.

For a quarter of a century he was too busy in New York to do much about it but in 1921 he came back to Chattanooga in an aggressive mood. He opened up with an address to the Kiwanis Club and thereafter he held meetings, organized committees, made speeches and had the Chattanooga *Times* pour out a stream of news stories and editorials demanding that Lookout Mountain be saved.

Eventually a corporation was formed to acquire the slopes of the mountain for public use. A good deal of the land was donated and $117,000 subscribed to purchase the rest, Ochs and his family putting up $34,000. The outcome was the acquisition of 2314 acres, which the corporation proposed to turn over to competent authority for preservation as public property forever. At first it was intended to give the land to the city, but since it was the scene of a battle of the Civil War it was at last decided that the national government was its proper custodian. Ochs did not live to see the end of the negotiation, but at last Congress accepted it and it is now the property of the people of the United States.

After it had been acquired, however, and before it had been transferred to public ownership, it was still difficult of access by automobile and the county authorities hesitated to spend the money to build a first-rate road to the top. Thereupon Ochs advanced the county $150,000 out of his own pocket, none of which he got back, or expected to.

This project was approaching completion when the fiftieth anniversary of Adolph Ochs's acquisition of the Chattanooga *Times* came around. The paper proposed to celebrate the occasion with a ninety-six-page edition, recounting the history of the region for that half century, and the publisher was invited to come down from New York. But Chattanooga realized that here was its opportunity to pay a fitting tribute to the man, and the city snatched the celebration out of the newspaper's hands. Instead of a mere anniversary, it became a three-day gala occasion with the whole town taking part and the paper more or less lost in the crowd.

There were dinners, luncheons, parties and processions of many kinds. They discharged orations at him in great numbers and with great fervor. They passed resolutions and gave him engrossed testimonials; they eulogized him on rostrums and cheered him in the streets and down at the city hall they officially decreed that he should be Citizen Emeritus of Chattanooga no matter where he might live.

Ochs was completely floored by the outburst. He had come down from New York expecting a pleasant time, but nothing like this. To emphasize it, his colleagues of the press seized the opportunity to pay their tribute and made it to some extent national. Newspapers far and wide published laudatory editorials and many of the greatest figures in American journalism wrote personal letters felicitating him on the anniversary and expressing their admiration. He took it, said Joseph Collins,[1] with a curiously detached air; he sat and listened attentively, but as if he were quite sure they were talking about somebody else and all the attention had been centered on him by mistake.

Nevertheless, he was deeply moved. If to "walk with kings nor lose the common touch" is one criterion of greatness, he could qualify; for the praise of the common people of his boyhood home touched him and irradiated him with a delight that no prince or potentate had ever inspired in his heart. It was no mere polite formula, it was the expression of his deepest feeling, when he said, in his speech of acknowledgment, "What greater glory can come to a man, what more beautiful crown, than the love and affection of neighbors, the expression of their confidence and esteem, and the assurance that one's citizenship has been useful?"

It was, indeed, an American idyll, this relation between the good

---

[1] In a letter to Mrs. Ochs, who had been unable to make the trip to Chattanooga.

citizen and the city that did not forget. Chattanooga wrote the epilogue when Ochs was in his grave. At the Point, on the crest of the mountain he did so much to save, the city has built out of native fieldstone a building designed to serve as a point of observation, a museum, and as a shelter for visitors against bad weather, and has dedicated it to the memory of Adolph Ochs.

II

He was a profoundly religious man but, like many of his type, he was somewhat exasperating to pietists. His theology was of the sketchiest and he was shaky on dogma. The psychology of the ascetic was beyond his comprehension. He helped build a temple named Emmanuel, but he was no Jacob, given to wrestling with angels. Religion to him was not a battlefield, but a sanctuary: "I am willing to believe the things that give peace, plenty and hope." He was not willing to believe the things that brought millions of spears around the green banner of the Prophet, that set swords flashing over the difference between Homoousian and Homoiousian, that reduced Germany to cannibalism in the Thirty Years' War.

From the strictly sectarian standpoint perhaps the lady in Jerusalem had reason for regarding him as a pretty dubious Jew. At any rate, there is no doubt at all that, Jew or no Jew, he cheerfully accepted the dictum of Christian St. James: "Pure religion and undefiled before God and the Father is this: to visit the fatherless and widows in their affliction and to keep himself unspotted from the world." A man who was kind to those less fortunate than himself and honest in his dealings with everyone he regarded as a good man; and he did not believe that a good man could be a bad Jew.

Theologically, this is flat heresy in any religion, but it is nevertheless one of the things that bring peace, plenty and hope, and the man who not only believes but practices it stands high in the estimation of his fellows, no matter what the learned doctors may say of him.

But Ochs did have one fixed and definite theological concept. He believed in God and the immortality of the soul. Among his papers

[287]

after his death was found a statement by the Rev. Dr. Knass, written in answer to the question, "How do you interpret the soul?" The sheet is creased and worn; obviously it has been read and reread. It is an affirmation of belief in immortality based not upon revelation or dogma of any kind but upon the same sort of hypothesis that sustains the doctrines of the conservation of energy and the conservation of matter. The paper is not dated, but Dr. Knass undoubtedly wrote before the doctrines of conservation had been as seriously undermined as they are today. Probably his reasoning satisfied Ochs, or he would not have preserved the paper so carefully.

The interesting thing in this connection is the fact that Ochs made the inquiry. He was predisposed to believe; nevertheless he consulted authority. Perhaps it means no more than that his faith wavered at times and needed strengthening; yet he was never the man—at least in other things—to put much reliance in authoritarian opinion. He was, however, a newspaperman, and it is second nature with a good newspaperman always to verify his information when it is possible to do so. No matter how strong your belief it never does any harm to check up when a specialist in the subject is available; on the nature of the soul, therefore, he consulted a theologian, and Dr. Knass's reply was so shrewdly adapted to a layman's manner of thinking that it evidently made a great impression.

The materialism of Thomas A. Edison did not satisfy him. He had a tremendous admiration for Edison—in which he was again the typical American—and regarded it as no small honor to be invited to the inventor's home. But Edison's atomic theory of the soul, which he expounded at length to Ochs, struck the publisher as rather more improbable than the ironbound dogma of the most orthodox theologians. The truth seems to be that in religion, as in everything else, Ochs proceeded as far as common sense would permit, but there he stuck, and neither speculative theology nor speculative science could carry him further. In this his life was remarkably consistent. Within the realm of the reasonable his intelligence was powerful and exact; but the reasonable was his boundary. Beyond it nothing could induce him to go, so one looks in vain for any of those inspirations of genius

that have immortalized great artists, great philosophers and great soldiers. A religion that does no more than make a man a good citizen
and a good neighbor is not the sort of faith that sets the world aflame;
but it satisfies an ordinary man of sense and who is to say that it does
not furnish him in times of crisis with the spiritual bulwark that he
needs?

III

The assertion that his life was consistently reasonable should not be
allowed to stand, however, without a slight modification. In 1934 the
thing that more than any other convinced the family that he was a
sick man was his abandonment of the one form of nonsense that had
always enchanted him, namely, a frolic with youngsters.

Ochs had established a summer home on Lake George fairly early
in his New York career. The house had been built by George Foster
Peabody; it was large and comfortable, but its only architectural distinction was an inscription over the living-room fireplace. There Peabody had had inscribed in Hebrew characters a Biblical quotation:
"Unless the Lord build the house, they labor in vain that build it."
It was a touch that delighted Ochs and he preserved it carefully.

But it took some preserving, as did the rest of the house in the early
days when all the children of the neighborhood used to gather there
for parties. Things might go well enough if the master of the house
were absent, but once he appeared the situation was out of hand
immediately.

Indeed, mothers and governesses endeavoring to instill in their
charges the principles of decorum and correct social usage had reason
to look upon him somewhat as the elders of Athens regarded Socrates,
as an incorrigible corrupter of youth. It was his delight to appear in
the middle of an afternoon party that up to that moment had been
proceeding in a dignified and even stately fashion and to produce
from his pockets, or perhaps from large paper bags, a fearful array of
horns, whistles, rattles and other noisemakers for distribution among
the guests along with a challenge to see what could be made of them,

a challenge that invariably was accepted with enthusiasm. Failing mechanical devices, he had been known to invite such an assemblage to a squealing contest and to out-squeal the best of them. Effie and her friends soon learned that there was no coping with such a situation; their only possible course was to beat a retreat as rapidly as possible and as far as possible until a general failure of breath brought back a reasonable degree of calm.

Not far from the Lake George place was one belonging to Marcella Sembrich, not only a Metropolitan Opera star, but a celebrated teacher of singing, whose custom it was to bring to her summer home a group of pupils to continue their training. These were usually girls with very definite possibilities for operatic careers—Sembrich did not waste her time on hopeless cases—and they were subjected to a drastic regimen intended to develop not the voice only but the mind to a true comprehension of great music.

But the singer was an old friend of the Ochs family and it became almost a matter of routine for her to bring a group of her girls over when the day's work was done for a buffet supper, or a picnic in the long summer evenings. If Ochs were present, it nearly always happened that without quite knowing how these girls, who had been practicing hard all day, found themselves singing, not celebrated arias, but some opus on about the musical level of "Alexander's Rag-Time Band." More than one voice that in later years was to thrill the Metropolitan has been heard on Lake George lustily caroling the beauties of the Wabash or Mobile Bay. And Ochs, who was frankly bored by opera, rejoiced mightily in this music. To do her justice, so, apparently, did Madame Sembrich; at least she usually laughed and let them go.

Whenever he was on holiday at such a place as Miami or Paris he delighted in the races. He had ridden a little himself, but he never claimed to be a true horseman; what drew him to the tracks was less horseflesh than the crowds, the movement, the gay costumes of the women and the gayer silks of the jockeys, the noise and excitement and general air of gaiety. That it was all to him a lot of cheerful nonsense is evidenced by the way he placed his bets—never after a serious study of form, but usually on some long shot because he liked his name, or his jockey's colors, or for some equally nonsensical reason. Occasionally one came home and then Ochs was fairly beside himself with delight. Once he placed a two-dollar bet on a rank outsider at Miami and the creature sailed in far ahead of the field, making Ochs's ticket worth $87.10. That stood out as a red-letter day in his memory as long as he lived. He cherished it above many a business deal that netted him a five-figure profit.

It is significant that he was a great friend of Marie Dressler, the comedienne whose fame rested upon her unparalleled ability to handle gay nonsense. She was of his party on his last holiday jaunt to Honolulu in 1931, and they were kindred spirits throughout the trip until a professional engagement recalled her to California.

All this, however, does not invalidate the assertion that he was, above all things, a man of common sense, for there is no more rigid test of common sense than knowing exactly when to kick over the traces and thumb one's nose at reason for a moment.

Moreover, while nonsense is the subject, it would be somewhat less than candid to fail to point out that, while no man knew better how to handle it when it was gay, solemn nonsense sometimes trapped Adolph Ochs. For instance, on his return from Honolulu he was entertained overnight by William Randolph Hearst at San Simeon. Ochs was under no illusions whatever about Hearst's character as a journalist or as a man; yet that fabulous establishment on the shores of the Pacific somehow hit a weak spot. Hearst evidently put himself out to be as affable as he could and he saw to it that Ochs should miss nothing of the splendor, the luxury and the ingenuity of the establishment. Ochs's usually steady judgment was shaken; after his return to New York he wrote Hearst a note of thanks that exceeded the requirements of politeness and almost eulogized the man.

Again, when Mussolini's supple and astute agent, Count Grandi, made his first visit to this country in that same year of 1931, Ochs was taken in by his suavity and his glib profession of sentiments that the Fascist regime at heart abhorred. True, he was not the only one taken in; so were all the dignitaries of New York City; so were bankers, industrialists, society people and politicians; so was Columbia University, which bestowed its academic honors on the Italian foreign minister. Yet for all that it is embarrassing to have to admit that Ochs gave a luncheon for Grandi at which he publicly referred to "the wisdom of breadth of your statesmanship, and your inspiring message of international relations—the advocacy of world peace and prosperity, to which you so sincerely and whole-heartedly pledge yourself." This, to the representative of a regime that was the mortal foe of the democracy in which Ochs's faith rested, and that cared not a straw for peace, is incontrovertible proof that for all his common sense the publisher of the *Times* was not invulnerable to certain forms of solemn nonsense.

IV

Sometimes a negative event illuminates character as well as a positive one; what a man does not do may tell as much about him as what he does. Pride in the act is not necessarily more significant than regret for the act that was omitted.

In 1931 the New York *World* went under the hammer and Ochs failed to prevent it. This in itself may mean little, but his bitter regret when it was all over means a great deal.

It was not deliberate on his part. He was in Honolulu at the critical moment and his first information about the event was contained in a cable from his son-in-law when the deed had already been done. Nevertheless, he was so disturbed that on his return he summoned a special meeting of his staff and explained the circumstances in detail. He seemed to take it for granted that his men would think the worse of him if they were left under the impression that he had deliberately let his chief competitor go down. As a matter of fact, he was not altogether wrong. Perhaps he exaggerated the general sense of his responsibility. Nobody could have blamed him, logically, yet there is no doubt that the *Times* men were a little relieved to learn that their chief had had no chance to act.[2]

---

[2] Among the Ochs papers is a memorandum on this conference written by Arthur Krock, a participant, who declares that he had never seen the publisher "so animated" in discussing any subject. He talked, says Krock, with the vigor one associates with thirty-three rather than with seventy-three. That he was deeply disturbed is beyond question.

To the biographer, however, the incident is valuable chiefly for its illumination of Ochs's attitude toward newspapers in general. If he had taken the view that a newspaper is simply a piece of property, his failure to act was perfectly correct. He had had no hand in bringing its troubles upon the *World* and not the slightest responsibility for its fate. Commercially, it was his chief competitor. The *Herald-Tribune*, as a Republican paper, served a clientele that the *Times* could not reach anyhow. Hearst's *American* was still playing to the sensation-lovers. But the *World* was actually taking some business that the *Times* might have hoped to secure. Its elimination, therefore, meant a real reduction in competition, which, from the commercial standpoint, was desirable.

But the *World* since the day when Pulitzer had abandoned his effort to outscream Hearst, had become a really great newspaper. Even after Joseph Pulitzer's death it had been brilliantly edited—perhaps, indeed, too brilliantly for its own good—and its courage and intellectual integrity were beyond debate. It was the spokesman of the liberal wing, as the *Times* was of the conservative wing, of the Democratic party.

Ochs was a profound believer in the right of every school of thought to have a hearing. He did not agree with the attitude of the *World* on a great many questions. He regarded some of its premises as unsound and many of its conclusions as misleading. Nevertheless, he knew it was intelligent and he believed it was honest; and it was his theory that the cause of good government is served by the expression of every honest and intelligent opinion, even though part of them may be mistaken. The *World* was an exponent of ideas, hence its existence was to the public benefit, even if some of its ideas were rejected by Adolph Ochs.

Undoubtedly he had another idea in mind, too. Intellectually the competition of the *World* was anything but damaging to the *Times*. On the contrary, an alert and vigorous adversary in the duel of wits is the best possible guarantee against the atrophy of one's own intellectual powers. With the *World* on the job, neither newsmen nor editorial writers on the *Times* dared begin to nod, as Ochs knew very well.

If they did, the World would show them up instantly and embarrassingly.

This was the view of a man who saw in a newspaper vastly more than merely a means of livelihood.

It was not Ochs's monopoly. In essence it was also the view of Joseph Pulitzer, the man who had made the World a great newspaper. But it was not, unfortunately, the view of his son, Herbert, who had inherited the property but not the temperament of the born newspaperman. Herbert Pulitzer had spent much of his life abroad. To him the newspaper was simply a source of income and when the income dwindled, his first care was not to save the institution but to save his fortune by getting rid of what threatened to become a serious drain upon it.

In August, 1930, Ochs was approached by Pulitzer quietly. At Pulitzer's suggestion they met neither at the Times nor at the World, but in a private suite at the Ritz-Carlton Hotel. Pulitzer astonished Ochs by offering him the World, morning and Sunday editions, to combine with the Times. He was talking in terms of $10,000,000.

At that and a subsequent interview Ochs tried to explain to him that he really had nothing to sell to the Times, for a newspaper is not like a piece of real estate that can be transferred by deed from one owner to another. If the Times bought the morning and Sunday World, what would it get? Not the good will, for that would go to the evening World, which was not to be included in the deal. Not much of the circulation, for the World had long been teaching its readers that the Times was ultraconservative, not at all representative of the things in which they believed. Not the advertising, for that follows circulation. The Times might hope to pick up at most some 75,000 additional readers, too small an increase to justify an advertising rate high enough to recover the $10,000,000 purchase price within any reasonable time.

Pulitzer, therefore, was offering nothing that Ochs could buy, nor could any other publisher buy it at anything like the price suggested. The bulk of the value of the property lay in its quality as an established institution; its traditions and history were worth more than its physical assets and if Pulitzer wanted to save his money the way to do it was to preserve the institution.

Ochs therefore would not think of purchasing, but if it was a matter of preserving the *World* as a going concern, he would be interested. If Pulitzer wanted to get out, the thing to do was to find a purchaser who would continue the paper under its own identity in the hope of restoring its profitability. Ochs's suggestion was a sale to a corporation formed by the men actively engaged in producing the paper; if such a scheme were worked out, Ochs would undertake to help finance it, although he stated frankly that $10,000,000 was too high a price.

He was wasting his breath. Pulitzer exhibited no interest in the suggestion. Later Arthur Hays Sulzberger went, on Ochs's advice, to another member of the group and renewed the suggestion, but without avail. Pulitzer simply lacked the newspaperman's comprehension of the nature of a newspaper. To him the *World* was his property and he saw no reason in law or in morals why he should not divest himself of it in any way he saw fit. The only obstacle was the will of Joseph Pulitzer, which fixed certain conditions governing the sale of the paper. It was necessary, therefore, to apply to the courts to have those conditions set aside before a sale could be effected.

No such application had been made when Ochs left for Honolulu, but while he was gone the Scripps-Howard newspaper chain made an offer. They had no earthly use for the morning *World*, but they decided that it would be worth their while to acquire the evening edition to combine it with their *Telegram*; to get it, they agreed to take over all three, morning, evening and Sunday, and to pay the Pulitzers $3,000,000 for the entire property. Surrogate Foley, before whom the matter came, hearing the Pulitzers' case and having before him no evidence to controvert it, set aside the provisions of the will and ordered the sale. It went through and the morning *World* promptly disappeared.

Ochs told his staff that he would always regret not having been in New York at the time of the hearing. He said he would have gone before the surrogate as an expert witness to swear that the property as a going concern was worth much more than the price offered. He would have undertaken to raise as much as was offered, $3,000,000, provided the property were turned over to men who would maintain it and he would have set the total value at not less than $5,000,000. That would have blocked the sale and probably would have saved the *World*.

But he was in Honolulu. His regrets, therefore, were vain, but they do show his attitude toward the newspaper as an institution. They explain, also, a provision in his own will charging his executors in the most solemn terms "to perpetuate *The New York Times* as an institution charged with a high public duty," not merely as a profit-making corporation.[3]

[3] This provision throws so strong a light on the character of the man that its essential passages are here set on record in the testator's own words: "FIFTY-THIRD . . . my executors and trustees are vested with the control of the New York Times Company. I do not in any wise intend to limit or control their discretion or to impose, directly or indirectly, any limitation or restriction on the shares of stock given to them in trust or on the disposition of the said shares. . . . I am satisfied that my executors and trustees without any recommendations or suggestions from me will exercise their control of the shares of stock of the company to perpetuate *The New York Times* as an institution charged with a high public duty, and that they will carry forward and render completely effective my endeavor to maintain *The New York Times* as an independent newspaper, entirely fearless, free of ulterior influence, and unselfishly devoted to the public welfare without regard to individual advantage or ambition, the claims of party politics, or the voice of religious or personal prejudice or predilection.

"I trust its editorial page may continue to reflect the best informed thought of the country, honest in every line, more than fair and courteous to those who may sincerely differ with its views.

"I trust its news columns may continue fairly to present, without recognizing friend or foe, the news of the day—'all the news that's fit to print'—and to present it impartially, reflecting all shades of opinion.

"I trust its business departments may continue to conform to the highest standards of business ethics and that all persons associated or connected with any of the departments of *The New York Times* organization may be treated justly and generously.

"Realizing that *The New York Times* is an institution impressed with a public interest, I express the wish, which I trust my executors and trustees will be able to carry out, that no disposition of the controlling shares of the stock of The New York Times Company be made either during the continuance of the trust or upon ultimate distribution, except as a unit, as I am satisfied that the best interest and traditions of *The Times* will be most completely served and safeguarded by such disposition."

The following paragraph of the will applies the same restrictions to the control of the Chattanooga *Times*.

V

It cannot be too strongly emphasized that Adolph Ochs was not a seer. He never cast a horoscope or gazed into a crystal ball—that is, seriously; it would have been just like him to visit every fortuneteller at Coney Island if someone in a gay party had suggested fortunetelling as an amusement. But while he had no mystic gift of prophecy, he did have unusual foresight, as every man successful in business in a large way must have. Give him accurate information as to existing facts and he could deduce the probable course of events with great shrewdness.

This is as a rule a highly valuable gift, but it did him no good at all in the year 1933. In January of that year President Hindenburg made Adolf Hitler chancellor of the German Reich; in March the Reichstag passed the Enabling Act that gave the chancellor virtually supreme power; and what little was not included in the act, Hitler promptly seized.

In common with most Americans Ochs had ignored the Austrian corporal up to the moment of his accession to the chancellery. This is sometimes cited as proof of the stupidity of the Americans, but in reality it was a judgment based on experience. Hitler was nothing new to any man familiar with the development of the United States. The Know-Nothing movement, the Abolition movement, the Ku Klux movement—that is, the Ku Kluxism of the twentieth century—had all produced men as fanatical, violent and bloody-minded as the Austrian. They did little damage, however, because they attained little power. The leaders of such movements might have been spectacularly successful up to a point; but always there had been a point at which the common sense of the American people revolted. They defeated William Wirt, they hanged John Brown, they jailed D. C. Stephenson. Ochs himself had heard Tom Watson, of Georgia, screaming his vituperation of Jews and Catholics. It was annoying, but it was not really important, because in the end the voters had taken care of Tom.

Therefore when Hitler began proclaiming his doctrine of hate he had almost no effect on sensible Americans, including Ochs. They were aware that Germany had set up a democratic system. They were aware that in this country the democratic system had invariably drawn the fangs of such creatures before they went too far, and they assumed that it would do likewise in Germany. It was a logical assumption, neither stupid nor unreasonable on the basis of the known facts.

The trouble with it was that there was one fact unknown to most Americans, certainly unknown to Ochs, that invalidated the reasoning. This was the fact that the establishment of democracy in Germany was a sham. The masses had little faith in it, while there were certain classes filled with violent and bitter hatred of it. A few Germans made an honest and earnest effort to make the system work; and it was upon these that most Americans centered their attention.

It was inevitable that one who was himself a man of good will should do this. Ochs, for example, had supported the war against Prussian militarism with all his strength, yet his attitude toward the Germans as a people was anything but one of vindictive hatred. Germany was the land of his ancestors. From Germany his parents had brought and had taught to him as a child a great store of legend and tradition, most of it kindly, much of it merry, all of it charming. How could he hate a land that he had been brought up to regard as a sort of magic realm, afflicted with certain ogres and robber knights, to be sure, but inhabited in the main by people who were kind and good?

He didn't hate it. When his visits to Europe and the reports of his men there made it impossible to ignore the rising tide of bitterness, he refused to attribute it to a deep-seated hatred of the democracies and all they stood for; he accepted, instead, the thesis of the German spokesmen, that it was all based on the injustices of the Treaty of Versailles.

To Ochs's mind the worst injustice in that treaty was the vagueness of the clauses relating to the reparations Germany was to pay. For years this problem haunted his mind. Mention has been made of his conversations on the subject with Poincaré, MacDonald and Alfonso of Spain, but these were only three out of dozens of talks he had with statesmen, financiers and industrialists all over the world. He traveled, he talked, he wrote innumerable letters, he suggested devices, he argued and he pleaded, but he got exactly nowhere.

Perhaps the basic difficulty was that few men appreciate—or then appreciated—the significance of scale in economic operations. When the figures are of astronomical size, the devices that work well enough when dimes and pennies are involved fail to operate at all. Coolidge's famous remark, "They hired the money, didn't they?" expressed the view of the average man. They didn't hire the money. They never got a dollar, nor did they want one. Ten billion dollars was not what we lent Europe; ten billion dollars was merely an expression measuring the size of our shipments of goods to the Allies. But when the time came to pay, we demanded the expression, not replacement of the goods. The lend-lease arrangement of recent years indicates that we may have learned the lesson; but it took twenty years and another war to teach us. Ochs couldn't do it.

As regards German reparations the thing was even worse for it was further removed from the experience and habits of thought of the average man. Therefore with regard to this question what he was accustomed to consider ordinary common sense was in reality fantastic nonsense; and when anyone did talk common sense his argument struck the average man as completely crazy.

What could one do in such a situation? Again and again, in this country, France and England, Ochs found statesmen who understood perfectly what he was talking about and who agreed with most of his arguments. But they were elected officials. They knew that they could solve the reparations problem with relative ease; but they also knew that though they spoke with the tongues of men and of angels they could never explain the solution to their constituents, and their political careers would end abruptly at the next election.

In the end, of course, the reparations question solved itself as an economic problem. There was no way of paying and no way of collecting, so the whole business was dropped and remained only as a source of bitterness and recrimination, not as a financial transaction.

But by that time Ochs and other farsighted men were beginning to realize, to their horror, that reparations and, indeed, the whole Treaty of Versailles had been mere masks to cover the operation of forces not amenable to reason because their aims were not consonant with existence in a reasonable world. The doctrine of the master race was far more potent in Germany than the doctrine of democracy; and against the idea of the *Herrenvolk* no sort of conciliation was effective.

Not many perceived this clearly as early as 1933, but Ochs did, and it took the heart out of him. He who had seemed to be possessed of the spirit of eternal youth became an old man suddenly. It would be reckless to assert that it shortened his life, for seventy-four years of such intensive living as he had done are enough to wear down the strongest physical frame; but there is no doubt whatever that his realization of what lay ahead clouded, if it did not shorten, his days.

He did not live to witness the worst horrors of the Nazi regime in Germany, but he had only to glance around him to realize something of what must happen when democracy failed and a mountebank seized power. Had we not our own merchants of hate, bawling up and down the land, attacking science, attacking learning, doing their best to instigate pogroms against Catholics, Jews, Negroes, aliens and every other relatively weak minority? At Mer Rouge, Louisiana, not long before, the powers of darkness, working in darkness, had executed two men by the delicate process of running a steam roller over them. If such bestiality dared emerge into the light of day, was it hard to predict the horror of Dachau? It was not hard for Adolph Ochs; it was all too sorrowfully easy.

Once, far back in the golden days, he had paid a visit to the little village near Frankfurt where Effie's grandfather had lived. He was a physician practicing in Frankfurt, but, being a Jew, he was not allowed to live there, so he had established his residence in the village just outside the town. But this drop of bitterness did not spoil Adolph Ochs's sentimental pleasure in the visit, and when he discovered an old peasant woman who remembered the Weiss family his delight overflowed. He asked the privilege of doing something for the village as a memorial to the doctor, and the elders, after consulting the priest, decided that what they most needed was a bell for the village church. It was promptly supplied and the donor thereafter thought with mingled amusement and pleasure of a memorial to a Jewish doctor summoning faithful Catholics to mass. Surely, the old hates were dying out in these better days. Surely, since they were praying to the doctor's God, it was better to have them pray in a ritual strange to him than not have them pray at all.

What had happened to that bell he did not know. It was entirely possible that, some time after 1914, the German army had melted its bronze and worked it into shell bands to be fired at American troops. Even if it were so, it was the work of Prussian militarists, not of the simple villagers. Ochs never regretted the bell.

But now Germany was led by a man whose avowed purpose it was to convert the German people, including those villagers, into fiends such as those who drove the steam roller at Mer Rouge. Moreover he was doing it, not furtively and in fear of the law as it was done in Louisiana, but openly, boastfully, blasphemously demanding that he be praised for doing it. And Germany was succumbing. If that great people could be so poisoned, what assurance remained that any nation was invulnerable? Already the evil thing was wriggling into the United States and who could say with confidence exactly how deadly was the danger to our own country?

No, the gift of foresight was not an unmixed blessing to an American patriot in those days, for worse, much worse, was to come. Adolph Ochs realized it and it is small wonder that the knowledge sent his blithe spirit into an eclipse harder to bear than all his physical infirmities. It was more than fifty years since he had written his mother, from the office of the ill-fated Chattanooga *Dispatch* of his ambition "to make for you all a comfortable home where want is unknown and send my brothers and sisters on their different roads rejoicing."

For half a century he had achieved that ambition brilliantly, and now the affectionate hope had passed from his brothers and sisters to his grandchildren and to his nieces and nephews, but it was no less strong, no less ardent. But where was the excuse for rejoicing along the roads that these young people must travel? He could not see it, and he was heartsick. There were days when his depression deepened until he was convinced that all the labor of a lifetime was to be frustrated at last by forces utterly beyond his control and that he would end a defeated man.

Blows fell upon him thick and fast in these latter days. Two years earlier Jules, the valet, had dropped dead in his presence. He had had Jules for a quarter of a century, quarreling with him, frequently exasperated by him, yet developing a strong affection for one who, with all his quirks, was a faithful servant.

The end came at Lake George and an embarrassment developed. Jules, a Frenchman by birth, was a Catholic but it developed that he had rarely, if ever, attended mass at the village church and the priest was so suspicious of his piety that at first he refused him burial in holy ground. Ochs appealed the case to no less a personage than his old friend, Cardinal Hayes, and won his point; but in the church the priest delivered a discourse so bristling with references to purgatory and hell that at the grave after the body had been lowered Ochs suddenly produced a book from his pocket and read the Jewish burial service. The Catholic gravedigger hastily crossed himself, but Jules was interred, not only religiously, but with the ritual of two religions.

The year 1934 was a period of strange silence in Ochs's life. The good talker said little. The lover of cheerful clatter sat in silence. The bold optimist shrank from contemplation of the future. The sunny life seemed closing in shadows, shadows everywhere, which those closest to him could do little to lift.

In March, 1935, came the last heavy blow. Louis Wiley, who had seemed to be recovering satisfactorily from a surgical operation, died suddenly from a cerebral thrombosis. This snapped the last link with the brave days of old, for Van Anda, still surviving, had come into the organization ten years after Wiley. Ochs was left alone.

But it was more than that. Wiley's death meant the loss at once of a tower of strength and a great solace. The dwarfish figure was more than a business manager; he was a superbly competent newspaperman in any department. His news sense was excellent; he had written some and had uncovered many more of the best news stories the *Times* had ever carried; and his tremendous acquaintance among people who made news rendered his advice invaluable. "I do not suppose there was a more popular person in the two hemispheres," said the editor of the London *Times*, commenting on his death. The loss of such a man is a serious blow to any newspaper.

Yet his professional services were far from being the only thing that Ochs valued in Wiley; his gay good humor was worth almost if not quite as much to a man who loved gaiety but whose burdens sometimes crushed him into depression. Wiley amused Ochs and cheered him; the blackest mood could not long withstand this sprightly presence. In 1896 Wiley had started their association by battering down one of Ochs's sternest resolutions, that to add no item to the payroll until the deficit had been reduced, and in the forty-nine years they had worked together he had learned to love the man. Now with the darkness gathering around him his need of Louis Wiley may have seemed to him greater than it had ever been before; and in that moment Wiley was gone.

It is small wonder that at the funeral many noted with concern how haggard and drawn Mr. Ochs seemed to be. His appearance was not deceptive; he was a man struck another heavy blow when he was already down.

VI

But he was not to go out in darkness and gloom. Even before Wiley's death the clouds had begun to lift to some extent, and even after that event his physical condition continued to improve, and with the improvement some share of his old spirit came back.

Medical men say this is not unusual in such cases, but they are cautious about advancing an explanation. Rabbi Wise would have agreed that it is not unusual, but he would have been prompt and forthright with an explanation. He would have pointed out that it is written of the God of Moses and Abraham that sometimes He repents of having dealt sternly with His servant and suddenly, when it is least expected, substitutes grace for the rod.

Be that as it may, when spring came back again that year the sick man's interest in life suddenly revived. As the sun came north each day he felt stronger and each day the black pessimism of recent months receded.

There was no logic in it. Events were soon to prove that the appearance of physical restoration was deceptive, and the things that had weighed upon his mind were worse, not better. Not for another year was the country really to begin the long climb out of the depression; while in the world at large the powers of darkness were to rage unchecked for four years longer. Nevertheless, in the spring of 1935 Adolph Ochs began to recover his belief in "the things that bring peace, plenty and hope."

Perhaps that very foresight which had lately been a curse to him was sharpened until it could pierce beyond 1939. Certain it is that he made up his mind that the evil he dreaded would somewhere, at some time, be challenged and checked; and once the conscience of mankind was roused against it, he had no doubt of the result. So a gleam of the old hope pierced through the clouds, and with it came a reflection of the old delight in a world in which a man who plays a manful part does not labor in vain.

With the lengthening of the days his thoughts turned back to Chattanooga. Spring comes early in Tennessee, and when April arrived he knew how the misty green on the sides of Lookout was already deepening, how the dogwood buds were swelling, how presently every dark thicket would blaze with the glory of laurel and rhododendron; while down in the town along the residence streets every lawn would be aglitter with daffodils and forsythia. A great yearning to be there again rose in his heart, an ache to be back among the old scenes where his life's work had begun, to walk along the sunny streets, speaking to old friends who could remember him not as the world-famous publisher but as one of their own, a participant in their struggles, a sharer in their triumphs, a good neighbor and a good friend. There he would find heartsease, there he knew was peace.

The doctors pursed their lips and looked doubtful, the family protested, but the homing instinct was too strong to be denied. To placate Effie he promised to take a trained nurse and a valet with him, and to report to her by telephone every day, but the last touch of the projected arrangement was his own. He decreed that his granddaughter, Marian, did not know Chattanooga as well as she should; he would therefore take her along to point out to her himself the places that he remembered and loved. He would travel as he had always delighted to travel, attended by youth, eager to see all that was worth seeing, eager to savor life to the full.

So they set out, arriving in Chattanooga on Sunday, April 7, 1935. Ochs was in high feather as they arrived at the old home, then occupied by his sister, Mrs. Harry Adler. Members of the family and friends who dropped in during the day remarked with pleased astonishment on his good spirits; so bubbling over was he with life and laughter that it was hard to believe that he had ever suffered a day's illness. Toward the end of that Sunday he faithfully discharged his promise by calling his wife on the telephone. He told her, with evident sincerity, that for all his seventy-seven years he had never felt better in his life.

Monday morning found him in the same mood. He went to the office of the Chattanooga *Times* and plunged into shoptalk with the avidity of a man of half his years. First he went through the place with a cheery greeting for everyone he met; then he closeted himself with Adolph Shelby Ochs, the general manager of the paper, and became so interested in details that he had to be reminded of the arrival of the lunch hour. Then with his brother, Milton, Lapsley G. Walker, the editor, R. F. Walker, of the staff, and Miss Cunningham, the nurse, he walked to a coffee shop a block from the office, where the editor left them. As he turned away Walker noticed that the chief seemed unsteady on his feet, but he attributed it to the weakness of a convalescent and thought no more of it.

The others entered the coffee shop, and took seats, Ochs still chatting pleasantly. Silence fell as the menus were passed, but no one noticed anything unusual until Milton Ochs asked what his brother would have. Getting no answer, he repeated the question and looked up from the card. Adolph Ochs was slumped in his chair, unconscious.

Miss Cunningham promptly administered a hypodermic, an ambulance was summoned and the stricken man was removed to Newell's

Sanitarium, where oxygen treatment was applied, but without success. He died at 4:10 that afternoon, without regaining consciousness.

It was such an end as any man of sense would choose—swift, painless, with no long night watches or agonizing farewells. To adapt the phrase of a literary critic, it reminds one of the quiet withdrawal, at the evening's end, of a great man from a company whom he has entertained magnificently.

Every business house in Chattanooga closed during the funeral and every factory wheel stood still.

The legislature of Tennessee suspended business and stood silent as the hour struck.

When the body was brought back to New York the Republican mayor proclaimed a day of mourning.

The Democratic President of the United States and his wife sent a magnificent wreath.

The leader of the Socialist party paid public tribute to the fairness of the great conservative.

The chattering of the telegraph wires of the Associated Press was hushed for two minutes all over the continent.

Tributes from the illustrious of every nation on the globe poured in.

And the printer mistook him for "the little man who went about turning off the lights."

None of them were wrong. Every tribute paid to Adolph Simon Ochs as he lay dead was amply justified. One may include in this even the great words spoken over the bier in Temple Emanu-El on Fifth Avenue. "Who shall ascend into the hill of the Lord?" intoned the Rev. Dr. Goldenson. "He that hath clean hands and a pure heart; who hath not lifted up his soul unto vanity, nor sworn deceitfully." It was all true. The great publisher, lauded by the great, who knew his genius; the good man mourned by the small, who knew his generosity; the able craftsman marked by the printer, who knew his skill—he was all these.

But he was in addition to all these the last, or nearly the last, representative of a type that only America has produced in numbers and that America is not likely to see again. He was one of the strong men who in the latter half of the nineteenth century riveted together the fabric of American civilization—not without heat, not without error, not without grime, sweat, anger, oaths and blows, but withal so firmly that it has withstood two of the most tremendous assaults in human history.

The strong men worked for themselves, to be sure, and some of them were unscrupulous; but the really great among them have always recognized that power cannot rightfully be exercised unless the responsibility to which it is linked is assumed. It was Adolph Ochs's distinction among the Titans that he made this conspicuously clear. Freedom of the press represents power; but no man may exercise that power rightfully unless he accepts the responsibility that goes with it—the responsibility to tell the truth as far as it is humanly possible to know the truth, without deviation for his own benefit, or that of his party, his sect or his friends.

There have been other men who equaled or surpassed his organizing ability, his news sense, his resourcefulness and his driving energy; but no publisher in American journalism has surpassed his sense of responsibility to his country, to his readers and to his men. It is this, not his technical triumphs or his financial success, that gives him his rank among the mighty, making him one of the truly great figures of American journalism.

He served the truth. Being human, he could not serve it perfectly. At times he was misinformed, at times he was deceived, at times his judgment failed and he deceived himself; but he never lied, which is the final test of a servant of the truth.

"Willing to believe the things that give peace, plenty and hope," he nevertheless faced resolutely the bitter truth when what it gave was war, want and despair. He not only served but, in Bunyan's phrase, he was valiant for truth; so none with faith to believe that valor finally has its reward will doubt that at 4:10 in the afternoon of April 8, 1935, "all the trumpets sounded for him on the other side."

INDEX

[309]

INDEX

INDEX

[311]

INDEX

INDEX

Set in Linotype Electra
Format by A. W. Rushmore
Composition by Westcott and Thomson, Inc.
Printed and bound by The Haddon Craftsmen
Published by HARPER & BROTHERS
New York and London